WALK SCOTLAND

Walk Scotland
A Guidebook for All Seasons

Bruce Sandison

MAINSTREAM
PUBLISHING
EDINBURGH AND LONDON

This edition, 2005

Copyright © Bruce Sandison, 2001
All rights reserved
The moral right of the author has been asserted

First published in Great Britain in 2001 by
MAINSTREAM PUBLISHING COMPANY (EDINBURGH) LTD
7 Albany Street
Edinburgh EH1 3UG

ISBN 1 84018 959 2

A catalogue record for this book is available from the British Library

Typeset in Berkeley and Gill Condensed
Printed and bound in Great Britain by
Antony Rowe Ltd, Chippenham, Wiltshire

FOR ANN

Blow, west wind, by the lonely mound,
And murmur, summer streams —
There is no need of other sound
To soothe my lady's dreams.

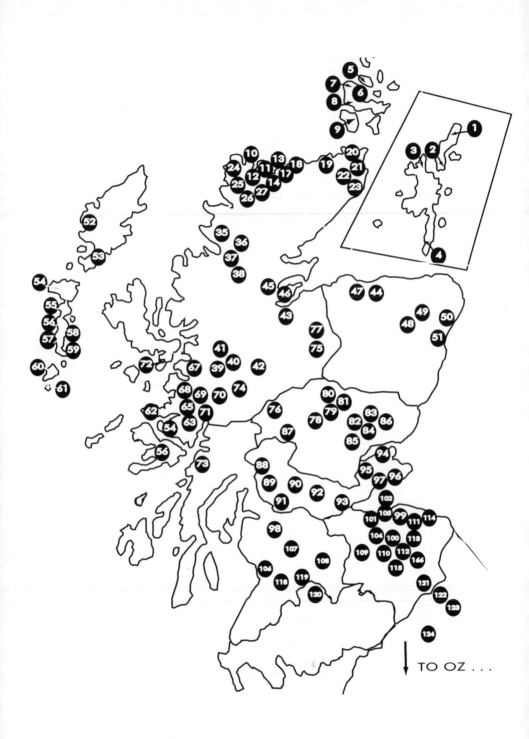

TO OZ . . .

CONTENTS

PREFACE

This is a book about the land I love. Our mountains and moorlands make us what we are. Every creature, human or animal, depends upon that land for survival. Therefore, whatever hurts Scotland's environment hurts us all.

In our brief stewardship of this irreplaceable treasure, let us strive to preserve its integrity. When we are gone, let there be no sign of our passing other than the kindly imprint of our care. This is our duty to future generations. There is no room for compromise.

Bruce Sandison
Tongue, Sutherland
March, 2001

I. MUCKLE FLUGGA

Angst may bedevil the international rugby scene, but there is one pitch where serenity reigns: Scotland's most northerly ground, at the head of Burra Firth on the Island of Unst in Shetland. Well, I think peace reigns supreme. There could be problems with Unst golfers, because the wildflower-rich links are also home to Scotland's most northerly golf course. I suppose there are rules to avoid conflict, such as 'Players should not tee off when a goal is being kicked', or 'No set scrums on the greens'.

Thomas Stevenson 'teed off' from Unst in 1854. He had been given the task of building a lighthouse on the island of Muckle Flugga, which lies between mainland Unst and Out Stack, the most northerly speck of UK territory. The lighthouse cost £32,378 15s 5d to build, expressed in proper, pre-decimal money. I particularly like the Presbyterian 5d. Would that the members of our new Scottish Parliament were so financially meticulous! Now that the lighthouse is unmanned, what about using it as a punishment centre for Caledonian MPs who stray from the straight and narrow?

Burra Firth has a history of battles, apart from bashing balls around in rugby rucks or on bumpy fairways. The firth is enclosed by headlands: to the west, Hermaness (657ft), and to the east, Saxa Vord (935ft). Tradition has it that two giants lived there, Herman and Saxa, both of whom fell in love with a mermaid named Utsta. The rivals became so jealous of each other that they started chucking huge boulders across the firth, creating such a din that a local witch intervened. She buried Saxa beneath a cover of green grass and turned Herman into a cloud of mist. Bad news, witches.

My partner and I bumped into Herman during our last visit. One moment it was bright and clear and the next he had enveloped us in his clammy white cloak. With 500-foot cliffs only a step to the left, knifed by isolated stacks and ravine-line geos, we decided it was time for a pause, coffee and some serious compass and map work. Far better safe than sorry. When the mist lifted, almost as quickly as it had descended, we found ourselves dangerously close to the edge, sharing the sandy top with a gathering of firework-beaked puffins.

Hermaness is a National Nature Reserve and you will find it on OS Map 1, Shetland, Yell and Unst, second series, Scale 1:50,000. The A89086 road ends at Burra Firth, and from there an unnamed road leads to a car park on the east side of the firth at The Noss (Grid Ref: 613149). Park here, drag on the stomping boots and set off on a glorious six-mile adventure exploring the reserve and its wildlife. After half a mile, you will arrive at the point where the Burn of Winnaswarta Dale crosses the path (Grid Ref: 610157).

Turn left here and follow the line of the stream westwards, up the hill over peat moorland peopled with acrimonious 'bonxie', the Shetland name for the piratical great skua. These huge birds are fearless in defence of their offspring and their territorial rights. Those who have not yet met Mr Bonxie may scorn advice to carry a stick to ward off aerial attack, but believe me, it is all true, so be warned. But these birds are a wonderful sight, as are the many thousands of other seabirds to be seen along the way: gannet, guillemot, black guillemot, Arctic skua, razorbill, kittiwake, fulmar and puffin.

When you reach the cliffs, turn north and trek on over easier ground until you eventually catch your first glimpse of Muckle Flugga near the Greing (Grid Ref: 601180). There is something quintessentially Scottish about the name 'Muckle Flugga'. It seems to me to encapsulate the very essence of my native land, its diversity, history and culture, a place which every Scot should see at least once before Auld Nick finally carts them off. Like learning and performing 'Tam O'Shanter', word perfect, before a baying gang of Burns Supper aficionados. Just something that has to be done, if you are to call yourself a Scot.

Having ogled Muckle Flugga, plod along the track to the top of the Hermaness Hill (Grid Ref: 605177). The way home is due south via a well-marked path, eased over the soggiest chunks by excellent duckboard walkways. As I write, I glow with the memory of Stevenson's proud tower fingering the sky above seabird-whitened cliffs, where cold Atlantic waves dash endlessly against the broken, black rocks. Rehearse the words 'Muckle Flugga'. You have to go.

2. THINGS THAT GO BUMP ON YELL

Crossing from Toft on mainland Shetland to Ulsta on the Island of Yell can sometimes be a pain in 'the buttocks', and this is the name given to the turbulent stretch of water in Yell Sound between the uninhabited island of Bigga and the ferry terminal at Ulsta. The journey takes about 20 minutes and on a fine day it is a wonderful experience – sky-blue seas crested with white-topped waves, backed by golden moors and green hills. But when the wind howls and the sea roars, it is easy to understand how it got its name.

Yell is the largest of Shetland's north isles: 17 miles long by up to seven miles wide, with a deeply indented coastline of about 100 miles in length. The island is home to 1,000 souls, most of whom live in the coastal communities of Setter, Mid Yell, Camb, Sellafirth, Gutcher, Cullivoe, Burravoe, Houlland and Ulsta. The interior of Yell is uninhabited, a magnificent, trackless, loch-scattered wilderness of incomparable beauty.

My ancestors came from Shetland and the islanders are an independent, individualistic race. I remember once discussing the question of home rule for Scotland with an acquaintance in Lerwick. My friend was less than impressed: 'It would make no difference to us,' he said, 'being ruled from Edinburgh or London. The one would be every bit as bad as the other.' Even in these troubled times of European Union quotas, fishing is a mainstay of the island economy and is deeply embedded in its history. A monument at Gloup in north Yell commemorates the deaths of 58 Yell men caught at sea in a sudden, terrible storm on the night of 20 July 1881. The tragedy left in its wake 34 widows and 85 fatherless children.

Yell is splendid walking country. You may come and go as you please, and there is little of the angst that so often bedevils hill walking in mainland Scotland. The people are welcoming and friendly, always ready to help whenever and wherever they can. This is immediately apparent when visiting the emporium of R. Robertson & Son at Ulsta. Tommy Robertson sells everything, from provisions to petrol, car insurance to craft products.

One of my favourite Yell walks is along the north shore of Whale Firth to the deserted village of Vollister, unmarked on the OS Map but located at Grid Ref: 475939. Use OS Map 1, Shetland, Yell and Unst, and OS Map 2, Shetland, Whalsay, second series, Scale 1:50,000, to follow the route. Drive north from Ulsta on the A968 and park on the farm access road at Windhouse (Grid Ref: 492918) at the head of the firth. Before setting off, visit the Windhouse, Yell's most notable ruin. The house is reputed to be haunted, not by one ghost but by a whole family of them: the Lady in Silk, the ghost of a woman whose skeleton, with a broken neck, was discovered under the floorboards at the foot of the main staircase; the Man in Black, a tall spectre dressed in a black cloak and noted for his ability to walk through walls; the ghost of a child whose remains were found built into the kitchen wall; and, to keep them all company, the ghost of a black dog.

A track leads north from Windhouse, above the firth, crossing Brocken Burn on the gentle slopes of Muckle Swart Houll (110m). The moor is rich in wildlife, including great skua, which mercilessly dive-bomb the unwary traveller. Watch out also for acrobatic Arctic skua, and whimbrel and golden plover piping plaintively from sphagnum tussocks.

After about a mile you will see the ruins of the village ahead of you on the hill overlooking the firth. Vollister was cleared, reinhabited and then cleared again in the later years of the nineteenth century, when the last residents finally gave up the unequal struggle to wrest a living from the acid soil. All that remains are their broken dwellings and a rusty boat-mooring ring in a rock by the shore.

West across Whale Firth, on the Herra, the position is very different. Witness the fine crofting lands around Grimister. Indeed, a well-known Yell rhyme notes the obvious prosperity of the Herra: 'North-a-Voe for poverty, South-a-Voe for pride, Basta for a pretty lass, The Herra for a bride.'

Follow the burn up to Loch of Vollister (Grid Ref: 478943), famous for large, dour trout, then cross Muckle Swart Houll to the east to find Loch of Windhouse at Grid Ref: 496942. The outlet burn from the loch will point you to a good track that leads back to the farm. The whole expedition takes around three hours, more if you happily linger along the way. To be on the safe side, however, avoid arriving back at the Windhouse after dark. You never can tell who might be waiting there to greet you.

3. SKELBERRY, SHETLAND

The Shetland Isles have provided home and haven for world travellers for more than 4,000 years. At Jarlshof near Sumburgh Airport, there is evidence of continuous occupation through the Stone Age, Bronze Age and Iron Age down to the days of Viking domination. Early writers referred to Shetland and Iceland as 'Ultima Thule'. In the fourth century BC, Pytheas of Marseilles, astronomer and geographer, sailed 'six days from north Britain' to reach them.

These remote northern lands are a wild scatter of more than a hundred islands resting in the storm-tossed bosom of the Atlantic Ocean and covering an area of more than 550 square miles. The largest is Mainland and the other principal islands are Yell, Unst, Fetlar, Bressay and Whalsay. They are an endless delight of sunlight and serenity, guarded by huge, seabird-clad crags, fringed with white sandy beaches. The moorlands are silvered with more than 300 freshwater lochs peopled by Arctic skua, red-throated diver and golden plover.

A walk of outstanding beauty and interest is from Skelberry in North Mainland over the moors to Lang Clodie Loch. It is a long walk, tough and definitely compass-and-map country. When you climb onto the moor an amazing vista opens. Scattered granite boulders glisten in the sun; golden plover flit and pipe over rough peat hags. Scootie Allan, the Shetland name for Arctic skua, tumble and twist in stunning aerial mock combat. Thread your way across the moor round peat banks, past a string of dark-blue trout-filled lochs and lochans with magical names: Roer Water, Maadle Swankie, Tonga and Muckle Lunga, Many Crooks, Moshella and the Loch of the Grey Ewe. But the most dramatic of all is the lovely Birka Water, 700 yards long by 300 yards wide, easier to measure in extent than to describe its beauty. Birka is crystal-clear and at the east end there is a sandy beach which makes a perfect picnic spot. Opposite the beach is a magnificent waterfall, dropping from high crags along the south shore. I first saw it after heavy rain, on a warm, sunny afternoon, full, silver and thunderous, tumbling sparkling into the waters of the loch below, sending urgent wavelets rippling over the calm surface.

The last time I passed, I walked round the loch to the foot of the falls and then climbed slowly to a tiny, narrow lochan at the top. As I reached the crest, my head level with the outlet of the falls, I found myself eyeball to eyeball with a red-throated diver, the 'rain goose' of the Shetlands. The bird was a yard away. As more of my bulk appeared, the graceful creature gave a wink of welcome and splashed noisily skywards in search of a less busy feeding place.

Birka collects together all the waters from the lochs on the north slope of Ronas Hill, the highest point on Shetland, and hurries them seawards down a splendid outlet burn on the west shore; a narrow, boulder-strewn stream, chattering and singing in the summer air. Far below, on a green plateau, tiny Lang Clodie Loch gathers the flow into her arms before shooting it out over red-ragged cliffs into the waiting Atlantic.

As I walked home in the evening, I paused and looked back, trying to fix the memory of the scents and sounds of these moorlands in my mind. As I write, they are still as fresh and startlingly clear as they were on that memorable sunny Shetland day.

Find your way round using OS Map 1, Shetland, Yell and Unst, second series, Scale 1:50,000. Park the car just before the houses at Skelberry. There is a gate on your left, leading down through a grass park to the foot of the hill. Cross the burn and climb the gully. Walk westwards, keeping

Roer Water on your left. Take frequent bearings to check direction or you may find yourself going too far north. Pass between Tonga and Swankie Waters, then walk in a straight line on to Birka. If you get it right, you should arrive at the sandy beach.

Walk round the north shore of Birka to reach the waterfall, crossing the outlet burn on the way. Climb the waterfall to say hello to my red-throated diver friend, then return to the outlet burn. Follow the outlet burn down the narrow defile to the cliff-top plateau and Lang Clodie Loch. Stay well back from the edge of the cliffs.

Return the same way but, if you feel adventurous, angle south past Sandy Water and Swabie Water to climb Ronas Hill. The way down follows the east shoulder of Ronas Hill and leads to a track that will take you back to the A970 and north to your car. Start of walk Grid Ref: 362862; access onto hill Grid Ref: 360863; Roer Water Grid Ref: 335864; route between Tonga Water and Maadle Swankie Grid Ref: 322872; Birka Water Grid Ref: 316875; Birka Waterfall Grid Ref: 315872; Birka outlet burn Grid Ref: 316875; Lang Clodie Loch Grid Ref: 312878.

4. SHETLAND CRUBS AND HUMLIBANDS

The Shetland accent makes music out of words. When Ann and I were there a couple of weeks ago, my friend Rae Phillips gave me a copy of *The Shetland Dictionary*, inscribed: 'Aa du needs ta ken aboot kabes, humlibands and crubs.' Which, translated, means: 'All you need to know about how to row Shetland boats and about small dry-stone-built shelters used for growing cabbage plants.' As an angler, I was fascinated by kabes and humlibands. A kabe is a sturdy, thick wooden post, used instead of a rollock. Humlibands are looped leather thongs attached to oars, which are slung over the kabe; thus allowing the oarsman to row without fear of losing an oar overboard; a matter of considerable importance, given the savage weather often encountered during fishing expeditions in these wild parts.

The remains of stone crubs lie scattered round the islands; by the shore, on the moor, located in fertile patches of soil and limestone enclaves. Although they are seldom used today, not so very long ago they were vital to ensure a constant supply of fresh vegetables. The harvest of the land and the sea is, and always has been, the central part of Shetland culture.

There is no 'best' time to visit these magical northern isles. Shetland is always welcoming. Its overwhelming beauty instantly ensnares the soul. June is captivating, when the islands awaken from the grip of winter to embrace long summer days when midnight is as bright as dawn; the simmer dim, the twilight of a Shetland summer evening.

We stayed in a self-catering flat near Okraquoy a few miles south from the Shetland capital of Lerwick. From our window we looked out over sheep-dotted fields, across the sparkling blue sea to the majestic, jagged cliffs of the Mills of the Ord on the island of Bressay. There were wonderful walks from our front door and we rarely needed the car.

Use OS Map 4, Shetland, South Mainland, second series, Scale 1:50,000, to find your way round. Okraquoy is at Grid Ref: 438317. One morning, we tramped north to find the trig point on Coall Head (64m) at Grid Ref: 441338, only four miles there and back, but an amazing adventure every step of the way. We were greeted at Bay of Okraquoy (Grid Ref: 439314) by a symphony orchestra of seals; black bewhiskered heads eyeing us cautiously, paralleling our passage along the shore.

The little headland at Trumba (Grid Ref: 440319) was decked out in a glorious carpet of light blue squill. Yellow flag nodded by tiny ochre-coloured burns. In one small corner by a stream we found squill, tormentil, marsh orchid, spotted orchid, lousewort, lesser celandine, white and lilac cuckoo flower, sorrel, red campion, sea rocket, silverweed and milkwort, all busily going about their business in happy unison.

Along the path we were enchanted by the birds we saw: wren, twite, oyster catcher, ringed plover, fulmar, hoodie crow, kittiwake, black-backed gull, Arctic tern, piratical Great skua and Arctic skua, curlew and whimbrel. The most difficult part of the journey is keeping going. There is an endless compulsion to stand and stare, a childlike enticement to touch beachside flotsam, to examine rusty iron and upturned boats. We beach-combed Bay of Fladdabister (Grid Ref: 437324) and climbed up to have lunch amidst the ruins of old limekilns on the headland. They were in use until the 1930s. Now, they make the perfect dining-room; exclusive, comfortable, grass-lined hollows, sheltered from the wind with a place to rest back and mind. Listen. Sea-sound and gull cry will ease your spirit. Feel the heartbeat of time passing.

The route north climbs past Gardie Taing (Grid Ref: 440328) to The Valder and Stack of Pulli (Grid Ref: 441331). Keep back from the edge, particularly in high winds or wet weather. It is a long way down to Davy Jones's locker. The caves here are amongst the most spectacular in Shetland. At the trig point on The Coall, pause, forever. The vista that unfolds is unforgettable.

The return journey can be varied by hiking due west for a mile and a half to climb the Sheens of Breitos (224m) at Grid Ref: 429338 and then walking south down the ridge to regain Okraquoy, a grand moorland walk. But Ann and I could not resist the call of the sea. We retraced our outward route and said hello again to the seals and birds and wildflowers, whilst searching for yet more kabes, humlibands and crubs.

5. ROUSAY CAIRNS

Orkney contains some of the most important archaeological monuments in Europe: the Stone Age village of Skara Brae; the dramatic Standing Stones of Stenness; the Ring of Brogar and the magnificent Chambered Tomb of Maes Howe. Given the enormous number of Orcadian Neolithic sites, I often wonder just how many people lived in Orkney 5,000 years ago? I build up a mental picture of busy farmer-fishermen tending sparse crops. Tousle-haired boys wrestling in play on white sand beaches. Heavy-breasted women grinding corn warmed by Neolithic sun, nursing babies, chiding scavenging dogs. There must have been a thriving community of several hundred souls in these northern isles at that time.

There is little evidence of the earliest settlers in northern Scotland, Mesolithic men, other than their middens. But their descendants left their mark particularly by the manner in which they buried their dead in great chambered tombs. These massive structures are scattered throughout the Highlands and Islands, memorials of when, to survive, a community had to work together. I think we have more to learn from them than they could from us.

The Island of Rousay, the 'Holy Isle', has more than its fair share of these monuments and an easy coastal walk passes the most impressive. The first part of the trip is by sea, from the pier at Tingwall on Mainland, over Eynhallow Sound by the island of Wyre to the little harbour at Brinyan. Craggy shores encompass Rousay. Most of the hinterland is gently hilled and there is a fine viewpoint on the highest peak, High Brae of Camps, a modest 244m above sea level. High Brae is easily climbed from the road that circles Rousay.

Orkney consists of almost 90 islands, some 30 of which are inhabited, and most can be seen from High Brae. Northwards lie Westray and Papa Westray, the wild rocks of North Ronaldsay and long straggle of Sandray. East are Egilsay, Eaday, Stronsay and Shapinsay, with Auskerry in the distance. South, across Mainland, crowd the gentle hills of Hoy.

The road round Rousay is numbered with bureaucratic thoroughness. You would imagine that, being a single road, it would have a single designation.

Not so. At the pier it is the B9065. Where it joins a loop, right and left, it becomes the B9064. A minibus plies the route in an anticlockwise direction, taking 45 minutes to complete the journey. The driver will introduce you to the life and times of Rousay, past and present, and this will greatly prepare you for the walk. Leave the bus at Mid Howe and follow the signposts for the Westness Walk, which lead to the brochs and chambered cairn of Mid Howe. At first sight you might be forgiven for thinking that Mid Howe was an old Orcadian cattle byre: drystane walls separated into cubicles. The structure is 32m long by 13m wide and the burial chamber is 23m. There are 12 cells, 6 on each side, and one side has platforms. Twenty-five skeletons were found here along with well-preserved pottery.

The path leaves Mid Howe and wends its way along the shoreline overlooking Eynhallow and the Church of the Holy Isle. These are fierce waters, where long arms of Atlantic and North Sea race through dangerous narrows with amazing force. Fulmars sweep by. In spring and summer the path is bright with wildflowers. Orkney is devoid of foxes, squirrels, deer and badgers, but if you have your wits about you there is always the chance of seeing an otter. I decided years ago that if I were reincarnated I would choose to return as an otter; footloose and fancy free, the outdoor life, as much walking as one could wish for and a protected species into the bargain. Who could ask for more?

The path eventually comes back to the main road, but this is a relative statement: expect possibly two or three vehicles an hour. Knowe of Lairo, a long, four-horned chambered cairn, is approached by the track that leads left from the road past the schoolhouse at Frotoft. It was probably constructed over a considerable period, bits being added at different times. The cairn extends in a long mound for a distance of 180ft and there is an 18-foot long entrance passage leading to three burial chambers. Nearby is another chambered cairn, Knowe of Yarso, a stalled cairn with four compartments, first explored in 1934 when the remains of 20 adults and one child were found. They were well prepared and provisioned for their last journey: '. . . 30 individual red-deer, some sheep and a dog. Relics included fragments of food-vessel and beaker pottery, four arrowheads and more than 60 other flint implements and five bone tools.'

The last of the Rousay monuments is Blackhammar, close to Yarso Cairn, another stalled burial chamber divided into 14 stalls, measuring 13m by 1.8m in width. I wonder if they sang or chanted when they buried their loved ones? How did they mourn? What incantations were performed over the sleeping bodies?

You will need OS Map 6, Orkney – Mainland, second series, Scale 1:50,000. Rousay Ferry Grid Ref: 403228; Brinyan Pier Grid Ref: 436275;

start of walk Grid Ref: 375310; Mid Howe Cairn Grid Ref: 371308; Yarso Cairn Grid Ref: 404281; Lairo Cairn Grid Ref: 414277; Blackhammar Cairn Grid Ref: 425275; High Brae of Camps Grid Ref: 419290.

6. ORKNEY AND THE GLOUP

The earth belongs unto the Lord and all that it contains
Except the Clyde and Western Isles
They're Caledonian MacBrayne's

This old rhyme will require revision when Calmac take over from P&O the running of the northern isles ferry services. What about: 'Except the Clyde and Scottish Isles'? Still, they'd better check before using it. The Pentland Firth is stormy enough as it is without ancient mariners making matters worse by offending Him.

The first time The Manager and I crossed the broken waters between Scrabster in Caithness and Stromness in Orkney, our car was hoisted on board the ferry by a rope sling. I can still hear the thud as it landed none too gently on the deck. Today, cars roll on and roll off in comfort. But it is a wondrous journey, regardless of weather conditions. I never travel this way without feeling a sense of excitement and ensuing adventure. Beyond the red cliffs of Roy lies a magical land of fertile fields and heather moorlands, fringed by some of the most majestic cliffs in the world. Arriving is light and easy. Leaving is hard. Join me in a five-mile walk on the wild side, along the dramatic coastline of the Deerness peninsula, a few miles southeast of Orkney's ancient capital, Kirkwall. You will need Ordnance Survey Map 6, Orkney Mainland, second series, Scale 1:50,000 to find your way round. And a compass. There are good tracks, but should a mist descend it is easy to become disorientated.

At the end of the A960 road from Kirkwall drive on, following signposts to The Gloup, and to the Mull of Head Nature Reserve car park at Grid Ref: 588075. Two hundred yards east from the car park will bring you to two well-constructed viewing platforms, where you can gulp at The Gloup. This is a sea cave that has, after thousands of years of attack by the waves, fallen in on itself. The result is a long, dark, gash in the cliff, arched by a land bridge at the seaward end, which has left an 24-metre deep, spray-foamed chasm. At this point, it is not only dogs that should be kept safely on the lead, but children also.

The springy turf overlaying the 370 million-year-old red sandstone rock is carpeted with wildflowers. Springtime brings into bloom delicate banks of primrose. Grass of Parnassus, thrift, lovage, meadow rue and oyster plants nod their welcomes by the margin of the track. As a boy I remember watching rare fulmars here, sweeping the cliff edge in stiff-winged flight. They have prospered mightily since then.

This is a walk for lovers. There are a number of kissing-gates along the way, leading deep into this paradise garden. Stride north from The Gloup to find Brough of Deerness (Grid Ref: 597080) after an easy sea-salt one-mile stroll. A muddy track leads to the top and the ruins of a Celtic chapel. Take care, because the track is narrow and intimidating. Caution is required, particularly in wet or stormy weather. Otherwise, you might find yourself exchanging eternal pleasantries with the previous occupants.

Hike on round Mull Head to Chip of Mull, a small bite out of the cliff at Grid Ref: 592098, and continue west along the cliff edge. At the fence line at Grid Ref: 585090, tramp west for a further half-mile to 'where the kissing had to stop' for 200 of God's humble servants. A monument here (Grid Ref: 571080) commemorates the fate of Covenanter prisoners being transported to the colonies aboard the *Crown of London*, on 10 December 1679. A few months earlier, on 22 June, they had surrendered after the Battle of Bothwell Brig to the Duke of Monmouth and Bloody Claverhouse, commander of the King's dread dragoons. Shackled together, the covenanters finally met their Maker when the *Crown of London* was wrecked in a storm in Deer Sound.

Retrace sombre footsteps to the last red kissing-gate and follow the track downhill to the car park. But it is hard to be sombre in Orkney. There is an energy about the islands and an all-embracing peace that defies dullness, exemplified in the music of Sir Peter Maxwell Davies, Orkney's adopted composer, and the late George Mackay Brown, who sang Orkney's praise in verse. Caledonian MacBrayne will have to row hard to establish their right to a permanent share of this enduring heritage.

* The Ferry service to the isles was in fact awarded to North Link Ferries and not to Valmac.

7. SKARA BRAE

You need good sea legs for Orkney walking. Not because the hills are high or hikes taxing, but just to get you safely over the Pentland Firth. I remember one journey with horror. House-high waves, mad walls of tormented, flying spray, roared in from all quarters. Sea gulls screamed derision through the storm. My five-year-old son, Blair, and I wedged together topside, trying to pretend it was all good fun. In spite of that violent journey across Europe's wildest waters, the magic of the Orcades has held us enthralled ever since and the journey from mainland Scotland is not always so stormy. We have often sailed millpond-calm amidst myriad sea birds, chased and chivvied by porpoise and gannet, lazing sunburnt past sentinel stacks, barely aware of time passing.

One of our favourite Orkney walks starts at the Bay of Skaill in Sandwick on the west coast of Mainland. The bay is a crescent of shining sand washed by green-fringed Atlantic waves. My first golden retriever, Jean, learned to swim there. She was a highly bred bundle of nerves, and required 'persuasion' before undertaking any venture which was faintly dangerous. And, as far as she was concerned, water looked mighty dangerous. I waded in, holding her in my arms, and she swam ashore. Jean loved water ever after.

Nestling in the sand dunes at the south end of the bay is the Neolithic village of Skara Brae. Five thousand years ago these stone houses must have resounded with the laughter and chatter of farmer-fishermen and their families. The dwellings are wonderfully preserved, after lying for centuries undisturbed under marram-covered dunes. A huge storm uncovered the remains of ten houses and they have been excavated to reveal fireplaces, complete with adjacent seat, flagstone box beds, dressers and wall shelves.

Leave Skaill Bay from behind Skara Brae and climb little Ward Hill, over soft, springy sea-turf specked with wildflowers. The rare Scottish primrose, Primula scotica, graces these cliff-tops. Kittiwakes, guillemots, razorbills and fulmars squawk and squabble on dramatic crags. The songs of wheatears, meadow pipits and larks sparkle in the crystal air, accompanied as always by the sound of the restless sea. From the hill, eastwards, Loch Stenness and Loch Harray sweep the moor with blue. These are two of Orkney's famous trout lochs. Fishermen-filled boats drift the skerry-strewn shallows in endless pursuit of beautifully shaped pink-fleshed wild brown trout. Fish weighing more than 17lb have been caught there and anglers come from all over the world to explore these lime-rich waters.

Close to the deep inlet of Bor Wick, a jagged scar in the cliff, is Broch of Borwick, an Iron Age fort on top of the hill: evidence that competition for land and fear of attack by invaders demanded a secure refuge. This did not prevent the Vikings from acquiring Orkney, as is evident from its placenames. 'Skaill', for instance, is the Norse word for the house of a

Viking chief; generally situated close to a good beach and longship landing place and surrounded by fertile lands. The Norsemen plundered at will throughout Shetland, Orkney, Ireland and mainland Britain until their power was broken at the Battle of Largs in 1261. But even then, Orkney remained part of Norway. Eventually, the islands were pledged to Scotland in 1465 as security for the payment of the dowry when King James III married Margaret, daughter of King Christian of Norway.

However, when walking along these cliffs it is not Vikings you have to fear. A more immediate danger threatens the unwary. Between Yesnaby and Neban Point the moor is owned by a colony of Arctic skuas. During the breeding season they guard their territory furiously and they dive fearlessly, shrieking with anger, on intruders.

A mighty sea stack, the Castle of Yesnaby, has been knifed from the mainland by thousands of years' Atlantic attack. Nearby there is an outcrop of even older rock, the starting point of the fault known as the 'Uranium Corridor'. Lunch at the viewpoint on Neban Point, lingering above the waves, watching the changing colours on Ward Hill, the highest peak on the Island of Hoy.

This is an easy walk and it will take about four hours, depending upon how long you spend at Skara Brae and how often you stop and stare. As always when on a cliff walk, keep well back from the edge. Remember that the cliffs are friable and subject to erosion. Park at Bay of Skaill and follow the signs through the dunes to Skara Brae. Walk south from Skara Brae up Ward Hill and follow the cliff path on to Neban Point. Return to the car park the same way. There and back is a distance of about eight miles. Good walking shoes are required and it is advisable to arrive at Skara Brae before 10.30 a.m. After that time, the village gets uncomfortably busy with tourists.

Use OS Map 6, Orkney Mainland, second series, Scale 1:50,000. Start point at Bay of Skaill Grid Ref: 236194; Skara Brae Grid Ref: 230187; Hill of Borwick Grid Ref: 223165; Castle Yesnaby Grid Ref: 217134; Neban Point Grid Ref: 216132.

8. MARWICK HEAD

A sea-salt walk this morning, to Kitchener's Memorial on Mainland Orkney, nine miles enlivened by gull-cry and flung spray from cold Atlantic breakers beating on black-scarred cliffs. However, begin the day with a quick jaunt to the Brough of Birsay, a small island off the northwest coast. Plan your arrival at Point of Buckquoy, the start point, three hours after high tide when it is possible to walk dry-shod to Birsay over an exposed concrete causeway. One hour is sufficient time to examine the remains of the Viking banqueting hall on the island and to visit the small museum.

You need OS Map 6, Orkney Mainland, second series, Scale 1:50,000, to find your way round. Point of Buckquoy is at Grid Ref: 243284. After a bit of robbing and pillaging on Birsay, return to Buckquoy to inspect the impressive ruins of the home of Patrick Stewart, one of Orkney's most notorious and barbaric despots. Earl Patrick terrorised his people, through both high taxation and physical abuse. When he was imprisoned in Edinburgh for his alleged crimes, his son raised a rebellion in 1615 to secure his father's release. Patrick was released, permanently. James VI had him executed.

Leave the red sandstone ruins and cross the bridge in the village that leads south to fields bordering the sea. These wildflower-carpeted links riot with colour during spring and early summer. At the end of the links cross a fence and follow a rising track which climbs gradually up to Marwick Head and Kitchener's Memorial (Grid Ref: 257252). Marwick Head is a RSPB nature reserve noted for Arctic and Great skua, and for the 40,000 seabirds that nest there from May to July. During the breeding season Great skua, 'bonxies', are fearless in defending their territories. Wear a hat, carry a stick, and you won't come to any harm.

Horatio Herbert Kitchener, immortalised in the First World War recruiting poster 'Your Country Needs You', was not so lucky. On 5 June 1916, three weeks before his first hundred thousand volunteer soldiers went 'over the top' into the hellish Battle of the Somme, the hero of the relief of Khartoum and Commander of the British forces during the Boer War was drowned off Marwick Head. Kitchener had sailed from Scapa Flow aboard the cruiser HMS *Hampshire*, bound for Russia. That evening, amidst a violent storm, his ship struck a German mine. All but 12 of the vessel's crew perished. It is reported that Kitchener was last seen on deck, 'calm and courageous' as the ship went down. His body was never recovered. His monument is, in my opinion, ugly and incongruous; a squat tower perched 86m above the sea, with all the visual and romantic appeal of a fairground helter-skelter. Our Imperial ancestors knew how to muck up a view. Leave the sad memorial and trek downhill to the fishermen's cottages and the old chapel at Marwick Bay (Grid Ref: 259243). It is now time for lunch and, on a hot day, if you are feeling brave, an icy splash in the crystal-clear shallows.

Return to Point of Buckquoy via another RSPB reserve at the Loons marshes, where there is a 'hide' (Grid Ref: 245242). Linger and look out for a wide variety of birds. Continue along a quiet, narrow road, the B9056, to find the cemetery at Grid Ref: 246268. A right-of-way here leads north over the fields to Point of Buckquoy.

If you have time and inclination for more, step north again from Buckquoy along a cliff path to reach Skipi Geo (Grid Ref: 248284) where there is an Arctic tern colony. On the edge of the inlet a huge whale rib is set into the ground, a dramatic reminder of Orkney's fishing heritage. Just the place to practise your sea-shanties.

9. HOY AND WARD HILL

Considerate parents gave me a small grand piano for my twenty-first birthday, and each night before I go to bed I play Beethoven. He never wins. After decades of mortal combat he always loses. Night after night I commit murder. One night, I discovered Peter Maxwell Davies lurking under a volume of Mozart and thought I would give him a bash. The work was 'Stevie's Ferry to Hoy', a haunting, beautiful melody. Not that I ever mastered the piece, but I recognise it and that's all that matters to me. Peter Maxwell Davies made his home on Orkney and is a mainstay of the Orcadian Annual Festival of Music. Arrange your visit in June and hear a hundred glorious voices ringing through the old red sandstone Cathedral of St Magnus in Kirkwall.

The Island of Hoy is an Orcadian enigma. It is unlike the rest of Orkney, more akin in character to the sweeping hills and moors of Sutherland. Hoy, the Norse word for 'high', is mountainous, almost roadless and absolutely majestic. Ward Hill, the highest peak, is only 477m but, because it rises so suddenly from sea level, it looks daunting. Ferries run from Stromness through Clestrain Sound to Burra Sound and the pier at Moness on Hoy. From the pier, there are a number of walks that vary in length between 5 and 16 miles. All have one thing in common: magnificent, unspoiled scenery and rarely another soul along the way.

A circular walk from Moness leads westwards from the ferry through Cuilags and Ward Hill, past Sandy Loch to the small village of Rackwick. wildflowers abound: sundew, butterwort, milkwort, trefoil, woodrush, bog asphodel and dog violet. Where the path meets a narrow single-track road, turn left and walk across the hill to Moness.

By the corrie of Nowt Bield and the ridge of Dwarfie Hamars is the

Dwarfie Stane. This is a huge sandstone block, a Neolithic grave measuring 8.5m long, 4.3m wide and 2.4m foot deep. Richard Feacham described it as:

> A passage and two cells have been cut in it, or hollowed out of it. The passage is seven foot six inches long, two foot six inches wide and two foot ten inches high. A square block of stone lying just outside the entrance was originally used to stop the entrance.

This burial chamber is unusual because most chambered tombs of the period were built above ground, rather than hollowed out of a convenient rock. Avoid the temptation of trying to crawl in; twentieth-century man is far too large. Walk back to the main road – well, the only road on the island – and down onto the beach. This is the quickest way back to the pier.

For a bird's-eye view of Hoy and, on a clear day, half of the north of Scotland, climb Ward Hill. After passing Sandy Loch, turn south and follow the line of Water Glen up to the summit. This is an easy climb and an amazing panorama waits. Sutherland mountains line the horizon: Foinaven, Arkle, Ben More Assynt, Ben Hope and the ragged ridge of Ben Loyal. North, in a magical multicoloured blue-and-silver carpet, lie the islands of Shapinsay, Rousay, Eday, Stronsay, Sandray and Westray. Pentland skerries guard the eastern approach to the firth. Across turbulent seas lies the deserted island of Stroma, flanked by Duncansby Head and the massive Caithness cliffs of Dunnet. Descend from Ward Hill down the edge of Howes of Quayana, a steep, ragged ridge of corries to White Glen and the Moness track.

For the boy or girl who likes a 'proper walk', two miles past Sandy Loch bear half-right and climb by Berrie Dale onto Grut Fea and across the plateau to view the famous Old Man of Hoy, a great stack rising 137m from the sea to the cliff-top. The moor here is home to hen harriers, merlins, buzzards, peregrines, and golden plovers. Great skuas greet invaders angrily, dive-bombing walkers in mighty swoops of flapping dark-brown wings.

As the ferry pulls away from Moness pier, hum a few bars of 'Stevie's Ferry' in gratitude. If you don't know the tune, fear not. I will be happy to play it for you at the drop of a quaver, provided you are prepared to take the risk of listening.

You will need OS Map 7, Pentland Firth, second series, Scale 1:50,000. Stromness Grid Ref: 255090; Moness Pier Grid Ref: 245039; Sandy Loch Grid Ref: 219030; Water Glen Grid Ref: 220025; Ward Hill Grid Ref: 229023; Howes of Quayana Grid Ref: 235020; White Glen Grid Ref:

242019; The Dwarfie Stane Grid Ref: 244006; Rackwick Grid Ref: 202992; Berrie Dale Grid Ref: 200015; Old Man of Hoy Grid Ref: 177008.

10. FARAID HEAD

Add spring to your step this morning. Escape for a few days from the torrent of political hogwash currently engulfing us and flee to the far north of Scotland. There, in private amidst the 'large religion of the hills', contemplate on how you should cast your precious vote in the next elections to the Scottish Parliament. Seek advice from the locals: firework-beaked puffins, kittiwakes, fulmars, guillemots, cormorants, grey seals, golden eagles, white-tailed eagles, buzzards, peregrines, coal-black ravens, otters and red deer. Ask the purple orchids, spotted orchids, mountain aven, mountain everlasting, shy primrose and Primula scotica where you should place your cross. They really know how to decipher a politician's manifesto.

The 'manifesto' for this nine-mile journey is OS Map 9, Cape Wrath, second series, Scale 1:50,000 and your start point is in the township of Durness (Grid Ref: 403677). Park by the community centre. Gavin Clarke built a work of art in its own right here, the dry-stone wall, from Bettyhill. Provision yourself for your journey at another 'work of art' in the village, Mrs Mackay's emporium.

Leave the car park and turn left towards Balnakeil. After 91m, bear north on to a track which leads over the fields to Aodann Mhor and the broken cliffs at Seanachsteal, where there are the remains of a Pictish fort (Grid Ref: 407697). More recent ruins are found as you progress further north along the cliffs to Faraid Head (Grid Ref: 390718): concrete huts and fortifications built during the Second World War. Why haven't these unhappy eyesores been removed? We are talking serious cliffs here, up to 91m in height. Keep back from the edge. There are splendid views south to two famous racehorse mountains, Foinaven (908m) and Arkle (787m). Both cuddies were great winners for the punters and for their owner, the Duke of Westminster. Westward lies the Parbh Peninsula and Cape Wrath, the Vikings' turning point on the route of their annual summer rape, rob and pillage cruises to our shores.

The well-marked path turns south at Faraid Head to reach one of the most perfect golden strands on planet Earth: Balnakeil Beach, one mile long, backed by high sand dunes and ultra busy if there are more than half a dozen people walking its margin. This is a favourite windsurfing and surfboarding location, providing you are neoprene-clad. At Balnakeil itself (Grid Ref: 391686), stop in the seventeenth-century churchyard and pay your respects to Rob Donn, the Gaelic 'Rabbie Burns' who is buried there.

Follow the road west now to the golf course and have a look at the famous ninth hole, a shot across the Atlantic where players have to reach the green by striking their balls across a wave-lashed cove (Grid Ref: 388688). Behind the clubhouse you will find a sandy track that leads round the side of the hill to a miraculous little water, Loch Lanlish (Grid Ref: 385683). This holds some of the most wonderful and difficult to catch wild brown trout in Europe.

Loch Lanlish is where I stock up on golf balls. It borders the sixth fairway and is an easy slice from the tee. I rarely manage to tempt the Lanlish trout, but I haven't bought a golf ball for years. They are all recovered from the loch during my fishing trips. The south end of Lanlish is a botanist's paradise. Mind where you tread. Leave the loch by following the fence line and climb gently to the site of the Dun overlooking the azure waters of deep Loch Borralie (Grid Ref: 385676).

Tramp east from the Dun down to the south end of Loch Croispol (Grid Ref: 390677). Shortly after leaving Croispol, you will find a track that directs you north to Balnakeil Craft Village. Have your wallet handy. The real prize here is the studio of Lotte Globb, a ceramicist of international renown. Lotte uses local materials to colour her work, which seems to me to express the very soul of my native land. Suitably laden from the studio shop, return to the start point along the minor road, a distance of about half-a-mile. If you have time, also visit the Smoo Caves (Grid Ref: 420677): 6m long, 4m wide and containing a waterfall 24m high in the inner cave. You will be in good company. Sir Walter Scott visited the caves during a tour of the far north. In 1826 he wrote three letters to the *Edinburgh Weekly Journal* in defence of the Scottish £1 banknote, entitled 'Thoughts on proposed change of currency'. Read them prior to casting your vote. They might add additional spring to your political currency.

I I. INN MOINE

This is the story of Inn Moine, built by 'The Mannie on the Hill', the largely unlamented George Granville Leveson-Gower, Marquis of Stafford and First Duke of Sutherland (1785–1833). His monstrous statue stands on

Beinn a' Bhragaidh (394m), towering above the town of Golspie on the shores of the cold North Sea. The Duke stares seaward, his back turned forever on the people he betrayed. Leveson-Gower was one of the richest and most influential men in Europe and he married Elizabeth Gordon, Countess of Sutherland (1766–1839). From 1810 onwards, through their agents, William Young, Patrick Sellar and James Loch, the pair set about 'improving' their vast landholdings in the far north of Scotland. Their purpose was to clear the land of people to make way for sheep, and in the execution of this policy they were unconscionably ruthless, demonstrating an almost complete disregard for the lives of those evicted. Little or no provision was made for the destitute, and the perpetrators, supported by local ministers, claimed that the clearances were in the people's best interest. News of what was happening gradually filtered south and James Loch rushed to defend his boss by publishing in 1820 a 'full account' of the 'improvements'. This fuelled the fire of public concern, expressed by a Staffordshire farmer, Thomas Bakewell. He wrote a 145-page rebuttal of Loch's whitewash job. General David Stewart of Garth was also outraged by Loch's duplicity. The general said: 'It is certain that there is no recent instance in which so much unmerited suffering has produced so little compassion.'

Inn Moine was, in my opinion, built as an attempt to redress the balance of public opinion. The tiny structure, measuring barely 7.3m by 3.6m, still stands at the side of the lonely track between the Kyle of Tongue and Loch Hope. It is a ruin now, bypassed by the realignment of the present A838 Tongue to Durness road, but in its day it was an exemplary public relations stunt. The Duke financed the construction of a road over the Moine and the Inn was erected for travellers crossing the moor. Ironically, the Inn's only guests now are sheep, but a fading plaque on the east gable, written by the loquacious Loch, reminds us that the Inn and road were made at the sole expense of his illustrious master for purely altruistic motives.

Inn Moine looks south towards Ben Hope (926m), Scotland's most northerly Munro, and the crenellated ridge of Ben Loyal (763m), the 'Queen of Scottish Mountains'. To the north lies the modest, gently rounded summit of Ben Hutig (408m) and this little hill offers a splendid view of the surrounding countryside and an invigorating moorland tramp.

You will need OS Map 10, Strathnaver, second series, Scale 1:50,000, to find your way round. Inn Moine itself is just off this map and may be found on OS Map 9, Cape Wrath at Grid Ref: 519601. However, it is impossible to miss the building. It is still the only structure on the moor.

Start the day by the bridge over Strath Melness Burn at Lubinvullin (Grid Ref: 568646,) close to the white sands of Strathan beach. A good track leads northwest up the hill from the road, reaching Loch na h-Uamhachd (Grid Ref: 556658) after approximately one mile. From there the going gets rough and should not be underestimated. Find the best route you can among the broken peat hags and heather banks.

Follow the inlet stream of the loch to little Loch nan Clach Geala (Grid Ref: 551656), then trudge up to the triangulation pillar on the top of Ben Hutig (Grid Ref: 539653). Leave the hill by descending the long southeast ridge. After a stiff walk of one-and-a-half miles you should pick up the line of an excellent peat road at Grid Ref: 548632 which leads easily back to West Strathan and the start point at Lubinvullin. Total distance covered, five miles. Time there and back, approximately three hours.

Choose a fine day for this expedition because its real joy lies in the mountain and moorland panorama along the way, and the outstanding array of wildlife: golden plovers, curlews, greenshanks, dunlins, red-throated divers, buzzards; sphagnum moss, tormentil, butterwort, sundew, bog asphodel, bog myrtle and spotted orchid. Spare a thought also for the people who used to live and work in the glens and straths of North Sutherland, and for their sad fate.

End your journey with a visit to a more robust, thriving inn, The Craggan at Melness, one of Scotland's best-kept secrets. The Craggan is perfectly situated on a hill overlooking Tongue Bay and Rabbit Islands and offers good food, good company and a relaxed welcome. Gaelic is the preferred language – and don't mention 'The Mannie on the Hill'. In these airts, to this day, he is *persona non grata*.

12. WINDS OF HOPE

Climbing Ben Hope (1,139m), our near neighbour and Scotland's most northerly Munro, is obligatory if you are a member of Clan Sandison. This applies to dogs as well as humans. All of our dogs have climbed it. I explained this to the latest addition to our tribe, Hareton, a scurrilous seven-month-old Yorkshire terrier. He is the successor to Heathcliff, erstwhile 'Lord of the Hills', who now lies at rest on the slopes of Ben More Assynt after 13 glorious years in the hill-walking business. 'Hareton,' I said as I hauled on my boots, 'you will just have to get used to it. This is the way it is going to be, always. Really, it's great fun, and just think, your first-ever Munro!' He seemed to understand and licked my hand in agreement. Flashing me a hideous white-toothed grin, he bounded off after his mistress who was waiting with his lead, whereupon they set off up the track and disappeared from view.

You will need OS Map 9, Cape Wrath, second series, Scale 1:50,000 for this adventure. Ben Hope is user-friendly and approachable, a comfortable amble over a two-mile long gentle ridge to the summit. Indeed, many climbing books suggest that Ben Hope and its near-companion, Ben Klibreck (961m), comprise a good day out; scale Hope in the morning then canter up Klibreck in the afternoon; just to properly stretch the legs, you understand. If you are keen to bag Munros in short order, this is eminently practicable.

But these peaks deserve much more than a quick up-and-down dash, particularly Ben Hope, which is one of my favourite mountains. On a fine day half of Scotland is visible from the top of Ben Hope. Most people climb Ben Hope from the farm shed, where the Dubh-loch na Beirine stream bustles under the road on its way to enter the south end of Loch Hope (Grid Ref: 462478). There is a noticeboard here advising that this is the 'way up'.

'Up' is the operative word: an unremitting slog on a muddy, narrow track to a break in the crags on the west face of the mountain. Thereafter, up again, without respite, to gain the rock-strewn summit (Grid Ref: 478501). I prefer to tackle Ben Hope the old way, as described by W.A. Poucher in his book *The Scottish Peaks*, published by Constable in 1965 and reviewed then as being the most comprehensive guide available: 'could hardly be bettered'. Poucher's route is longer, but is a much more pleasant and attractive way of spending a day out in the wilds of northwest Sutherland.

Another reason for using the old route, rather than the currently annotated way, at least for me, is the danger of setting a precedent. What is at the moment suggested could well become, by habit, the only allowable way; a thin-edged wedge into the concept of our responsible right of freedom to roam where we will in our native land. I don't like noticeboards, or their instructions.

Start your journey near the dramatic ruins of Dun Dornaigil Broch (Grid Ref: 458450), constructed by our Pictish ancestors some 2000 years ago on a green bank overlooking the Strathmore River. A track climbs east from Alltnacaillich Farm to a splendid waterfall (Grid Ref: 466455) on the Allt ma Caillich burn, the 'burn of the old woman', where there is a plaque on a rock commemorating the death on the hill of a young stalker.

Continue east from here to gain the summit of Carn-achaid (Grid Ref: 474447), the round-shouldered southernmost top of the Ben Hope massif. Now hike north along the broad ridge to reach Creag Riabhach (Grid Ref: 480474) and, after a further mile and a half, complete the final ascent up to the trig point and cairn on the top of Ben Hope itself. We had lunch at the cairn, where we were joined by a curious snow bunting and, on the way down, were surprised by a brace of ptarmigan, winter-white and almost invisible when stationary. A golden eagle circled overhead, quartering its territory on the lookout for unwary rodents or anything else on offer. A herd of red deer hinds and young stags marked our progress. We dropped down the base of the long line of Leitir Mhuiseil (Grid Ref: 470480) and followed the track along the bottom of the cliffs to regain the waterfall. As the sun dipped west behind the bulk of Foinaven (909m) casting dark shadows over the steel-grey waters of Loch Hope, evening echoes chummed us home. Back at the Broch, Hareton was still going strong. All dog, ready for more. I thought, Heathcliff would have been proud of his offspring.

13. THE KYLE OF TONGUE

Vigorous physical and mental activity this morning: an action-packed, drive, park and hike expedition around the Kyle of Tongue in North Sutherland in the 'Land of Clan Mackay'. This adventure lasts all day and you should pack OS Map No.10, Strathnaver, second series, Scale 1:50,000, lunch, stout boots, wet weather gear and repellent to ward off marauding midges.

Begin at the west end of the Kyle near Melness cemetery (Grid Ref: 574592). To the south of the cemetery is a grassy eminence, the site of a 6,000-year-old Neolithic settlement. The inhabitants were hunter-gatherers and shellfish was an important part of their diet. Excavations have revealed the remains of implements and pottery fragments. Some of their food – cockles, mussels, whelks and oysters – may still be found to the south of the cemetery wall.

Drive south down the west shore of the Kyle, and park near Kinloch at Grid Ref: 555531. On the hill to the west is Dun na Maigh, an excellent example of a broch: dry-stone towers constructed about the time of the birth of Christ. The walls of Dun na Maigh are 4.8m thick and the internal staircase, built into the wall, is clearly visible. Nearby (Grid Ref: 550525), on the north side of the Moine Path, are the remains of a chambered cairn, a burial place for Neolithic notables.

Examples of Bronze Age cup marks and sculptured stones come next at Grid Ref: 562525. There is a quarry on the east side of the road where, beneath the boughs of a birch tree, you will find a large boulder. Careful examination should reveal 18 cup markings which were probably of religious significance to their makers. A step further north brings you to another boulder inscribed with a remarkable set of intersecting lines.

Continue north and park at Grid Ref: 565530 on the brow of the hill overlooking Loch Hakel. This is the start point for a two-hour hike east to Druim na Coub (Grid Ref: 565520), where Clan Mackay and Clan Sutherland fought a furious battle in 1433, a blood-and-guts, broadsword and axe fight to the death. Then hike southwest to the remains of a 4,000-year-old Bronze Age settlement at Grid Ref: 570517, surrounded by the humps of 30 burial cists. One cist is exposed. You will find it near an obvious cairn of white stones.

Return to the southeast shore of Loch Hakel and the huge stone opposite the small, scrub-covered island. On the top of this stone you will discover the most perfect set of cup-and-ring markings in Europe: 30 cups, 11 of which are surrounded by inscribed rings. On the island itself is the Giranan, the tumbled remains of a Celtic fort, built about 2,500 years ago. Wade over and have a look. The perfect place for lunch.

The beach by the island was the scene of another fight in March 1746. A party of Jacobites, the survivors of a sea-battle fought in the Kyle of Tongue between the French sloop *Le Prince Charles* and the government frigate *Sheerness*, were ambushed here and forced to surrender. Before doing so they threw gold coins, destined for the Jacobite army at Inverness, into the loch. Some of these coins were still being found in 1840. Watch out for anything glinting in the heather.

Return anti-clockwise round the loch, enjoying views of Ben Loyal (764m) to the east, and drive north to park at Grid Ref: 585547 near the entrance to Ribigill Farm. A short walk east brings you to the remains of Scrabster Village, which was emptied of its people during the nineteenth-century Sutherland Clearances. All that remains are the outlines of their dwellings and the heaps of stones they gathered to enable them to cultivate their small fields.

A memorial to Ewen Robertson (1842–95), the 'Bard of the Clearances', stands nearby and bears these prophetic lines: 'In place of sheep, there will be people, cattle in the shieling in place of stags.' Look around the busy community of Tongue, at peat-smoke drifting lazily above cottage and croft. Spare a thought for these sad souls, forced by thoughtless human greed to abandon their native land.

End the day with a quick canter up to Castle Varrich which overlooks the village and the Kyle; a dramatic, Clan Mackay fortress, 10 metres high with 1.5 metre-thick walls. You will now be ready for rest and recuperation and, perhaps, a less-than-Neolithic cup of something that cheers. Find this in the comfort of the Ben Loyal Hotel in Tongue, or with Hamish Mackay amidst the happy ambience of the Craggan Inn across the Kyle.

14. HIKING WITH VIKINGS

No snow is good news for us. We live in a cottage at the end of a broken track which quickly becomes impassible to vehicles when the white stuff falls. I am told by those in authority in our household that walking up the hill, beast-of-burden-laden with shopping, is 'good for me'. I suppose it is, but so far this winter, these events have been mercifully few. We are lucky to be able to live and work in the wilds of north Sutherland. From our home in Tongue, we may step out from our front door straight into the wilderness. Dramatic mountains are our constant companions. Ben Loyal, Ben Hee and Ben Hope semi-circle the southern horizon. Less than an hour's drive brings us to more majestic peaks: Ben Klibreck, Cranstackie, Foinaven, Arkle and Ben Stack.

Our companions are the great raptors that live nearby. Hardly a week passes without us seeing a golden eagle above Sgor Chaonasaid (708m), the most northerly summit of Ben Loyal. Yesterday, as I tramped up the hill with my granddaughter Jessica, I pointed out an eagle. 'No, granddad,' the seven-year-old replied. 'It's a buzzard.' She was right. Jessica is always right. A couple of years back, during a huge storm, my wife Ann watched a pair of white-tailed eagles catching and eating seagulls that had been whisked into the shelter of our little glen.

Ann and I celebrated the new millennium by following one of our favourite walks; the one we promise ourselves we will hike every day, but somehow never seem to have time to do so. Find your way round using OS Map 10, Strathnaver, second series, Scale 1:50,000. The immediate predecessor of the current edition of this map had a picture on the front showing Castle Varrich, which we visited during our walk. The only trouble was that it had been printed back-to-front. This picture has since been replaced with a new shot, the right way round, of Strathy Point Lighthouse.

Park in the village (Grid Ref: 591566) across the road from the excellent Ben Loyal Hotel. Just past the Royal Bank of Scotland building, you will find a signpost pointing to Castle Varrich. The ruined castle dominates the village and the golden sands of the Kyle of Tongue. It pinpricks the sky on a craggy knoll at the north end of An Garbh-chnoc (124m). During our New Year walk, once clear of civilisation, Ann unleashed the 'hound from hell', Hareton, her ferocious Yorkshire terrier, who immediately hoofed it in hot pursuit of a rabbit.

The track leads down the slope to the margins of the Rhian Burn, bustling busily north to greet the shallow waters of the Kyle. The stream is surrounded by natural woodlands and is crossed by a wooden bridge. Blue tits, wrens and finches flit amongst the bare branches in search of insects and anything else to fortify them against the cauld January blast. The well-trodden path ahead used to be very muddy, but recently railway sleepers have been laid over the soggiest parts.

A few minutes after leaving the shelter of the forest, the track climbs steeply up to the old castle (Grid Ref: 580568). The ruins are in surprisingly good condition, given that they have sat there for more than 400 years. Castle Varrich used to be a Clan Mackay stronghold, although it was probably used even earlier by Vikings. They arrived in these airts towards the end of the ninth century. Castle Varrich is a simple square tower with an entrance on the north side, facing out across the Kyle Causeway to Rabbit Islands and Eilean nan Ron. Whilst sitting on a window lintel in the castle, I often wonder about the previous owners. Did some Norse granny take her granddaughter up the hill, talking about wildlife, whilst her husband staggered along behind with the weekend groceries? Did he remember to bring the front-door key with him, or had he left it in the longship? Still, there and back to the shore is only half an hour, with or without messages.

It is easy to extend this outing into a much longer day, and great fun to do so. From the castle, an obvious track climbs south round the shoulder of the adjacent cliff. This is the start of a splendid walk along the west side of the hill. Climb to the summit of An Garbh-chnoc (Grid Ref: 584559) and then continue south to reach Garbh Chnoc (Grid Ref: 570540). Return to the minor road past the north shore of Lochan na Cuilce (Grid Ref: 576535), then walk back to Tongue in time for tea and bickies in the village shop.

15. BEN LOYAL

A royal salute this morning, for Ben Loyal (784m), 'Queen of Scottish Mountains', in northwest Sutherland. Her Majesty is not tall by Munro standards, but she is mighty enough to make you catch a breath or two. Her dramatic crenellated ridge is one of the best-known mountain profiles in Scotland, gloriously crowned with four principal peaks. There are three subsidiary tops and this sublime ridge gracefully holds court over the crofting community of Tongue, by the yellow sands of the shallow Kyle. The name 'loyal' is most likely derived from the Gaelic word *high*, meaning 'law', hence the 'Mountain of the Lawgiving', a place where laws were made and proclaimed. The westerly outrider-peak of Ben Loyal is Sgor a'Chleirich, which may be translated from the Gaelic word *leircachail*, meaning 'clerical', or *cleireach*, meaning 'clerk'. Clan Mackay, who still rule in these lands, needed constant reminding that they should be law-abiding, which they rarely were.

Most lawful visitors climb Ben Loyal from the north, from Tongue, the shortest route to the summit. Park at Grid Ref: 584548 (OS Map 10, Strathnaver, second series, Scale 1:50,000), drag on the boots and follow the road past Ribigill Farm onto the moor. Within two miles you will reach a steading at Cunside (Grid Ref: 584515), crouched below the black tower of Sgor Chaonasaid (708m), Loyal's most northerly peak. After a further half-mile, gaining height over soggy ground between Ben Hiet and Sgor Chaonasaid, head southeast into Bealach Clais nan Ceap.

An obvious, steep, gully (Grid Ref: 585500) points the way up Sgor Chaonasaid. The track by the side of a peat-stained bubbling burn is muddy and well-tramped. Along the way, look out for the rusty remains of an aeroplane that crashed here during the Second World War. On the plateau, you will see the distinctive rock-cap of An Caisteal, the summit, half a mile ahead, with tiny Loch na Creige Riabhaich in a hollow on your left. Although the loch lies at an altitude of 518m, it contains very pretty wild brown trout. If you, as my wife and I do, carry telescopic fishing rods, this is the place to use them to catch supper.

The summit is surrounded on three sides by steep crags, but is easily gained from the north by a grassy slope. Enjoy the view; round-shouldered Ben Hope (926m), Scotland's most northerly Munro to the west, with Foinaven (908m) and grey Arkle (787m) beyond; Loch Loyal and Loch Craggie lie to the east. They are backed by the gold-and-purple wilderness of the Flow Country, pinnacled by Ben Klibreck (961m), Ben Griam Beg (580m), Ben Griam Mor (590m) and the distinctive cone of Morven (868m) in Caithness. To the north, across the broken waters of the Pentland Firth, lies Ward Hill (479m) on the Island of Hoy in Orkney.

Whilst the route described above is the quickest way to the top, it is not, in my view, the most pleasant. A more exciting expedition can encompass the main peaks during the course of a marvellous day out. Park opposite the Ben Loyal Hotel in Tongue and catch the post bus to Lairg. This leaves the village at about 9.25 a.m. Get off just before Inchkinloch (Grid Ref: 600444), at the south end of Loch Loyal. Angle north uphill to Loch na Beiste (Grid Ref: 589459) – where you will also find accommodating brown trout – and continue via Glas-choire Beag to the top of Cam an Tionail (714m), Ben Loyal's south peak.

An invigorating step north again, down and up, will bring you to the top of steep-sided Sgor a'Chleirich (615m). Immediately below the summit, on Druim na Coup, is the site of a bloody battle in 1431 between Clan Sutherland and Clan Mackay. The Sutherland men were routed, leaving more than 1,000 warriors dead in the heather. Return from Sgor a'Chleirich and climb to An Caisteal. The way ahead now is to go over Sgor a'Bhatain (700m) to the eagle's eyrie of Sgor Chaonasaid. Descend from Sgor Chaonasaid by the route described earlier to the main road and walk back to Tongue.

It will be unusual if, during the course of the day, you do not see golden eagles and you will almost certainly meet buzzards, ravens and peregrines. Amidst the high tops there are pretty blue banks of wild thyme and a host of other mountain and moorland plants. Red deer are abundant and you may catch a glimpse of a wildcat or fox. Back at base, catch a glimpse of either the Ben Loyal Hotel bar or the famous 'Brass Tap', with its sturdy stone floor and open fireplace, up the road in the Tongue Hotel.

16. BORGIE FOREST MEMORIAL WALK

'The Mannie on the Hill', a monument to the Duke of Sutherland, towers over the town of Golspie. The Duke obtained immortal fame during the nineteenth century by ruthlessly evicting 16,000 of his tenants to make way for more profitable sheep. Many find this constant reminder of the dreadful Sutherland Clearances to be deeply offensive but, in spite of all protest, the Duke remains firmly on his lofty pedestal. Plans are afoot to erect an alternative monument on a hill overlooking Helmsdale, to the north of Golspie, to commemorate the people who lost their homes and livelihoods to the Duke's rapacious 'improvements'. Preliminary drawings indicate that it will be a very grand affair, depicting a family clustered together, forlorn and helpless, facing an uncertain future. For me, however, the most significant monument of the Clearances is more modest, and more poignant for being so. It may be found at the entrance to the Borgie Forest in North Sutherland; a dry-stone wall at the centre of a small wood of native trees. The wall is built of stones collected from buildings abandoned during the Clearances. Local children planted 200 of the trees and the name of each child will be inscribed on a plaque by each tree.

Visit this unique memorial during a wonderful forest and moorland walk covering a distance of ten miles. You will need OS Map 10, Strathnaver, second series, Scale 1:50,000 to find your way round, although the majority of the route is along well-made forest tracks. Park off the A836 Thurso to Durness road at Grid Ref: 679580 and tramp south into the forest. It was planted on land gifted to the nation by the then Duke of Sutherland, to provide homes and work for 'heroes' who had survived the First World War.

After four easy miles, the track swings right (Grid Ref: 669515). At the end of the track, march on between the trees to reach a gate through the deer fence which leads onto the moor. To the south, Beinn Stumanadh (527m) and Creag Dubh (441m) guard the horizon. Ben Loyal (764m) and Ben Hope (927m) tower to the west. Pick your way north across the golden moor to Grid Ref: 655540, then angle northwest to meet the Borgie River.

An attractive suspension bridge crosses the stream (Grid Ref: 653546). If the river is in spate, it is worth turning south here and following the track for ten minutes to the Borgie Falls. Climb the path by the river to see the falls from above. The river hosts good numbers of salmon and there is every chance of catching a glimpse of them leaping upstream. Lunchtime!

Return to the suspension bridge and continue north, re-entering the forest at Grid Ref: 657551 via a gate and cattle grid. The river is on your right and the most pleasant route home is to cut into the forest and follow the west bank downstream. This provides more opportunities for seeing 'The King of Fish', salmon salar, going about his lawful business. The Borgie Forest is also unique in the wide variety of mushrooms and toadstools along its banks and amongst the trees. However, unless you are an expert, leave them to get on with their lawful business in peace as well. But they are spectacularly colourful.

The streamside track is muddy in places and eventually brings you to a small, wildflower-rich meadow (Grid Ref: 664578). Walk up to the cottage on your left to regain the forest track. Continue north now, to reach the children's millennium forest and the magnificent dry-stone wall (Grid Ref: 664585). Follow the circular path, Celtic in design, to the centre. There is an all-pervading sense of calm, as though life itself sprang from the old stones.

Recent tree-felling east of the track has exposed a short trail that had been a favourite hike for The Manager and me, particularly on windy days. But even now, we walk this way because it passes an irresistible bench by the riverside. There is a small memorial plaque on the back of the bench containing lines written by one of my great heroes, Hugh MacDiarmid. They always bring a lump to my throat when I read them:

> The rose of all the world is not for me
> I want for my part
> Only the little white rose of Scotland
> That smells sharp and sweet – and breaks the heart.

This is what my native land means to me.

17. GOING WILD IN SKERRAY

Grab your hiking boots and OS Map 10, Strathnaver, second series, Scale 1:50,000 and come with me on a magical journey along the jagged cliffs bounding Skerray in North Sutherland. Skerray means, literally, 'between the rocks and the sea' and this dramatic 11-mile walk will capture your soul. Your marine companions will be whales, dolphins and grey seals. Stiff-winged fulmars glide effortlessly by. Sea eagles may mark your progress. Scottish primroses, thrift and squill brighten the way.

The route brings you close to little Island Neave and its much grander neighbour, Eilean nan Ron (Island Roan) (Grid Ref: 640655), a North Coast 'St Kilda' lying one mile offshore from Skerray harbour. The halfway point of this walk is the deserted township of Sletell, where sheep now wander amidst the ruins of buildings once loud with the sound of children's laughter. The population of Skerray today amounts to less than 100, but it is a thriving, bustling place, as aware of its future as it is proud of its past.

Park by the post office in Lotts (Grid Ref: 674624), one of the 11 townships that comprise this coastal crofting community. There is a lot to do and see in Lotts. Two ruined houses scheduled for demolition have been marvellously restored, complete with thatched roofs. One is a vibrant museum and historical centre; the other is Jimson's, an Aladdin's cave of a shop, which could do serious damage to your chequebook. Adjacent to Jimson's is a small garden centre with a big reputation. The star of the show is a unique, world-famous chrysanthemum, rooted in Skerray and known as the Highland White Dream. Native trees – elm, ash, aspen, whitebeam, holly, pine and rowan – are grown from locally harvested seeds. Heathers, alpine plants and herbs scent the air. In nearby Borgie Forest a spiral path is being formed, based upon a Celtic design and leading to a magnificent dry-stone wall shaped like the stem of a leaf.

From Jimson's, walk south past the village hall and the red-roofed Free Church building until you come to the graveyard overlooking Torrisdale Bay (Grid Ref: 677621). Amongst the tall stones gathered here lies Alexander Macbeth, a Skerray man who died at the age of 97. Alexander was the first man to join the 93rd Sutherland Highlanders when the regiment was raised in Strathnaver in 1800 and he fought at the Battle of Waterloo.

After visiting the cemetery, turn left up the road signposted to Aird. At the last house, step out onto the hill and follow the cliff west. After two miles, the route descends to Skerray harbour (Grid Ref: 660638), guarded by Island Neave. The ruined building with the tall chimney is all that is left of the old Skerray shop. It used to house a bakery as well and in the early years of the last century it was supplied by sea from Orkney. For more than a hundred years, boats entering the harbour have used the chimney as a marker-point to find safe passage through the skerries to the quay.

As you climb from the harbour onto the cliff again, there are stunning views out to Island Roan. Although the island was probably inhabited during Neolithic and Pictish times, there is little evidence of these early settlers. However, in 1820, three families, evicted from their mainland homes during the Sutherland Clearances, moved to the island and built new homes for themselves. Eventually, 12 families, approximately 90 people, lived and worked on Island Roan as crofter-fishermen.

Two world wars and a decline in the prosperity of the fishing industry sealed the island's fate. By 1938, only 12 people remained. On 6 December, on a cold, clear, moonlight night, the last inhabitants left. But even now, those who once lived there yearn for the old ways: 'Although life was hard on Eilean nan Ron, we had food, fire and friendship, and when you have that nothing else really matters.'

Tramp on now, down past Lamigo Bay (Grid Ref: 650634) and Port an t-Strathan (Grid Ref: 644635). Sletell lies one mile ahead. Have your lunch looking out to Rabbit Islands and the golden sands of Tongue Bay. Walk home following the old track from Sletell that leads back to the main road at Loch Modsarie (Grid Ref: 646617). Go round the head of the loch and hike one and a half miles northeast across the moor to regain Lotts – the end of an unforgettable journey through Skerray, the magical land between the rocks and the sea.

18. LORD OF THE MOORS

Every dog must have its day. Even Heathcliff. Heathcliff and I enjoy a relationship based entirely upon mutual distrust. I know that the moment my back is turned he will be up to no good. He knows that the moment Ann's back is turned I will give him a less than dog-user-friendly pat in payment. We exist together in an uneasy state of armed neutrality, constantly on the alert for angst. Heathcliff goes everywhere with his mistress: up mountains; dinner parties; shopping; over soggy moors; bed; concerts; on beach walks; on holiday; the library; fishing expeditions; business meetings; and, on one unforgettable occasion, a wild, uncontrolled terrier race at a Game Fair. In the car, the brute travels stylishly, draped muffler-like round Ann's neck, his beady black eyes scanning the horizon in search of trouble.

Ann's strict rule, when Heathcliff was a lad, was that he must always be kept on the lead out-of-doors, even although we lived in a remote area in the north of Scotland. The need to do so became apparent after his first, and only, encounter with a sheep on the shores of Loch Treig near Fort

William. The dog had done another runner and I had spent an hour screaming over the hill, yelling, Cathy-like, 'Heathcliff, Heathcliff!' before I found him. A tup had trapped him in a tiny cove. Heathcliff, who detests water, was soaking wet and yapping plaintively; perched on a bare, wave-lashed rock a yard from the bank, faced by a hissing angry monster that would not go away. I recovered the poor beast and, after a pat, bore him back to his distressed owner. Ever since then, when sheep appear Heathcliff disappears, pronto, whether he is on the lead or not.

Which is why there is never any problem about birthday presents. Ann insists her little darling's birthday should include a decent walk. Before the statutory birthday cake, complete with candles, a once-a-year treat, properly served with Heathcliff, feet on the table, napkin round his neck, munching happily. The damn brute knows, too, almost to the minute, when the event is to take place. And also, on that day at least he is pretty safe from my tender love and care.

This year on his birthday we took Heathcliff on one of our favourite walks, between the mouth of the River Borgie and the mouth of the River Naver in north Sutherland. The walk combines the best of all worlds: a mile or so along a wonderfully deserted beach as well as a happy scramble over heather-topped Lewisian gneiss. There is something for everyone: wildflowers and geological formations for Ann, a wide variety of birdlife and prehistoric monuments for me, rabbits, hares and the chance of a quick roll in a dead seagull for Heathcliff. Pack OS Map 10, Strathnaver, second series, Scale 1:50,000 to follow the route.

We parked just before the Borgie hurries into Torrisdale Bay, where a small bridge crosses the river at Crossburn (Grid Ref: 681611). Wide, empty white sands lie ahead, dotted with oystercatchers, and we followed a winding track up onto the raised beach above the sea (Grid Ref: 684612). This is the site of mainland Britain's most northerly football ground, although the changing-room and goalposts have long since been blown away.

Aim for the left, lower, side of the hill. There is a small stream here and after crossing it you should find a track leading to the summit. The most instantly significant feature here is the windswept juniper. It has been uniquely moulded over the rocky landscape. There is also a profusion of wildflowers, including several rare species. The soil is lime-rich, enhanced by gale-shredded shells being distributed on the hill by seabirds. These plants, like the juniper, have also adapted to survival in their harsh environment. Many are dwarf species, hugging the ground for safety.

Once up, continue for a few hundred yards to find Loch Druim an Duin (Grid Ref:691611). If you are an angler and enjoy trout for breakfast, this is the place to catch them. You may also catch a glimpse here of red-throated diver and perhaps a shy otter. In winter, when the surface of the loch is frozen, otter footprints can be seen, as well as the sites of their 'play-slides'.

Leave the loch and climb gently to the edge of the cliff (Grid Ref: 697611) overlooking the mouth of the River Naver and the township of Bettyhill. The narrow strips of land on the side of the hill below Bettyhill are memorials to the Strathnaver Clearances of the early years of the nineteenth century. Families evicted from the fertile strath were each allocated a single plot upon which to live and support themselves. Evidence of the dwellings of previous inhabitants lie on the raised beach by the riverbank: hut circles built 5,000 years ago by Neolithic men. There are more than 20, buried in the sand, circular in shape and in all probability similar in style to the famous site of Skara Brae in Orkney. View them from the eyrie of another building, erected about the time of the birth of Christ, the Invernaver Broch; in its original form, 12m high and 12m in circumference. The ruins are still impressive today and provide welcome shelter during stormy weather.

Descend from the Broch to the raised beach and walk back to the start point along the golden beach. Meeting other people along the way is the exception rather than the rule. You will, however, be 'chummed' offshore by curious bewhiskered grey seals, and, overhead, by ominous black ravens. There and back takes about two hours, depending upon how long you linger. Just about far enough to give a small Yorkshire terrier a happy birthday.

19. FORSS CLIFFS

There is a 'Nelson Touch' to the lounge of Forss House Hotel in Caithness, an oak fire-surround made out of wood from HMS *Britain*, Nelson's flagship. At least, that is what the brass plaque claims, but search as I might, I can find no confirmation of this alleged fact, or indeed any indication that Nelson ever sailed in such a vessel. An HMS *Britannia* took part in the Battle of Trafalgar (1805), but she, 'a dull sailer', was the flagship of Lord Northesk. Of HMS *Britain* I wat not. Far more certain is the provenance of the cast of the salmon above the fireplace, a huge fish weighing 42 1b and caught on 14 August 1954, by David Coupar. This mighty salmon was taken from the Corner Pool, a narrow, deep pool, a couple of minutes' walk from the ivy-clad walls of the hotel. Landing it must have been a battle of similar proportions to the sea-fight off Cape St Vincent in which Britain's most famous sailor died.

Leave the hotel and cross the lawn to the gate overlooking the river. A convenient seat here gives a fine view of Falls Pool. After heavy rain, when the river thunders seawards, silver salmon leap the torrent on their headlong journey to upstream spawning grounds. A flight of steps leads to the foot of the falls and set into the wall of the cliff is another plaque, marking the resting place of the previous owner of the Forss, C.E. Radclyffe.

Otters fish the pool and prey on salmon lying below the falls. At daybreak, I have watched an otter catch a fish here and unceremoniously bustle it into the shallows to feast. Yellow wagtail flit amidst myriad flies and best bib-and-tuckered dippers hunt for aquatic insects, molluscs and small fish in the fast-flowing current. There is an old mill by the stream, long disused, a listed building, which was sedately degenerating into sad ruin but is now being restored. Return to the top of the steps and, skirting the hotel, walk down to the Corner Pool. Cross the wooden bridge and head north. An easy, wildflower-strewn mile will bring you to the mouth of the river at Crosskirk Bay. The broken waters of the Pentland Firth surge over black-scarred rocks, dashing salt spray against million-year-old cliffs. The stark cry of kittiwakes and fulmars fills the air and the dark, bewhiskered heads of grey seals mark your coming.

On the greensward above the bay stand the remains of one of the oldest places of worship in Scotland, St Mary's Chapel, dating from the twelfth century. The structure is now roofless, but the nave and chancel are well preserved, measuring approximately 5m by 3.3m. The surrounding tombstones guard the ruins where the holy men of the 'Land of Cat' once sang and prayed. Close by is the site of St Mary's Well, where they slaked their earthly thirst. More modern buildings cluster at the outfall of the river; a fishing bothy and the grey stones of a snuff mill, once powered by the stream; busily reducing tobacco to snuff for more than a century, legally and illegally. During the Middle Ages Caithness was a law unto itself, and smuggling was a common practice. Where better to offload contraband from passing vessels, wines, spirits and tobacco, than in the remote confines of rocky Crosskirk Bay?

From Crosskirk, follow the ragged coastline northeast along Ushat Head. The clifftop abounds with sea-pink, scentless mayweed, rose-root, mountain thistle, common primrose, cowslip, vetch, thyme, birds-foot trefoil and that most lovely and unique of all our northern flowers, Primula scotica; a cluster of vibrant blooms, deep crimson in colour, centred with bright yellow.

A good Scots mile, after passing over a less-than-obvious raised beach, brings you to Brims Ness. Incorporated into the farm buildings by the shore are the remains of Brims Castle; one of the many Clan Sinclair castles and strongholds scattered throughout Caithness from the Ord to the North Sea. The only battles that take place here today are on the crests of the waves that roll down from Iceland; Brims Ness is a favourite location for surfing competitions.

Walk south from Brims and take the first exit on your right. This peaceful country lane will lead you comfortably back to the Forss House Hotel in good time for a rewarding, refreshing draught; well-supported by Horatio Nelson's ancient timbers and under the glassy, circumspect gaze of Mr Coupar's wondrous fish.

20. DUNNET HEAD

General George Armstrong Custer's ancestors on his mother's side were Caithness people, from the small town of Castletown which overlooks the broken waters of the Pentland Firth. When Custer and 211 men of the US 7th Cavalry fell at the Battle of the Little Bighorn on 25 June 1876, did he think of his Scottish antecedents? Sitting Bull, who commanded the Indian army, later recounted Custer's last stand: 'The Long Hair stood like a sheaf of corn with all the ears fallen around him. He laughed. He had fired his last shot.' The general and his companions died with their boots on.

Drag your boots on this morning and stand with me by the lighthouse at Dunnet Head (91m), the northernmost point of mainland Scotland. The red cliffs of Hoy on Orkney scar the northern horizon. The Merry Men of Mey, where the cold waters of the Atlantic meet the grey North Sea, dance frenetically even on the calmest of days. The air is loud with the cry of kittiwakes and fulmars. Gannets dive and feed in crystal-pristine depths. During winter months, there is always the chance of spotting Great northern divers, Iceland gulls and Glaucous gulls.

The tourist route to Dunnet Head by car is along the B856, a tortuous, winding road leading to the top from the gentle levels of St John's Loch and the old church in Dunnet Village. The church was built in the sixteenth century and Timothy Pont, the Scottish cartographer, was appointed minister in 1601. Pont surveyed most of Scotland during his life, 'visiting even the most remote and savage districts of the kingdom.' Many of the maps he laboriously compiled are presently housed in the National Library of Scotland in Edinburgh, where they have recently been scanned into a computer system.

Avoid the tourist route and scan instead OS Map 12, Thurso, Wick and Surrounding Area, second series, Scale 1:50,000 to find our route to the lighthouse, built around 1832 by Thomas Stevenson, the father of Robert Louis Stevenson, one of Scotland's best-loved writers. Park at Grid Ref: 209713 in West Dunnet and find the peat track leading steeply over the moor past the House of the Northern Gate. This dramatic, isolated, clifftop dwelling used to be the home of the late Commander and Lady Vyner, famous for making Sheffield steel and an assortment of knives and forks. Lady Vyner was a friend and companion of the Queen Mum, who used to visit the House of the Northern Gate. The Queen Mum fell in love with the area and subsequently bought and renovated the old Castle of Barrogill, which was renamed 'Castle of Mey'. The original structure was built between 1566 and 1572 by George, 4th Earl of Caithness and the restoration has carefully preserved many features of the ancient Z-plan tower; corbelled turrets, great hall and gaping gun holes.

Our track now descends to a sheltered, sandy beach and climbs again on to the cliff top. There are vertigo-inducing glances down to the sea along the way, where white-fringed, green waves dash endlessly against the Old Red Sandstone black-scarred rocks. In wild weather, flung spume from these waves splashes the path and it is important that you keep back from the edge. Stay safe on the narrow path and detour inland when the wind howls. A not unknown occurrence in these airts.

At Grid Ref: 192725, step northeast to find little Loch of Bushta which can't be seen from the path. The south end is smooth and sandy and on warm days this is the perfect place for an invigorating splash. You will not be disturbed, other than by the red-throated divers that are invariably seen here. Return to the track and continue north, round the headland to the lighthouse, a distance of approximately three miles.

From the lighthouse, follow the road south down to Many Lochs, on your right at Grid Ref: 205752. Leave the road here and tramp the track at the south end of the first loch. After 15 minutes you will find yourself back in the wilderness; hiking over peat hags, heather banks, sphagnum tussocks and sweet-scented bog myrtle. March due south for one mile past Loch of Muirs to pick up another peat track at Grid Ref: 202732. This will lead you to the start point. There and back is a moderately taxing nine miles, but because the route is exposed and covers a deal of soggy going, be well shod and suitably clad. A compass and map are essential should a sudden mist descend. Avoid making this journey your 'last stand'.

21. SINCLAIR AND GIRNIGOE CASTLES

Puffin time this morning – the bird that is, not lungs – in Caithness, on a stark, clefted cliff close to Noss Head near Wick. To find 'Tammie', the dialect word for puffins, walk round the northeast stone wall enclosing Stevenson's lighthouse and bear quarter left to a dip in the hill. The promontory before you divides two geos, the local name for a steep-sided sea-inlet. Keep close to the left of the knoll and within a few yards find a narrow but safe natural stone seat overlooking a sheer drop of some 30m. Settle comfortably and watch.

Directly across from the seat, in the sandy soil surmounting the sandstone cliff, are a series of puffin burrows, now busy with firework-beaked parent birds feeding their single offspring. They do so for the first six to eight weeks of the fledgling's life. Thereafter, the adults, having done what they consider to be their duty, abandon the chick. The flightless, hungry little bird flaps one night to the edge of its burrow, then takes the quick route down to the sea – very much a case of sink or swim. Tough, being a burgeoning puffin.

Caithness cliffs are like sea-bird-filled tenements; loud with the squawk and squabble of stiff-winged fulmars, kittiwakes, guillemots, razorbills, black-backed gulls and marauding Great skuas. Springtime flowers riot on the clifftop and on the yellow sand dunes which scimitar nearby Sinclair's Bay: thrift, sea-pink and vetch; rare Primula scotica with its light-green leaves and vivid purple flower; sea rocket, sandwort, chickweed and hawkweed; field gentian, campion, wild pansy and knapweed. A good-to-be-alive time for all creatures great and small, where every step heralds the approach of long, light-filled summer days.

Start your walk at the tiny fishing village of Staxigoe, where my paternal grandfather was born and where my father's uncle had a small farm. In times past Staxigoe was an important harbour that could often be crowded with more than 70 boats. A few vessels still fish from Staxigoe, for lobster and crab, but its glory days are gone. You will need OS Map No 12, Thurso and Wick, second series, Scale 1:50,000 to see you round. Park at Grid Ref: 385524 and, skirting Field Farm, walk north along the edge of the cliffs. A comfortable, sea-salt-swept couple of miles brings you to Noss Head, the lighthouse and the puffin colony at Grid Ref: 388550.

Scurrilous scoundrels have described the Caithness climate as consisting of nine months of winter interspersed with three months of bad weather. Nothing could be further from the truth. Some of the hottest days I have known have been spent lazing on 'secret' Sandigoe beach, just along from Noss Head. The perfect place for a coffee break. Hike down to the sands and spend a few moments gazing in awe-struck wonder at the endless white-capped, blue-green waves sweeping the golden shore. There is also a good chance of seeing rock doves, rock pipits, shags, eider ducks and oystercatchers here.

Return to the clifftop and stalk out to the gaunt grey ruins of Sinclair and Girnigoe Castles (Grid Ref: 369550). The most notorious incumbent, George, the 4th Earl of Caithness, murdered his son, John Sinclair, here in 1576: 'Keiped in miserable captivity for the space of seven years.' John's alleged crime was that he failed to slaughter the inhabitants of the town of Dornoch, as he had been ordered to do by his outrageous father. The real reason, however, was probably that John had married a Sutherland Mackay and produced an heir before his father had managed to produce an heir more to his liking with his own new wife. John was deprived of food for a week, then given copious quantities of well-salted beef to eat. When he asked for water, it was refused and he died, choked by his own swelling tongue.

Your walk may be extended from the castles, north to Ackergill Tower (Grid Ref: 354547); used to billet the officers of Cromwell's army when they visited Caithness in the seventeenth century and now wondrously restored as an exclusive conference centre and luxurious retreat for busy business executives from around the world. The Tower also boasts the most northerly opera house in Britain. A step further brings you to the glorious sweep of Reiss Beach and the mouth of the River Wester (Grid Ref: 347576). Retracing your steps to the start point is no hardship. The whole walk, there and back, is 11 easy miles of constant delight.

22. CAMSTER CAIRNS AND LOCH WATTEN

Times ancient and modern today, in Caithness, with a visit to the 5,000-year-old Grey Cairns of Camster, followed by a hike round the shores of Loch Watten. The cairns are Neolithic burial sites where tribal leaders were laid to rest. The central chamber of the long-horned cairn is one of the most dramatic and atmospheric places I know. It is accessed, on hands and knees, by a 6-metre-long narrow corridor. I have often sat there and communed with the spirits of the builders of these astonishing monuments. The cairns were erected centuries before the pyramids of Egypt became even a twinkle in the beady eye of any Pharaoh.

Use OS Map No 12, Thurso and Dunbeath, second series, Scale 1:50,000 to find your way round. The Grey Cairns are easily located adjacent to the minor road between Watten and West Clyth at Grid Ref: 259452. They used to dominate the open moorland, but in the mid-1980s tax-avoidance forestry boys moved in and planted great swathes of Christmas trees nearby. An information panel explains essential details and wooden walkways have been laid across the bog to help keep your feet dry.

After leaving the cairns, drive north through Watten Village and park on the left of the road at Grid Ref: 250558, just before the railway level crossing. The walk round the loch is approximately seven miles and takes three hours, or longer depending upon how often and how long you stop to stand and stare. Tramp anti-clockwise. On the north side, and at the west end, avoid debilitating burns when necessary by a brief recourse to convenient railway bridges. Along the way, look out for the site of further burial cairns near Lynegar at Grid Ref: 227567.

However, the real joy of this walk, particularly during winter months, is the wide variety of birds. Caithness is like a Crewe Station for Arctic and Scandinavian feathered visitors. For them, it is the perfect short-haul winter holiday destination and they arrive in their thousands from October onwards. There are grey-lags and white-fronted geese, flocks of straight-necked whooper swans, wigeons, pochards, goldeneyes, tufted and long-tailed ducks. In hedgerows and stubble fields you will find redwings, fieldfares and bramblings. Other visitors include waxwings, redpolls, snowbuntings, dunlins, turnstones and purple sandpipers. Carrying binoculars is as essential as lugging along a packed lunch.

We lived in Caithness for 17 years in a house overlooking Loch Watten. An enduring memory of that time is the sound of birds 'talking' and 'chattering' to each other through long, cold winter nights. No human mind could ever conjure up such magical music. I would stand, shivering under the star-studded blue-black canopy of sky, bewitched by their cacophonous symphony. The ethereal song they sang was as old as time itself, unchanged for thousands of years and yet newborn, vibrant and mystical every time I listened. Another delight of this walk is the chance of seeing otters. The loch is full of delectable trout and is regularly visited by otters in search of food. One afternoon, near the west end of the loch, I watched a mother and her three cubs playing for half an hour by the water's edge. These graceful creatures are my favourite animals.

As you round the top end of the loch, known as 'Shearer's Pool', and walk down the south shore, stop by the red-roofed boathouse for lunch (Grid Ref: 212569). I remember once, when setting out for a fishing expedition from here, almost dying of fatigue and embarrassment. As I laboured over the starting rope of a recalcitrant outboard motor, my son, Blair, smiled knowingly from the shore. Eventually he said, 'Try turning on the petrol, Dad, I think you will find it makes a difference.'

Reach journey's end by the outlet burn, where the loch tumbles into a channel connected to the Wick River (Grid Ref: 248552). On the B870, hang a left and walk past Watten Lodge to regain the start point. The Scottish Executive has confirmed the international importance of Loch Watten as a bird sanctuary. Plans are afoot to recognise the water, along with four other Caithness lochs, as a European Special Protection Area. I am quite certain the builders of the Grey Cairns of Camster would approve, mightily.

23. WHALIGOE STEPS AND HILL OF YARROWS

Take a step down this morning, in fact 365 steps down, to reach Whaligoe Harbour on the east coast of Caithness, a few miles south from the county town of Wick. Captain David Brodie of Hopeville constructed these dramatic steps and the little harbour they serve in 1788. The steps cost £8 to build and Brodie's intention was to develop Whaligoe as a herring station. Attractive government bounties were paid on each vessel fishing and on every barrel of herring cured, and local businessmen were keen to exploit this largesse to their own advantage. The 'silver darlings' were the staple diet of Highland people then, eaten with tatties, and the early years of the nineteenth century saw the herring fishing industry expand dramatically. By 1840 more than 1200 boats were busy and Caithness was the most important herring fishery in Europe.

Find Whaligoe and the steps on OS Map 12, Thurso, Wick and Surrounding Area, second series, Scale 1:50,000, at Grid Ref: 321404. Turn east off the A9 Inverness–Wick road by a row of cottages. At the end of the row you will find a parking area. Walk round the large house on the edge of the 50-metre-high cliffs to reach the top of the steps. Descend with care. As you do so, think of fishwives coming the other way carrying wicker crans of herring on their heads. Savage entertainment. Thomas Telford (1757–1834), road builder and engineer, surveyed the Caithness fishing ports in 1790 on behalf of the British Fisheries Society to identify which ones could be expanded. He thought Whaligoe 'a dreadful place'. It is, in the true meaning of the word: 'producing great fear.'

In spite of their antiquity, the steps are in excellent repair. This is not by accident but by design, the design of a local lady, the late Mrs Juhle, who cared for them selflessly for several decades. Mrs Juhle reasoned that since Jesus was a fisherman there was every possibility that at His 'second coming' He might arrive at Whaligoe. She was determined that He would find the steps in a fit state to receive His feet. Since Mrs Juhle's time, the steps deteriorated and were in danger of becoming unusable. Now the work involved in their maintenance has been taken over by the Wick Heritage Society and the steps are again in safe hands. Visit the Society's outstanding museum in Wick. It will mightily enhance your understanding of Whaligoe and the great days of the Caithness herring fishing industry.

Climbing up the steps will make you catch your breath, but, once you have, travel even further back in time by visiting the astonishing array of Neolithic and Pictish monuments scattered around Warehouse Hill (Grid Ref: 309413). Begin at Garrywhin Cairn (Grid Ref: 313411), where human skeletons and pottery fragments were found. Hike now to Garrywhin Fort (Grid Ref: 314414) overlooking little Loch Watenan. The ruins crest the ridge and the entrance to the fort at the north end, through an 2.4-metre-thick wall, is considered to be the most impressive example of its kind in Scotland. To the east, at the bottom of the hill, are the famous Garrywhin Stone Rows (Grid Ref: 313413), consisting of a chambered cairn with six rows of slabs radiating southwest, the longest row being 61 metres in length.

From Garrywhin, strike northwest for one mile across the moor to reach the summit of the Hill of Yarrows (646 ft) at Grid Ref: 296428, for an overview of the country the Vikings called their 'Land of Cat'. On your way, you pass further Neolithic remains and a chambered cairn at Grid Ref: 304422 and another small loch, the Loch of Warehouse, at Grid Ref: 300424. This is the place to catch your own cat's supper, if you are so inclined and so blessed. There are some superb brown trout in the loch, but be warned, they are 'dour'.

The foreground view from the top of Hill of Yarrows is disfigured by commercial forestry, but lift up your eyes to the horizon and a splendid vista of moorland and water entraps the soul; to the north, a distant prospect of the Orkney Islands; east across a sparkling blue sea pegged with the black of oil drilling platforms. Return to Whaligoe by tramping two miles southeast;

in time for a quick dash down the A9 for rest and recuperation in the welcoming embrace of the Portland Arms Hotel at Lybster.

24. SILENCE AT SANDWOOD BAY

We don't have 'sleeping policemen' in our neck of the far north. Traffic calming is a more natural affair, provided free of charge by five donkeys. They patrol the middle of an eight-mile 'beat' of the A838 Bettyhill to Rhiconich road, assisted by assorted blackface and North Country Cheviot sheep, highland cattle and the occasional cuddie out for a post-prandial stroll. Believe me, these guys know how to slow traffic, a lot.

You will find Rhiconich at Grid Ref: 257524 on OS Map 9, Cape Wrath, second series, Scale 1:50,000. Hang a west here, signposted to Kinlochbervie on the B801. This busy fishing port is abbreviated locally to 'KLB'. It lies on the north shore of blue Loch Inchard, backed by dramatic mountains in the Reay Forest; the jagged ridge of Foinaven (908m), the long, grey shoulder of Arkle (787m) and graceful little Ben Stack (721m).

Drive past KLB to find Oldshoremore, Oldshore Beg and a series of magnificent, white sand, unspoilt beaches. Be calm. Linger awhile. There is a good caravan site at Oldshoremore, as well as plenty of B&Bs, guest houses and hotel accommodation. Relax here for a few days and discover the magnificent serenity of this special corner of northwest Sutherland. King Hakkon of Norway lingered awhile in Loch Inchard on his way to Largs in 1263 to have a serious chat with young Alexander III about who really was boss-man in the Western Isles. Hakkon's huge Viking fleet was virtually destroyed and retired to Orkney, where the Norwegian King died. The rest, as they say, is history.

Apart from the challenge of scaling the aforementioned peaks, all of which offer a tremendous day in the wilds, there is another hike here not to be missed; the walk out to Sandwood Bay (Grid Ref: 220653). These airts are now owned and carefully cared for by the John Muir Trust, who welcome responsible access. Support their work. When The Manager, my wife Ann, and I first tramped this way many years ago, we didn't see another soul. Fings is busier now at Sandwood, ever since our monarch-in-waiting, Bonnie Prince Charlie, gave the bay his imperatorial seal of approval by making a well-publicised visit. However, compared to the hiking hoards you encounter further south, Sandwood is deserted.

Park at Blairmore (Grid Ref: 195600). There and back to Sandwood is an easy eight miles, with a good track all the way. This makes the expedition a walk for all ages, particularly ideal for little legs. The bay is, in my opinion, the most beautiful in Scotland; two miles of golden sand washed clean by Atlantic waves born a thousand miles beyond the western horizon. Northwards, sand mingles with green and emerald hills that stride in an amazing array of stark, black cliffs towards the high point of Cape Wrath. To the south, the slender dark stack of Am Buachaille, 'the herdsman', guards the entrance to the bay. Behind the dunes, Sandwood Loch sparkles in summer sunlight, surrounded by green fields specked white with safely grazing sheep. If ever there was a place to find calm, then Sandwood Bay is that place.

At the end of our day, on our way home, The Manager and I often stop at the Rhiconich Hotel for rest and recuperation. Well, that's what I call it. Rhiconich also has a reputation for 'sleeping policemen', of the donkey sort. One Easter, a few years back, a crofter was herding his animals north towards Durness. Donkeys are not the kind of creatures that can be hurried and their master soon found he had a considerable convoy of vehicles in his wake. Undaunted, he and his donkeys plodded on, in the middle of the road, oblivious to the growing angst of the drivers in the cars behind. Horns were tooted and fists were shaken. Eventually, after about half an hour, the crofter left the animals to get on with it and wandered back to the lead car in the procession. The red-faced driver was but a microsecond away from serious donkey rage. As the crofter approached, the driver wound down the window and prepared to give him a piece or three of his mind. Before he could utter a word, however, the crofter bent down and spoke to him. With the ineffable politeness to be found only amongst members of Clan Mackay, he asked the driver, 'Excuse me, sir, but can you tell me, is this the way to Jerusalem?'

25. FOINAVEN

We were sitting, enveloped in mist, below Ceann Garbh (901m), the north top of the Foinaven Ridge in northwest Sutherland. Visibility was just about enough to steer a coffee cup mouthward. 'I hear voices,' said Ann. At these moments I find the best course is to pretend indifference. 'Listen, you must have heard that?' Not a whisper assaulted my senses. 'Are you deaf?' Still nothing. No sound other than the wind.

That's a lie, really. I could hear the roaring in my ears and my heart thumping after the long haul up the hill from Clach a'Bhoineid on the A838 Durness–Laxford Bridge road near Rhiconich. The way over the moor to the foot of the slope winds between blue lochans and black pools speckled with ankle-breaking peat bogs and damp holes. And we had stopped at Lochan Cul na Creige for our traditional morning fight. This ritual is supposed to be a pause for route planning, plotting the way ahead, and we rarely agree. It seemed to me that the best plan was to keep to the north side of the Loch na Claise Carnaich inlet stream, then cross the glen only when we were adjacent to where the crag steepened on the east side of Creag na Claise Carnaich, rather than cross the stream immediately and angle up the side of the hill to reach the same point.

My better half had arrived at exactly the same conclusion, but by the time we had finished 'discussing' the matter, we both believed that the other had decided upon exactly the opposite route. Neither of us wishing to further distress the other, we plodded uncomplaining up the soggy hillside, although by the time we stopped for a breather I had murder in my heart.

Foinaven (908m) is one of Scotland's most dramatic mountains, a few rocks short of a Munro, but absolutely magnificent. The classic approach is from Lone on the shores of Loch Stack. Walk in from the road at the south end of the loch, past Airdachuilinn, and continue on the stalkers' path by Arkle (757m) towards Creagan Meall Horn (729m). Below the summit of Creagan Meall Horn, leave the path and climb easily north to gain the start of the Foinaven ridge. Once up, you are confronted with the 'Black Tower', a tricky descent down loose scree and up again, but thereafter it is a joy all the way to Ganu Mor, the highest point on the ridge overlooking Strath Dionard and the green slopes of Cranstackie (800m) to the north. This is golden eagle and raven country. Not seeing them is the exception, rather than the rule. Inquisitive snow buntings sometimes join you for coffee.

And as for Ann's voices – she was right. Out of the mist came a line of men. As they approached, I heard one say to his companion: 'Thank God we didn't come up this way, it must be a killer.' Perspicacious, I mused, still panting. I guessed that this was one of John Ridgway's parties from Ardmore, where he runs his Adventure School. The leader, a fit-looking Aussie, gave us a cheery wave as he bounded by, but I nobbled one of the tail-enders. 'Could you give my cousin a message?' I asked. He looked at me as though I'd taken leave of my senses. 'When you pass Waterfall Cottage, pop in and ask him if he and Rita could come over next Saturday.' My cousin lives next door to John Ridgway. I suppose that if you come from London or Birmingham the last thing you'd expect atop a Scottish mountain is to be asked to issue dinner invitations. He agreed, suspiciously, and disappeared down the hill.

I felt better after that, good humour restored, and we continued our ascent to the top of Ceann Garbh and then on up the edge of the ridge to the twin cairns on Ganu Mor. The weather changed for the better too, opening up a stunning vista of grey-black cliffs, white cloud-filled corries and golden moorlands with the silver ribbon of the River Dionard below, winding seawards through the golden sands of the Kyle of Durness. The damnable thing about climbing mountains is that you have to come back down. I could have happily stayed forever in this dreamland.

We retraced our steps, stopping from time to time to drink from crystal-clear streams. The evening air was full of the sound of meadow pipits and curlews. As we approached the head of the inlet stream to Loch na Claise Carnaich and the route of our unpleasant earlier assent, unhesitatingly, and without a single word, we crossed to the other side.

Use Os Map 9, Cape Wrath, second series, Scale 1:50,000. Start point Grid Ref: 280546; Lochan Cul na Creige Grid Ref: 282532; inlet stream Grid Ref: 286530; Creag na Claise Carnaich Grid Ref: 295522; Cean Garbh Grid Ref: 314514; Gaun Mor Grid Ref: 316507.

26. GOING UP ON BEN STACK

Have a dizzy day out. Climb Ben Stack (721m) in northwest Sutherland. It is steep, steep, steep. On the final pull up to the summit, I stopped to catch my breath and admire the view. Instant vertigo ensued, more throat-catching than anything ever dreamed of by the film director Alfred Hitchcock. I peered back down into the lift-shaft of the faint track and shuffled closer to the security of a large moss-covered boulder.

Far below, snug in its green forest, lay the white-painted doll's house of Stack Lodge. The River Laxford ribboned west through the green strath to meet the broken seas of the Minch. The shoreline of Loch Stack zigzagged wildly round its leaden waters. A coal-black raven whisked by, croaking mockingly at my discomfiture. I could just make out the red dot of our car, parked by the shepherd's bothy on the Lairg to Scourie road.

I raised my eyes. To the north, shafts of silver sunlight pierced billowing clouds gathered above Foinaven (908m) and the grey bulk of Arkle (757m). Ben Hope, Ben Loyal, the Ben Griams and the peatlands of the Flow Country beckoned to the east. Southwest, across the golden moor to

Assynt, rose the mystical ridge of Quinag (808m), one of the most dramatic and wonderful of all Scottish mountains.

The landscape I surveyed had lain unchanged since the end of the last Ice Age. It is an old friend of mine. I looked out over a vast array of sparkling blue lochs and lochans, most of which I had explored during fishing expeditions with family and friends. On the moor, I noted the small, scrub-covered island in Loch a'Mhuirt, the 'Murder Loch'.

A man with a beautiful wife once lived on an island in the Murder Loch. Lord Reay coveted the woman, who rejected his advances. To gain possession of the woman, Reay had the husband murdered. As compensation for her loss, he gave her a loch nearby that is known to this day as Loch na Mnatha, the 'Woman's Loch'.

Many of the waters are unnamed on the Ordnance Survey map (Sheet 9, Cape Wrath, second series, Scale 1: 50,000), but they have local names: Boot Loch, Pound Loch, Otter Loch and Granddad's Loch. Granddad was an enormous trout of over 8 lbs in weight. I never managed to tempt Granddad to rise to my fly, no matter how carefully I presented it on the surface of the water above his lair by a red-decked rowan. And there is Mrs Little's Loch, where my six-year-old daughter caught her first brown trout. Begin your expedition at the shepherd's bothy (Grid Ref: 265437), where there is room to park the car. A good stalkers' track leaves the road here, winding up the west shoulder of Ben Stack. Follow the track until you arrive by a gatepost at Grid Ref: 259432 overlooking Loch na Seilge. Turn left and, with the inlet stream to Loch na Seilge on your right, begin the ascent of Ben Stack. Until you reach the first line of crags, the going is wet to downright soggy. The track is sometimes difficult to identify, but, with patience and concentration, you should have few problems and as you climb higher, the way ahead becomes obvious. If in doubt, angle to the north. Before the summit (Grid Ref: 269424) the climb eases, and there is a wide, grass-covered mini-plateau. From here, the last few hundred yards revert to being steep and the track narrows.

Because of the strength of the wind, The Manager and I approached the top on our hands and knees. For the same reason, discretion always being the better part of foolhardy valour, we did not traverse the short ridge to the second, lower, east summit.

Three hours should see you safely up and down, but it is easy to plan a longer expedition. Do this by obtaining a copy of Tom Strang's excellent guide, *Walk Sutherland*, published by the Scottish Tourist Board and available from most tourist offices. A splendid expedition is to hike the Ben Stack ridge and then continue east, descending from the mountain via the shoulder of Leathad na Stioma (Grid Ref: 284410) to regain the A838.

Ideally, however, to avoid the roadside hike back to the shepherd's bothy, you need a second car waiting.

Little Ben Stack dominates the wild highlands of the Reay Forest. It is the heart and soul of one of the most amazing and precious wilderness lands I know. This splendid mountain is nothing less than a glorious shout of unbridled joy, a shout that will echo unendingly throughout your life. Get there if you can.

27. ARKLE WALK

The controversial visit to the UK by Emperor Akihito of Japan reminded me of Scotland's Burma Road, a stalker's path in northwest Sutherland. Find it on OS Map 9, Cape Wrath, second series, Scale 1:50,000. The track starts on the north shore of Loch Stack at Lone (Grid Ref: 309422) and winds east through the wilderness for eight miles to reach Gobernuisgach Lodge (Grid Ref: 438418) in green Strath More. The original path was built long before its infamous East Asian railway namesake, but after the Second World War the track was widened. Those involved in completing this tortuous task christened the new way the 'Burma Road'.

The Burma Road gives easy access to three superb mountains: Arkle (787m), 'the hill of the level top'; Meall Horn (777m), 'the hill of the eagle'; and Sabhal Beag (732m), 'the hill of the little barn'. These peaks lie in the Reay Forest and those intending to walk this way, as a matter of courtesy, should announce their intent to the estate factor at Achfary (Tel: 01971 500221) prior to setting out. Park at Grid Ref: 297402 on the A838 Lairg/Laxford Bridge road and cross the inlet stream to Loch Stack. Follow the path northeast out to the bothy at Lone which is reached after a distance of one-and-a-half miles.

I prefer miles, feet and inches to kilometres, metres and centimetres. You know where you stand with feet. At least I do. I suppose it is because I was brought up using proper maps, scaled at one inch to the mile rather than the present insensitive 1:50,000 editions. I find it hard to learn these new-fangled European tricks. Rugby was never the same to me after they abolished the 25-yard line. I still swim in yards, not metres. I even hanker after a forpit of earth-spattered tatties, rather than hygienic pre-packed spuds in kilos. Munros are mountains over 3,000ft in height, not 914.4 metres. Corbetts are over 2,500ft, not 762.0 metres.

Arkle and its grand neighbour Foinaven (2,980 ft) (there, I feel better already) are as well known as racehorses as they are Highland summits. In equine form, Arkle and Foinaven both won the Grand National, much to the delight of thousands of happy punters. This thought brings a special spring to the steps of eager hillwalkers. To visit Arkle, hike north from Lone up the line of the Allt Horn burn for just over a mile, climbing through a little plantation of conifers onto the south shoulder of the mountain. Leave the comfort of the track at Grid Ref: 321432, where two tiny streams tumble down from Meall Aonghais (Grid Ref: 320445). Plod northwest up the hill, keeping well clear of the crags on your left. A mile and a half of heavy breathing will bring you safely to the cairn at the top of the south summit.

The summit is broad and scattered with broken, sparkling, quartzite rocks interspersed with delicate blue patches of wild thyme. But the way ahead round the scimitar ridge narrows as you make the final approach to the north top. Care is needed here in bad weather. There are sudden, ankle-breaking clefts that could catch you unawares. Concentrate. Watch where you put your feet. Arkle is a highly user-friendly mountain on a fine day, but in winter conditions, or in mist, unless you are an experienced hillwalker, it is best to keep off. In any case, the real pleasure of climbing the peak is to enjoy the view from the top. A misty summit and visibility of a few yards is but poor reward for the effort involved in getting there.

I could bang on a bit about the view and I think I will. It is, quite simply, one of the most outstanding vistas in all of Scotland, dominated by the fantastic ridge of Foinaven: Coir a' Chruiteir, the dark, knife-like slash of Cadha na Beucaich leading on to the promontories of A' Cheir Ghorm and Gaun Mor, the highest point on Foinaven. The corries to the north and west of Arkle cup blue waters: Loch an Easain Uaine (the loch of the green waterfall), Loch na Tuadh and scattered Loch an Tigh Shelg. As I gaze down at them, I remember happy days spent fishing there, the trout caught and the ones that got away. And, of course, I think of these treasures in comforting pounds and ounces.

28. ASSYNT ADVENTURE

I wish I had known the poet Norman MacCaig. His verses about Assynt, where he spent much of his life, are some of the finest ever written in the English language. He captures the soul of the land and its people. In 'A Man in Assynt', MacCaig asks:

Who owns this landscape?
Has owning anything to do with love?
For it and I have a love-affair, so nearly human
We even have quarrels.

There have been many quarrels in Assynt; from the days when Viking raiders visited these broken hills in search of food and slaves, to the time of the Highland clearances, when Assynt was emptied of people to make way for sheep. Much has changed today, not least of which being the famous 'victory' of the Assynt crofters, when they bought the land they worked and formed the North Assynt Estate, ushering in a new era of hope and certainty.

Our walk this morning follows the eastern boundary of that estate; from Tumore (Grid Ref: 185267) on the shores of Loch Assynt in the south, over the moor to Grid Ref: 156314 near Nedd in the north. This is a public right of way. Find the route on OS Map 15, Loch Assynt, second series, Scale 1:50,000. The path is well marked and easy to follow and there and back is an enchanting nine miles of pure joy. However, in wet weather, you may have to detour from the track to find suitable crossing places over the burns that tumble down from the vast bulk of Quinag (808m) which towers to the east. But they are narrow streams, so you will have no difficulty in jumping over – in any case, a damp foot or two is no real hardship to hardened hillwalkers like us, is it? Dogs is different, particularly our little Yorkshire terrier, Hareton. He hates water and has to be 'ferried' to safety by The Manager.

Norman MacCaig was also an angler. During his long life he tramped every inch of these hills in search of sport; although I suspect, like me, carrying a fishing rod was more of an excuse for being there, rather than a serious intention to remove red-spotted brown trout from their natural habitat. Nevertheless, returning to base with a couple of brace for breakfast is always welcome. Filleted and fried in oatmeal – the trout that is, not the angler – they make a meal fit for a king, or maybe even fit for the First Minister of the Scottish Parliament.

The start of the track is rather difficult to spot when driving, but look out for it just past Lochassynt Lodge. Take care when doing so, because this is a fast stretch of the A837 Ledmore–Lochinver road. Park on the wide verge on the south side. A signpost, which still manages to retain the word 'Nedd', points the way north. Cross the stile adjacent to the red-painted gate and tramp uphill to reach the Bealach Laeireag, 'the broad saddle', (Grid Ref: 191282).

The west face of Quinag is your constant companion; a magnificent sandstone ridge, spread out over a distance of two and a half miles, from jagged Spidean Coinich in the south to the rounded top of Sail Gorm in the north. As you descend from the Bealach, the Uidh an Leothaidh burn chatters busily on your left. Stopping to drink from such a stream, Norman MacCaig once wrote:

> Its water goes down my throat
> with a glassy coldness,
> like something suddenly remembered
> I drink
> its freezing vocabulary
> and half understand the purity
> of all beginnings.

A further mile or so brings you to Loch an Leothaid and its small western satellite, Loch Uidh na Larna. Resist the temptation to stop and fish. This will be more appropriate on the return journey. Follow the outlet stream from the loch down through natural woodlands of rowan and birch to reach the B869 Ullapool–Lochinver road. Lunch by the wooden bridge over the crystal-clear waters of the Abhainn Gleann Leireag.

Returning to the start point by the outward route adds to the pleasure of this splendid walk. There is the astonishing vista of the Quinag ridge to the east and, back at Loch an Leothaid, the happy business, if you are so disposed, of catching breakfast for the following morning. They won't be too heavy to carry home, averaging about 7oz in weight, but you couldn't buy finer fish anywhere.

However, the real prize comes as you regain the Bealach Leaireag and begin the final descent. The mountains of Assynt leap from their heather bed in a mighty hymn of praise, Canisp, Suilven and Conival. In their majestic presence, you 'half understand the purity of all beginnings'.

29. QUINAG IN ASSYNT

Macho I am not. Nor is Heathcliff, Ann's Yorkshire terrier. We were both worried, glued to a ridge flanked either side by 305-metre chasms. I tried reason: 'Listen, Heathcliff, we have come this far, what on earth is the point of going back now? Just don't look down. It's perfectly safe.' Secretly, I crossed my fingers. Inch-by-inch, his hairy face twisted into a hideous, white-toothed grin, the dog inched along the broken ridge. 'Come on, you can do it,' I exclaimed, encouragingly. Safely at my feet, Heathcliff rolled over onto his back, tongue lolling, legs in the air. I gathered him up and tucked him in my jersey. 'Wimp,' I muttered, relieved. The descent from Spidean Coinich on Quinag in North West Sutherland is exposed, but, with care, it presents no real problems. Unless you happen to be a Yorkshire terrier. Clutching the little dog, I caught up with my better half waiting anxiously below and after suitable admonitions regarding future good behaviour, we reformed and marched on towards Bealach a'Chornaidh.

Quinag is one of my favourite Scottish mountains, a dramatic, crenellated ridge, towering over Loch Assynt in the south and Kylesku to the north. Spidean Coinich gives Quinag its name. In Gaelic, *cuinneag* means water spout, and the jagged peak of Spidean Coinich closely resembles the pouring-lip of a gigantic water jug. The views across Assynt from the summit of Quinag are stunning; a magical mountain and moorland vista of sunlight and shadow, scattered with blue lochans margined by silver seas; a cathedral of endless skies encompassing a hillwalker's delight.

Above Loch Assynt are the famous Inchnadamph limestone caves: deep caverns where prehistoric human and animal remains have been found; and in the ravine of the Traligill River, the Vikings' 'Troll's Burn', an astonishing array of wildflowers: alpine saw-wort, purple and mountain saxifrage, mountain aven, and dark-red helleborine.

Use OS Map 15, Loch Assynt, second series, Scale 1:50,000 to find your way round. Park in the small quarry (Grid Ref: 233273) to the east of the A894 Skiag Bridge–Kylesku road. Cross the road and splodge over wet ground to reach the broad shoulder of Spidean Coinich at Grid Ref: 220270. The ascent of Quinag from here is easy going over huge stone pavements, degenerating into broken rocks before the summit. Nearing the top, keep to the left, away from the sheer cliffs guarding the eastern face of the mountain.

The way off the top of Spidean Coinich is not immediately obvious. Find it on the west side of the summit. Descend cautiously along a narrow track, down to Bealach a'Chornaidh. The climb to the subsidiary summit involves some deep breathing and scrambling but is perfectly safe. North of Spidean Coinich (Grid Ref: 207278), in sheltered corries, pockets of fine stone-weathered yellow sand lie scattered amidst gigantic boulders, etched with mauve and purple lichens.

You may skirt the next intermediate top (Grid Ref: 201279) and walk on towards Sail Gorm. Take care at Grid Ref: 197296, particularly in poor visibility, where the track runs very close to the edge of a precipitous gully. We lunched by the cairn on Sail Gorm, overlooking the graceful sweep of Kylesku Bridge, specked with speeding, Dinky toy cars. A snow bunting joined us and we chatted about this and that with the friendly bird, scatteing him crumbs as we talked. A bible-black raven soared by, eyeing us curiously, calling crossly, as ravens tend to do. The heather Isle of Lewis lined the western horizon and we dozed away a few lazy moments of absolute peace.

Leaving Sail Gorm, we retraced our steps to the saddle east of the subsidiary peak. From there, we walked out to Sail Garbh (Grid Ref: 209293), the highest point of the ridge, and then on to the end of the ridge to view the magnificent Barrel Buttresses at Grid Ref: 215299. Again retracing our steps, we returned to the saddle and angled across and down the shoulder of the subsidiary peak to Bealach a'Chornaidh (Grid Ref: 200285). From this point, above Lochan Bealach a'Chornaidh, look out for the faint path over the moor and follow it above the north side of the loch. This grows into a good stalker's path that leads comfortably back to the car park. The end of a memorable day.

30. CANISP

Canter up Canisp (846m) this morning. There and back is an easy four hours. Indeed, some hillwalking pundits suggest the walk is 'boring' and complain that dear old Canisp is just too gentle and good-natured to give hikers a sufficiently vigorous ride. Not me. I love Canisp.

It was the first Assynt peak my wife and I climbed and we did so to celebrate our twenty-fifth wedding anniversary. Nor did we reach the top on that initial April ascent, being driven back by serious snow and a howling gale. So, regardless of what alleged pundits might say, take care. Choose a good day and be fully prepared for your attempt. Assynt weather is notoriously fickle and being caught in a blizzard on any hill is no laughing matter.

You will need OS Map 15, Loch Assynt, second series, Scale: 1:50,000 to see you through the day. Park by Loch Awe at Grid Ref: 250159 on the A837 Ledmore Junction–Lochinver Road. A track leads down from the road to a foot bridge over the River Loanan, the outlet burn from Loch Awe which tumbles north for three miles to its meeting with windy Loch Assynt near Inchnadamph. The way to the top of Canisp is obvious, at least it is in fine weather; otherwise, you will need to use your compass. Cross the soggy moor to reach the north end of Loch na Gruagaich (Grid Ref: 244160) then squelch up the slowing rising wide shoulder of the hill. From this point the summit of Canisp is obscured, but it lies three miles northwest.

The reason you should choose a good day is because the ascent of Canisp opens up one of the most magnificent views in all of Scotland. Canisp may concede height to, among others, Ben More Assynt (998m), but it still provides an eagle-eye vista of the surrounding peaks: the sandstone shock of Suilven (731m), the Viking's 'Pillar Mountain', thrusting up from its Lewisian gneiss base; the triple tops of Quinag (808m), guarding the north shore of Loch Assynt; Conival (987m) and Ben More Assynt itself; and, to the east, the glorious peaks of the Inverpolly National Nature Reserve: Cul Mor (849m), Cul Beag (769m) and the distinctive, craggy crest of Stac Pollaidh (613m), keeping watch over the blue waters of Loch Sionascaig.

Small cairns dot the hill, but these are of little significance to route-finding. Just plot the most direct course to the summit. However, one of these stone piles has been shaped into a high-altitude 'cloche' and it contains and protects a very healthy rowan. The last time we passed, about two years ago, the tree was still doing well and German friends sent us a photograph of it, still thriving, last year. But I very much doubt it will ever reach a significant height, given the fearsome weather conditions it has to contend with.

Plod on over broken slabs of rock and deer grass mixed with heather and suddenly, almost without warning, you will find yourself on the summit (Grid Ref: 203188). There is a welcoming hollowed cairn in which to have lunch and from which to gape at the view. Suilven looks near enough to reach over and touch its highest point, Caisteal Liath.

If going up is spectacular, then, believe me, coming down is even nicer, not only for the compelling vista of mountains, lochs and moors, but also for the special pleasure of chumming the sparkling waters of Allt Mich Mhurchadh Gheir to their home in Loch na Gruagaich. Descend from the summit to Meall Diamhain and then drop down to the source of the burn, a small, unnamed lochan at Grid Ref: 220183. If you have supper in mind, and are carrying collapsible trout rods, as we do, then this is where to catch a brace of brightly red-speckled brown trout for the evening meal. Having done so, follow the growing stream past limestone outcrops rich with wildflowers and deep, clear pools, perfect for a skin-bare splash on a hot summer day.

Canisp is gentle and good-natured and it bids welcome to all shapes and sizes of walker, fit and not so fit, young and not so young. Canisp is a happy mountain, full of the sound of lark and meadow pipit, a mountain that casts a magic spell that draws you back, year after year. No matter how often we stalk its fine corners and secret corries, we always find some new, until then, hidden joy. This wonderful, great grey-shouldered hill is to us endlessly exciting. Never, ever, boring.

31. BEN MORE ASSYNT

The quickest way to clear any room in Castle Sandison is for my wife, Ann, to suggest a walk. Residents and visitors alike, with single accord, lunge for the nearest door, claiming compelling, urgent business. 'Mother's Walks', as they have become known, are renowned. They are synonymous with great pain, great distance, and great effort; indelibly stamped with wet feet, muddy trousers, torn jackets, bumps and bruises. One Christmas, in Northumberland, the tribe, full of Yuletide goodwill, succumbed to Ann's innocent suggestion of an afternoon walk. Pleading insanity, I managed to escape. The last I saw of them was a distant line of distraught figures, Ann leading, tramping through the snow towards the nearest river. Five hours later, worried, I got the car out and set off in search of my wife and children. They appeared through the night, wet, bedraggled and worn out, but happily safe and sound.

But undeniably, these walks are good for me and although I complain, moderately, I have to confess I really enjoy every step of the way. Well, most of them. Certainly, without Ann's encouragement I doubt I would be as fit as I am, and although I may not be able to tackle the more serious Scottish mountain assaults, I generally manage to get there eventually.

Which thought cheered me not a lot during a recent attack on Ben More Assynt (998m), the highest mountain in Sutherland. The most direct route is along the north bank of the Traligill River, past the famous Inchnadamph Limestone caves in Gleann Dubh, followed by an unrelenting, stiff climb up on to the shoulder below Conival (987m) and the Big Rock. The weather was cold, wet and windy, with low cloud obscuring our way ahead.

I persuaded Ann to try a less taxing, left-flanking movement, up Allt Poll an Droigh-inn burn, a tributary of the Traligill River, to more gently gain the plateau of Beinn an Fhurain. It seemed a good idea at the time, but the burn was in spate after three days of near-continuous rain and we tramped to the foot of the crags below Loch nan Cuaran before we could safely cross.

Once over, true to form, Ann started straight up to gain the ridge, but I insisted on a traverse below the crags to find an easier approach. Which led directly to a deep, dangerous gully. We climbed, Ann carrying her beloved companion, Heathcliff, over the most difficult, rocky section. My better half was not greatly amused by my path-finding ability, but, being too out-of-breath and too courteous to argue, she held her peace. Indeed, to this day, Ann has not reproached me, although at the time I noticed a steely glint in her blue eyes.

Approaching the top, we met a man and his daughter coming back down. The little girl, who was about eight years old, was sensibly tethered to her father by a 'lead'. As the pair passed, the man glanced at Heathcliff and said to Ann, 'Mine doesn't bark.' The remainder of the walk was magnificent, including the rough, exposed, rock-strewn ascent to Conival. At the top, the clouds cleared and we were rewarded with an unforgettable view of half of the north of Scotland. A treasured memory for the dream bank of the mind.

Coming back was even nicer, descending steeply to the Big Rock, then down the series of waterfalls that grow into the bubbling, crystal-clear Traligill River. As we tramped the last few soggy miles home to the car park near the Inchnadamph Hotel, I asked Ann if she had enjoyed her day. She smiled: 'There and back by candlelight, Bruce, well done. Can't wait to tell the children all about it.' Death, where is thy sting?

You need OS Map 15, Loch Assynt, second series, Scale 1:50,000. Start of walk Grid Ref: 261216; Glenbain Cottage Grid Ref: 264217; Beinn an Fhurain Grid Ref: 290218; Big Rock Grid Ref: 298209; Conival Grid Ref: 303199; Ben More Assynt Grid Ref: 320201.

Further information: The Sutherland Tourist Board, Tourist Information Office, The Square, Dornoch, Sutherland. Tel: 01862 810400; Fax: 0862 810644.

32. THE BONE CAVES OF ASSYNT

Nothing quickens the pulse more than the roar of a rutting stag, and never more so than when that sound is heard close-up and amplified by the walls of a prehistoric, limestone cave. Ann and her walking partner, Sue Fothergill, heard the beast when they were lunching in the second and the largest of the famous Allt nan Uamh 'Bone Caves'. The caves are situated on the slopes of Breabag (815m), to the east of A837 Ledmore to Lochinver road in Sutherland.

Sue was playing her recorder at the time, an adjunct of their walks together, and the sudden, primeval challenge of the red deer was entirely in keeping with the plaintiff, human sounds emanating from within the depths of their ancient shelter. Excavations in the caves have revealed the evidence of human habitation dating back to early post-glacial times, including the remains of bear, lynx, lemming and reindeer. No doubt these Mesolithic people also made music after a hard day's hunting and gathering in Assynt; secure in their cathedral-like home, crouched around their eternal fire; men, woman and children in close harmony with their environment. Did their spirits respond to Sue's song, and was it the first time music had echoed round these walls for 7000 years?

You will need OS Map 15, Assynt, second series, Scale 1:50,000 to find your way round. Start at the roadside at Grid Ref: 252179, where a track leads up the north bank of the Allt nan Uamh burn. There and back to the caves will take two hours. More time should be allowed, however, in order to enjoy the flora and fauna along the way. This is limestone country, particularly rich in wildflowers, including several rare species such as mountain saxifrage, mountain aven, globeflower, holly fern and serrated wintergreen.

Halfway up the burn, at Fuaran Allt nan Uamh (Grid Ref: 263178), 'the spring of the burn of the caves', you will find an astonishing, natural water garden; a wide, green sward, alive with a magical, crystal flow which quickly gathers into a tumbling stream. In the stillness of the glen the sound of other, unseen, underground streams can be heard, busy about their master's business in the soft limestone below.

The caves lie at the foot of a prominent limestone cliff and the ascent to the caves and the descent from them is steep and can be demanding. The track is narrow, one-person wide and built close into the side of the hill. Negotiate it with care and caution, particularly in wet weather. However, it is well constructed, marvellously camouflaged and an excellent example of environmentally friendly design.

Another excellent example of classic design is the sign of God's hand on the geological landscape of Assynt. The rocks of Assynt draw visitors and students of geology from all over the world, such is their renown; the oldest being Lewisian gneiss, which was formed in Precambrian times some 2,800 million years ago, followed by the Torridonian sandstone of mountains such as Suilven and Cul Mor. The best way to appreciate the geological history of Assynt is to go there and see for yourself; armed with the first-class guide prepared by D.R. Shelley which is based upon a 56-mile motor trail which takes you round all the significant sites. The guide is illustrated and divided into 18 sections, each one devoted to a particular place of geological interest. Obtain a copy of the guide from the Lochinver Tourist Information Centre, which also has, at the front of the building, a display and explanation of the principal rocks of Assynt: Lewisian gneiss, Torridonian sandstone, quartzite, limestone, pipe rock and Assynt marble.

For further walking adventure, consider extending the day into an assault on Breabag itself, a straightforward hike and an invigorating day out amidst the wilds of Sutherland. From the Bone Caves (Grid Ref: 267171), continue up the line of the burn then climb northeast to the little lochan at Grid Ref: 284178. Avoid the steep crags to the east by skirting round them to reach the summit plateau from the south.

From the summit of Breabag, a splendid view awaits. To the south, the long, grey shoulder of Canisp (846m) backed by the Viking's 'Pillar Mountain', Suilven (731m), and, in the distance, Cul Mor (849m), Ben More Coigach (743m) and the jagged spire of Stac Pollaodh (613m). To the east lie Conival (987m) and mighty Ben More Assynt (998m), the highest mountain in Sutherland.

The western panorama is dominated by the graceful, exciting shape of Quinag (808m), guarding blue Loch Assynt. And, in the distance, across the lands of the Assynt Crofters' Trust and the fractured, fjord-like coastline, the far horizon is darkened by a faint outline of the 'heather isles', Lewis and Harris in the Outer Hebrides.

33. BEN KLIBRECK

There are two Munros, Scottish mountains over 3,000 foot in height, in my backyard: Ben Hope (927m), 'the hill of the bay' and Ben Klibreck (961m), 'the hill of the speckled calf'. Munro-bashers on a tight schedule climb both in one day. Living so close to the peaks, my wife Ann and I can afford to adopt a more leisurely approach. Klibreck offers a designer-day out. There are a variety of routes to the summit and no matter which you choose, the beauty of this majestic peak will captivate you. Use OS Map 16, Lairg and Loch Shin, second series, Scale 1:50,000 to find your way around. The most direct and popular ascent to the trig point on Meall nan Con (961m) (Grid Ref: 586299) starts from Vagastie (Grid Ref: 535283) on the A836 Lairg–Tongue road. There and back takes about three hours.

An alternative, circular, tour begins near the village of Altnaharra at Klibreck Farm (Grid Ref: 588344), on the shores of Loch Naver. From the farm, climb steeply south to gain the subsidiary summit of Meall Ailein (721m) (Grid Ref: 613314). Once there, tramp south–southeast to reach Meall nan Con. Thereafter, continue south again to master Creag an Lochain (807m) (Grid Ref: 576280). Return to base by descending to Loch na Uan, reputed to hold monster wild brown trout, and follow the outlet stream north from the loch to regain Klibreck Farm. The total distance covered during the day is approximately nine miles.

However, with a modicum of pre-planning, those who enjoy a longer day out can mount a more thorough investigation of this splendid mountain by using the post bus to reach their start point. Park your car at the post office at Altnaharra (Grid Ref: 867354) in time to catch the bus, which arrives there from Tongue at about 10 a.m. Ask the driver to let you off at the Crask Inn (Grid Ref: 525248), a 15-minute drive further south.

Crask holds the UK record for the lowest temperature ever recorded, 29 °C. I remember it well. We were driving home past Crask that night and were frozen and snowed in for weeks thereafter. A step from Crask brings you to a bridge over the River Tirry, where a forestry track leads east up the north bank of the stream. Follow this track for two easy miles to Grid Ref: 568246, then climb northeast onto the lower shoulder of the Klibreck ridge.

The beauty of the mountain and the surrounding scenery unfolds as you gain height. Loch an Fhuarain, cupped in a dark corrie below the sheer sides of Creag an Lochain (807m) (Grid Ref: 576280). The blue chain of Loch a'Bhealaich and Loch Choire, feeding the River Mallart into one of Scotland's most notable salmon streams, the River Naver, a favourite fishing venue of HRH Prince Charles. The deer forest of Ben Armine lies to the east. Ben Loyal, Queen of Scottish Mountains, and Ben Hope rise to the north. In the distance, westwards, the sharp dramatic crest of Foinaven in Reay Forest.

From Creag an Lochain, tramp due north along the grassy ridge to greet the final hard pull up to the top of Ben Klibreck. Nearby, you will discover a substantial dry-stone shelter. Time for lunch. Loch Naver sparkles at the foot of the mountain, with the white shape of the Altnaharra Hotel guarding the head of the loch. Spare a thought for the people who lived there and were evicted from their homes during the monstrous Strathnaver Clearances in the early years of the nineteenth century. The first township to be cleared, at Grummore (Grid Ref: 610366), now hosts a caravan site. Look north and east also, to mark the tip of Ben Griam Beg (580m), the site of the highest Pictish hill fort in Scotland, and the Flow Country of

Caithness and East Sutherland; bounded by the mountains of Morven (706m), Smean (509m) and the grey Scarabens (626m).

Continue northeast from the summit, along the ridge to Meall Ailein (Grid Ref: 613314). From there, locate the stalkers' path which leads due north, back down the hill to Klibreck Farm on the shores of Loch Naver. Descend with care; the hill is very steep and can be dangerously slippery after rain. Walk back to the main road in time for a quick glance into the gillie's bar at the Altnaharra Hotel. The beer is splendid and the talk even more so. After a taxing 12-mile day, you deserve a reward!

34. BEN GRIAMS

Father's car broke down along the narrow, desolate road that winds over the moor from Kinbrace in the Strath of Kildonan to Syre in Strathnaver. He huffed and puffed under the bonnet whilst my mother, my brother and I kept quiet in the back of the car. Father was a short-tempered man at the best of times, and never more so than during a crisis.

Suddenly, out of the mist, a shepherd appeared on a rusty old bike, trailed by a rusty old sheepdog. He stopped and asked if he could be of assistance. Father, black to the eyeballs by then, grudgingly agreed. After a few moments the shepherd announced: 'Just you give it a turn when I give you the nod.' He nodded, Father turned the key and the engine sprang to life. Delighted, Father thanked him: 'You must be a mechanic,' he said. 'Oh, no,' came the reply, 'I am a Mackay from Strathnaver.' And with that, he mounted his bike and peddled off into the storm. That was 40 years ago, but I remember the incident every time I travel this way and I say a silent 'thank you' to our unknown saviour. The B871 is still one of the most lonely roads in Scotland and it lies on the edge of the internationally renowned Flow Country. The only refuge here is the Garvault Hotel, crouched in splendid isolation in the wilderness and noted in the Guinness Book of Records as being mainland Britain's most remote hotel.

In recent years, large tracts of the Flow Country of East Sutherland and Caithness have been devastated by tax-avoiding, blanket forestry which has irreparably damaged a landscape that had lain largely untouched by the hand of man since the last Ice Age. What remains is an irreplaceable treasure, a vital part of Scotland's natural heritage.I often tramp the Flow Country and one of my favourite areas for doing so is in Badanloch, to the north of the Garvault Hotel. The hotel is an unpretentious family affair, comfortable and well run, and it offers guests excellent value for money in accommodation and sustenance. It is a noted venue for anglers and lovers of wild places.

The river Helmsdale, one of Scotland's most productive and private salmon streams, rises from an interconnected series of lochs to the south of the hotel: Badanloch, Loch nan Clar and Loch Rimsdale. Ben Griam Mor (588m) and Ben Griam Beg (579m) dominate the northern horizon. Park at the Garvault Hotel and walk eastwards across the moor to pick up the stalker's path on the slopes of Ben Griam Mor. After about a mile, leave the path and climb to the summit of the mountain.

On the summit you will find a well-constructed stone armchair waiting to receive your weary limbs, and the view is magnificent. Ben Loyal and Ben Hope crown the western horizon, and the Reay Forest peaks: Foinaven, Stack and Arkle. To the north lies the Flow Country. As you descend northwards from Ben Griam Mor, plan your route ahead in order to avoid the dampest areas of the moor. It can be soggy and waterlogged and the going is often rough-to-miserable.

But the Flow Country is magnificent, in spite of the often adverse weather conditions. It is a land of sphagnum moss tussocks, golden plover, dunlin and greenshank, scattered with interdependent lochs and pools peopled by red-speckled trout, both black-throated and red-throated divers and playful otters.

Ben Griam Beg lies to the east of Loch Druim a'Chliabhain where there are the remains of a Pictish hill fort, the highest such hill fort in Europe. The outline of the fort is still easily discernible; a stone wall enclosing an area of 152m by 61m, with the entrance to the north. Small, circular stones with holes in the middle were discovered near the site some years ago. Perhaps they were used as weights for fishing-nets?

From the summit of Ben Griam Beg, descend northwest, walking round the north shore of Loch Druim a'Chliabhain, then due south to the boathouse on the west shore of the loch. Meet the stalker's path and walk back to Garvault. The last time Ann and I did this journey, we rested on our return journey by a small lochan. A greenshank joined us. He bobbed on a peat bank, piping plaintively: 'Oh dear me, oh dear me', the sure sign of an approaching storm. Moments later the skies opened with a vengeance. Hunched against the howling wind we staggered over the moor and completed the walk, cold, shivering, and drenched to the skin. Which was ample excuse for repairing to the warmth and comfort of the Garvault Hotel for urgent, well-earned refreshment.

Use OS Map 10, Strathnaver, Sheet no 17, Strath of Kildonan, second series, Scale 1:50,000 to follow the route. Garvault Hotel Grid Ref:

781386; Ben Griam Mor Grid Ref: 805390; Loch Coire nam Mang Grid Ref: 800405; Loch Druim a'Chliabhain Grid Ref: 810415; Ben Griam Beg Fort Grid Ref: 830413.

35. BEN MOR COIGACH

When our silver-wedding bells rang, Ann and I escaped to Coigach. Sun-drenched Caribbean strands were not for us, even if we could have afforded them. A Wester Ross cottage overlooking the Summer Isles was 'paradise enow'. We had a magical, memorable holiday, hillwalking and exploring the cliffs and moorlands with never a cross word uttered. As we watched the sun set over Badentarbat Bay and Tanera Mor, the decades slipped away and time stood still, captured in a seascape blaze of gold and silver. A migratory whale rose, spouting, close to shore; late-evening oyster-catchers piped plaintively; slow-eyed, black-faced sheep safely grazed; peat smoke scented the air. A good-to-be-alive day.

On our anniversary, a cold, wind-biting, snow-filled, April-raw day, hillwalking would have been foolhardy. So we packed our bags and hiked up the Kirkaig river to the Fionn Loch, 'the white loch', celebrating our arrival with hot coffee in the shelter of a lochside peat hag. It seemed the right thing to do. We have been returning ever since, captivated by the desolate beauty of the loch-scattered heather moors of the Rubha Mor peninsula; the golden beaches of Achnahaird and Garvie; and the mystical mountain wilderness, embraced between Loch Lurgainn and Loch Bad a'Ghaill and wave-capped Loch Broom.

Coigach means fifth, thus the area is a fifth part of the County of Ross. Years ago, during a Sutherland/Ross border dispute, two venerable Ross-shire men were given the task of walking the line. Their footsteps would prove the true boundary. Before setting off, they were warned by the local minister that their feet were on oath. At the end of the march, by Altnacealgach burn, the old men swore their feet had never once left Ross-shire soil, omitting to mention that before starting they had filled their shoes with earth from Balnagowan in Ross-shire. That is how Altnacealagch got its name: the burn of the cheat.

A tortuous, narrow road leads out to Achiltibuie and the Summer Isles from Drumruine on the A835 Ledmore Junction–Ullapool road. Coigach lies south of this track with the Inverpolly National Nature Reserve to the north. Some of Scotland's most splendid peaks bid welcome: Cul Mor (849m), Cul

Beag (769m), Stac Pollaidh (613m), and glorious Suilven (728m).

There is something for everyone here. Yellow sands for the bucket-and-spade brigade; sea fishing and fishing for sea-trout and wild brown trout; walking and climbing and the culinary delights of the Summer Isles Hotel. There is also a good pub with good food and excellent beer at Altandhu. Who needs more? Above all, at least for us, there is nothing to match the peace and beauty of the Coigach hills; Beinn an Eoinn (601m), 'the mountain of the birds'; Beinn nan Caorach 700m), 'the hill of the sheep'; Sgurr an Fhidhleir (696m), 'the hill of the fiddler'; and Ben Mor Coigach (743m) itself, 'the big hill of Coigach'. But they are not to be attempted lightly, because part of the way is exposed, particularly the approach along the narrow ridge to Speicin Coinnich, the mossy peak. A head for heights is essential, but with care, you should come to no harm.

Choose a good day for your assault to fully enjoy the views. You will not be disappointed. What these peaks may lack in height is more than compensated for by their rugged splendour and the magnificent vista they offer over the surrounding countryside from their tops. A traverse of all is one of the most spectacular walks in the northwest, a splendid, challenging day out, offering all that is best of Scotland.

Use OS Map 15, Loch Assynt, second series, Scale 1:50,000 to navigate your way round. Park at Achvraie, near the signpost to the Youth Hostel. Follow the faint track up the north side of Allt Ach a'Bhraighe burn to An t-Sail. Walk along the edge of the crags southeast, climbing steeply to Sgurr an Fhidhleir and Speicin Coinnich.

Return from Speicin Coinnich to Ben Mor Coigach, then follow the track west towards Garbh Choireachan. Angle downhill to the right, to the gorge above Allt na Coisiche. Follow the stream until about a half a mile above Culnacraig. Cross the burn and then follow the fence back to road. Turn north and walk back to Achvraie. Allow a full day and expect to cover about 12 miles.

Key points along the route: Rubha Mor Grid Ref: 985145; Altandhu Grid Ref: 984127; Summer Isles Hotel Grid Ref: 027081; Achvraie Grid Ref: 045059; An t-Sail Grid Ref: 070070; Sgurr and Fhidhleir Grid Ref: 095054; Speicin Coinnich Grid Ref: 106043; Ben Mor Coigach Grid Ref: 094043; Culnacraig Grid Ref: 066037.

36. STAC POLLAIDH

Time for tea before tackling Stac Pollaidh. We put the kettle on. Our self-catering cottage at Polbain in Coigach, the 'fifth part' of Ross-shire, overlooked Badentarbat Bay and the beautiful Summer Isles of Tanera Mor, Tanera Beg, Eilean Fada Mor and Eilean a'Char. Polbain is one of the townships that cling to the road along the Coigach shore. They begin in the south with Culnacraig, followed by Acheninve, Badenscallie and Polglass. Then Achiltibuie, with its famous Hydroponicum, a temperature-controlled tropical garden, Polbain itself and Altandhu. Finally, on the peatland and heather peninsula of Rubha Mor, at the end of the road, is the little hamlet of Reiff. These townships are reached after a tortuous, 40-minute drive north and west from Ullapool.

Stac Pollaidh (613m), 'the peak of the moss', is a small mountain with a big reputation. The ascent to the summit ridge is easily accomplished, but conquering either the east or the west peak requires a deal of care and a considerable degree of scrambling skill. The whole 600-yard length of the ridge is a continuous moonscape of jagged, broken and fractured sandstone slabs and stark pinnacles. The rock is often loose and friable and each handhold should be carefully tested prior to putting any reliance or weight on it. However, most of the obstacles that you will encounter can be safely avoided by skirting the base of the pinnacles, and just being on the ridge is an amazing experience, reward enough in itself for making the climb.

The view from the ridge is stunning. The mountains of the Inverpolly National Nature Reserve and Assynt crowd the north and east horizons: Cul Beag (769m), Cul Mor (849m), Suilven (731m), Canisp (846m), Quinag (808m), Conival (987m) and mighty Ben More Assynt (998m). At the foot of Stac Pollaidh, at the very heart of the Nature Reserve, lies Loch Sionascaig, one of Scotland's most beautiful and least known lochs. The loch is barely three miles across, but it has a shoreline that meanders round 17 miles of headlands, bays, secret corners and dramatic promontories. The loch is famous for its wildlife, particularly its wild brown trout. Some fish grow to prodigious proportions of more than 15lb in weight, although most of the residents are of modest size, weighing in the order of 8oz.

The southern outlook from Stac Pollaidh is just as dramatic as the view north, directly across Loch Lurgainn into the shadowy wilderness of glens and corries that is Ben Mor Coigach (743m), dominated by the jagged tooth of Sgurr an Fhidhleir (703m), the 'Fiddler's Ridge' that towers over the blue crochet of little Lochan Tuath. The eye is guided westward by the silver line of Loch Lurgainn, Loch Bad a'Ghail and Loch Osgaig to the golden sands of Achnahaird and the moorlands of Rubh Mor. Then, west again over the broken waters of the Minch to a distant prospect of the 'heather isle', Lewis, the long island of the Outer Hebrides.

The most popular route up Stac Pollaidh is from the car park at Grid Ref: 108096 on OS Map 15, Loch Assynt, second series, Scale 1:50,000. Don't follow this because the route has been trampled into a glutinous, ever-expanding quagmire which is now the object of repair and renovation. Instead, start from near Linneraineach Cottage (Grid Ref: 124091) where you should be able to park in an old quarry a few yards to the west of the cottage.

Cross the stile on the north side of the road then angle northwest up the hill towards the east peak of Stac Pollaidh, one mile ahead. A rocky, boulder-strewn plateau greets you upon arrival below the summit ridge. Catch your breath here, and the view, before joining and following the tourist route round to the northeast face of the mountain.

The final assault takes a zig-zag line which eventually deposits you close to the centre point of the summit ridge. Where you go from here is dependent upon your expertise and ability. For experienced hillwalkers the east peak is accessible with care, but the west peak is best admired from below by non-rock-climbers.

Depending upon how often you stop to gawp at the scenery, there and back from Linneraineach should take no more than three hours. This leaves plenty of time to end the day at glorious Garvie Bay (Grid Ref: 041138). Park where the River Oscaig rushes under the road at Grid Ref: 040130 and follow the west bank of the stream north, past Loch Garvie, to reach the bay.

For more information about this stunning area, contact the Highlands of Scotland Tourist Board, Peffery House, Strathpeffer, Ross-shire 1V14 9HA. Tel: 01997 421160, Fax: 01997 421168.

37. A WALK BY THE WHITE LOCH

Gairloch in Wester Ross is a bustling community. Each year, thousands of visitors flock to the world-famous Inverewe Gardens, begun in 1865 by Osgood Mackenzie and now containing more than 2,500 species of plants collected from round the world. Children bucket-and-spade on white sands and splash in clear waters warmed by the Gulf Stream. But the shores of Loch Gairloch were not always so peaceful. During the nineteenth century, famine and eviction brought devastation to the north. Whilst Lowland granaries bulged with grain, many in the Highlands starved. Families went barefoot, clothed in meal bags whilst Free Church ministers appealed in vain for help to Edinburgh and London. Lord Napier, leading a Royal Commission of inquiry into the state of the Highlands in 1882, reported: 'A state of misery, of wrong-doing, and patient long-suffering, without parallel in the history of our country.' When you walk the shore here or climb in the surrounding hills, remember these men, women and children, and how mainstream, 'enlightened', society callously ignored their plight.

Northeast from Gairloch lies one of Scotland's most beautiful lochs, Fionn, the white loch, in the heart of the Fisherfield Forest: 180 square miles of wilderness enfolding 35 mountains, 18 of which rise to more than 3,000ft in height. In his book, *A Hundred Years in the Highlands*, Osgood Mackenzie recounts seeing the most famous basket of wild trout ever recorded, taken from the Fionn Loch: 'The total weight of the 12 fish caught that twelfth of April by trolling was 87lb 12oz.'

There are several fine walks out to the Fionn Loch. It may be approached from the east from Drumchork near Aultbea via Loch Mich'ille Riabhaich, named after a sixteenth-century rogue who terrorised the area. From the north, you may walk in along the stalker's path which begins at Corrie Hallie near Dundonnell on the shores of Little Loch Broom. From the west, the Fionn Loch is reached from Poolewe, Loch Maree and Loch Kernsary. All of these routes can be found on OS Map 19, Gairloch and Ullapool, second series, Scale 1:50,000. Our favourite approach is from Poolewe (Grid Ref: 858808), along the banks of the River Ewe. At Inveran

(Grid Ref: 874786), at the south end of Loch Maree, the road turns northeast and climbs to reach Kernsary (Grid Ref: 894804) after a gentle mile and a half.

The National Trust for Scotland owns the land to the northwest and as you gain the first crest Loch Kernsary sparkles below, stroking the moor with long silver fingers. When we last passed this way, a graceful hind, belly-deep in yellow flag, drank delicately from the outlet stream.

As you climb higher, past Kernsary Lodge, majestic mountains crowd the view, including Martha's Peak. Martha, busy weaving whilst she tended her cattle, dropped a spindle. Trying to retrieve it, she fell to her death on the steep slope. The hill has been known by her name ever since. At Grid Ref: 893794, hang a right and tramp up the glen to find Old Boathouse Bay (Grid Ref: 945779) on the south shore of the Fionn Loch.

Climb the headland above Lochan Beannach Beag to enjoy one of the most stunning vistas in all of Scotland, encompassing the dramatic peaks of Ruadh Stac Mor, A'Mhaighdean, Beinn Tarsuinn and Mullach Coire Mhic Fhearchair. From Old Boathouse Bay, walk west for two miles to the end of the loch to reach New Boathouse Bay at Grid Ref: 928810, protected by the scrub-covered island of Eilean an Eich Bhain.

Before leaving the bay, look north across the loch towards Beinn a'Chaisgein Beag (680m). An old drover's track crosses the mountain here, leading down to the Fionn Loch. On the shores of the loch is the site of what must have been the remotest shop in Scotland; a welcome refuge for the herdsmen and their families as they cursed their black cattle on the long, arduous journey to the southern markets.

Return home by following the road south over Bad Bog back to Kernsary and Poolewe. You should allow a full day for this expedition, and the total distance, there and back, is approximately 14 miles. There are no serious problems along the way, other than the possibility of sore feet and weary legs towards the end of your expedition. You will, however, return with unforgettable memories for the dream-bank of the mind.

38. THE MOUNTAIN OF THE BIRDS

Beinn an Eoinn in Wester Ross is strictly for the birds and lovers of wild places. The Gaelic name means 'mountain of the birds', and this 854-metre peak is home to some of Scotland's most elusive species. Golden eagles nest amongst high corries in nearby Beinn Eighe Nature Reserve, feeding snow-downed chicks on carefully sized morsels of rabbit, hare and anything else stupid enough to move below their fierce gaze. Greenshanks pipe over hidden glens. Dippers splash in tumbling streams. Snow buntings, dotterels and ptarmigan haunt the high tops. Golden plover dance along the tracks and the hills are loud with the song of curlews, snipes and sandpipers.

When Ann and I tramped this way a few years ago, this wonderful wilderness was on its best behaviour; it was a long, cloudless summer day warmed by the July sun, cooled by soft southerly Atlantic breezes. We had parked the car by the hut near Loch Bad an Sgalaig and our destination was Beinn an Eoinn, Poca Buidhe and Loch na h-Oidhche, 'the loch of the night'. Civilisation lay ten miles distant at Gairloch. For the time being, however, we were alone amidst a mountain-and-moorland wonderland. Loch na h-Oidhche is cradled between Beinn an Eoinn to the east and Baosbheinn, 'the wizards' mountain', to the west and from the road their dark slopes look intimidating. Both are substantial mountains, just below 3,000ft; but beside their overbearing neighbours, they become mere children.

Slioch spears northwards above the blue waters of Loch Maree, backed by a mad thrust of Fisherfield peaks. Torridon peaks line the southern horizon in splendid array: Beinn Alligin, 'the mountain of beauty'; Beinn Dearag, 'the great rocky peak'; Cam na Feola, 'the hill of the flesh'; and, rising above them all, the sheer, black, north face of Liathach, 'the grey one'.

We crossed the little wooden bridge over the outlet burn of Am Feur Loch and hiked south. Well, Ann and I crossed the bridge. My golden retriever, Breac, dashed straight into the stream and had to be dragged protesting from his early morning swim. Heathcliff, Ann's scurrilous Yorkshire terrier, stayed close to heel; he has a long memory and ingrained distrust of water after almost drowning in a remote Sutherland lochan. We caught a second breath as the stony path climbed between Meall a Ghlas Leothaid and Meall Lochan a'Chleirich to round Meall na Meine. It was wet and rough-going, down the slope to the valley of Abhainn a'Gharb Choire, the outlet stream from Loch na h-Oidhche. We rested, watching the black-and-white flash of a dipper darting amongst tiny waterfalls. Breac resumed his interrupted swim and charged upstream as we walked on, Beinn an Eionn tamed in height by our rising approach.

A final valley and slow climb brought us to a flat, boulder-scattered plateau and the shining levels of Loch nah-Oidhche. The slopes of Beinn an Eoinn rise steeply from the shore and a path runs down the east bank. But to fully appreciate this mystical land, climb the north shoulder of the hill and walk the wide ridge to the summit at the south end.

The most startling aspect of the view is the sudden shock of the first sight of Ruadh Stac Mor (1,008m), Sail Mor (980m), and the famous Triple Buttress of A'Chonneach, an amazing, uncompromising howl of mountain pleasure, scarred and screed to the shores of lonely Loch Coire Mhic Fhearchair, cupped in its bosom. Beinn Eighe, Liathach, Slioch and the Fisherfield summits crowd round with golden moorlands brushing their feet, ribboned with silver streams, specked blue with lochs; a Bach-like cathedral world of spire and steeple, a glorious hymn of praise to nature.

Descending from Beinn an Eoinn, we spent the night in the bothy at Poca Buidhe at the south end of Loch na h-Oidhche, close to the yellow stone. In days gone by, the hollow below this huge boulder used to provide shelter for 'fishers, stalkers and other liars'. Now, nearby, there is a comfortable, well-equipped bothy.

The following morning, we walked south from Poca Buidhe across wide granite pavements and over rough, trackless moors. For two hours we tramped in solitude, the silence broken only by startled deer, to a tiny water between Sail Mor and Cam na Feola called Loch nan Cabar, where we caught lunch. Bearing our prize back to Poca Buidhe, we cooked the small fish and ate royally. In the warm afternoon sun, with rising trout stippling the surface of Loch na h-Oidhche, the sense of peace was a tangible presence. You feel small and insignificant and yet, more surely than words can explain, you know that you are also an important part of this timeless beauty, with as much right to be there as ravens, deer or wild cats. If the hills and mountains of my native land mean anything, then this is what they mean to me.

Use OS Map 19, Gairloch and Ullapool, second series, Scale 1:50,000. Loch Bad an Sgalaig Grid Ref: 854713; start point Grid Ref: 856721; Loch na h-Oidhche Grid Ref: 890887; Beinn an Eoinn Grid Ref: 905646; Poca Buidhe Grid Ref: 899644.

39. BOTHERED BY BOTHIES

I know I am going to regret saying this, but I have mixed feelings about mountain bothies. To me they are unwelcome 'focal points', attracting public attention to some of Scotland's most fragile areas. It could be argued that by writing about these places I am equally guilty, but bothies relentlessly concentrate the mind and many walkers plan their expeditions round bothy locations. Thus, the very things which draw us to the hills – silence and solitude – are degraded.

A ruined croft building near where I live in Tongue in northwest Sutherland has recently been made into a bothy. The surrounding hills are modest, easily accessible from the road, and I have walked this way for years without seeing another soul. Now, the yellow-cagoule pack is appearing in ever-increasing numbers and only because of the presence of this bothy. There may be some rationale for a bothy at the end of a gut-bursting hike into the wilds, although I don't think so, but what is the point of a bothy 15 minutes from a main road? Even more pointless when you consider that there is an excellent Youth Hostel by the Kyle of Tongue and inexpensive accommodation of all kinds, including a camp site, in the township itself.

This is not to denigrate the work of organisations like the Mountain Bothy Association (MBA). They are motivated by the highest ideals: companionship, courtesy and respect for individual rights; and MBA members give unstintingly of their time and labour on behalf of others. The problem lies not in the work of the MBA, but in how others use, or frequently misuse, the facilities that the association provides.

Be that as it may, I would be the first to admit that I have tumbled gratefully into the shelter of a bothy on a stormy day, thankful for the comfort it provided and I suppose that bothies have a part to play in 'the large religion' of the hills. My only concern is that bothies might become the first step down the road to the provision of 'proper facilities' in the wilderness.

The work of the MBA was featured some years ago in the series 'Discover Scotland', published by the *Sunday Mail*, including details and a photograph of A'Chuil bothy in Glendessarry, one of the few bothies I have visited. My wife and I stumbled upon it whilst tramping the hills to the south of the River Dessarry, which drains into the head of Loch Arkaig. It was raining. After all, it was Lochaber and Lochaber has one of the highest rainfall levels in Scotland. But it was user-friendly rain, interspersed with bouts of warm sunshine, and we were having a splendid day. Most walkers here make for the heady heights of Sgurr na Ciche (1,040m). We were intent upon an easy ridge walk, from Carn Mor (829m), east by Meall nan Spardan (650m) to Monadh Gorm (448m). overlooking the spot where supporters of Bonnie Prince Charlie chucked barrels of French gold into Loch Arkaig in 1746. And if you believe that, you will believe anything. I know my Highland lairds and the possibility of their passing up the chance of an easy buck, then or now, beggars belief. A similar story is told about Loch Hakel in Sutherland, also involving barrels of French gold. The thing these stories have most in common is that not a penny piece of treasure was ever recovered.

I have no regard for BPC, but he must have had strong lungs and a great pair of legs. The area is littered with memorials to places where he hid or slept: on Sgurr na Ciche; above Glenfinnan; in a cave on Sail Chaorainn (1,002m) and various other points east, west and south. Given the number of locks of hair and bits of his kilt he left behind as presents to his supporters, BPC must have arrived back in France bald and bollock naked.

Park at the gate at the head of Loch Arkaig. Follow the track up the north bank of the river to Upper Glendessarry. Descend to cross the river, with care, by a disintegrating bridge. Climb southwest on Meall nan Spardan to Carn Mor. Walk east to Monadh Gorm and return to the start point by Strathan. The walk will take five hours; the distance is approximately 11 miles.

The summit of Carn Mor is one of the finest viewpoints in Lochaber, and on a clear day, it is an unforgettable experience. The four-mile walk east to Monadh Gorm extends this pleasure mightily, easy-going over peat and heather tussocks with green Glendessarry to the north and the silver ribbon of the River Pean to the south. Bog cotton whispers in the wind by tiny dark pools and the only difficulty is negotiating a deer fence across the hill beyond Meall nan Spardan.

The descent from Monadh Gorm to the farm at Strathan and Loch Arkaig is steep and tiresome and should be approached with caution, particularly in wet or misty conditions. Once down, the crystal water of the River Dessarry offers refreshment fit for a king and no doubt, in times past, a recalcitrant, fugitive prince.

Use OS Map 40, Loch Shiel, second series, Scale 1:50,000. Start point Grid Ref: 988915; Glendessarry Lodge Grid Ref: 968926; Upper Glendessarry Grid Ref: 951931; River Dessarry crossing Grid Ref: 944929; Carn Mor Grid Ref: 9029 10; Meall nan Spardan Grid Ref: 920920; Monadh Gorm Grid Ref: 961915; Strathan Grid Ref: 978915.

40. FRAOCH BHEINN AND LOCH ARKAIG

Hareton bagged his first Munro at the age of nine months, Ben Hope (926m), the most northerly mountain in Scotland which rises above the 'magical' 3,000 foot mark. As I explained to him at the time, 'We all have to begin somewhere, Hareton, and Ben Hope is as good a place to start as any.' It was a considerable undertaking for a tiny Yorkshire terrier and I confess that I carried him part of the way. But he made it in good style and since then, as a hillwalker, he has never looked back.

His predecessor, Heathcliff, who is now 'asleep' on the lower slopes of Ben More Assynt (998m), was also a great walker. He could go for hours across the hills and at the end of the day still be ready for more. Heathcliff was absolutely tireless and tramped miles with us during the 13 years of his life. So, in spite of being a golden-retriever man, I have come to admire the tenacity of Yorkshire terriers. I suppose I have to – if I value my life, that is, because Hareton is the apple of my hiking-companion's eye, 'She Who Must Be Obeyed'.

A highly user-friendly hill for little legs, human and canine, guards the west shore of Loch Arkaig in Lochaber; Fraoch Bheinn (856m), a creditable Corbett, being a mountain above 2,500ft but below 3,000ft in height. It is dominated by more substantial cousins, Sgurr na Ciche (1,040m) and Sgurr nan Coireachan (95.3m) to the west, and Sgurr nan Coireachan (955m) and Sgurr Thuilm (964m) to the south. Nevertheless, this mountain is ideal for those less inclined to dizzy heights and it provides a superb view of these adjacent peaks.

It also provides a history lesson, because this is Clan Cameron country; a clan which was 'out' with their chief, 'Gentle Lochiel', during Bonnie Prince Charlie's disastrous 1745 Rebellion. Jenny Cameron, who lived here in Glendessarry, was with her husband at Glenfinnan when Lochiel and BPC raised their standard at the start of this sad affair. Clan Cameron paid dearly for their trouble. After the Battle of Culloden (1746), Butcher Cumberland's troops ravished Lochaber. Lochiel's fine house at Achnacarry was burnt to the ground whilst he watched helplessly from a nearby hill.

Start your journey up Fraoch Bheinn more hopefully from Strathan. Park at the end of the road along the north shore of Loch Arkaig, just before the entrance to Strathan Farm. Walk the road to the beginning of the stalkers' path that leads north from Glendessarry into Glen Kingie. Find this location at Grid Ref: 979916 on OS Map 40, Loch Shiel, second series, Scale 1:50,000. The broad shoulder of the Fraoch Bheinn rises ahead and the route to the summit is easy to follow. However, as always, watch out for sudden changes in the weather. Be properly equipped and prepared to cope with all eventualities. Lochaber can be devious.

The wide summit ridge of the mountain drops steeply to the east into the glen of the Dearg Allt burn and, to the west, into the glen of Feith a'Chicheanais. Avoid the edge, particularly in mist, and you will come to no harm. Return from the summit towards Strathan by the same route, but at Grid Ref: 984935, descend west to the Feith a'Chicheanais burn. Cross the stream to find the stalkers' path on the west bank and follow it down to Glendessarry Lodge. From here, tramp southwest for one mile to arrive back at your start point at Loch Arkaig.

Which is where having a good nose comes in handy. Sniff about round the shores of the loch in search of gold. During the '45 Rebellion, BPC's French allies sent money to support his struggle in Scotland. Bullion was landed at Loch Nevis to the west, and lugged over the hills through the rugged pass of Mam na Cloich Airde and down Glendessarry to Loch Arkaig. However, depending upon how you view these matters, fortunately or unfortunately, by this time the dispirited BPC was on his way back to France.

Some believe that those who received the gold buried it somewhere nearby for future use, while others claim that the cash was chucked into the loch; which, ever since, has made Loch Arkaig one of the most popular fishing venues in Scotland. Still, whatever the truth, there is no harm in looking, particularly when you can employ the eager senses of a vibrant Yorkshire terrier to help in that task. 'Hareton!'

41. CEANNACROC FOREST

Get physical this morning to prepare for Sunday, Valentine's Day. Two Lotharios of that name, a bishop and a priest, were martyred near Rome on 14 February in about the year AD 270. Wonder if they were served breakfast in bed before dashing off to meet their maker? I doubt it. The Romans also paid homage to their god Lupercalia, the begetter of fecundity, on the same day. Priests cut thongs from the skins of sacrificed animals and marched through the crowds beating swooning females with them, thus enhancing the women's capacity to bear good little Roman soldiers, or so they said.

Swoon with your beloved high above Loch Cluanie, amidst the vast wilderness that is the Ceannacroc Forest. Pack OS Map 34, Fort Augustus, second series, Scale 1:50,000 to find your way round. An earlier, skirted, hiker in these airts did not have the benefit of guidance from the Ordnance Survey: Bonnie Prince Charlie, fleeing from government troops after his defeat at the Battle of Culloden. He knew these hills intimately. A cave here, at Grid Ref: 139155, is reputed to have been used by the fugitive prince. It lies between the peaks of Tigh Mor na Seilge (929m) to the north and Sail Chaorainn (1002m) to the south. Not much room for passion, though, even if BPC had been so inclined.

The route up to the first top, Carn Ghluasaid (957m) (Grid Ref: 146125), might also leave you passionless. It involves an unrelenting ascent from the car park at Lundie (Grid Ref: 145104), on the 230m contour, to the summit in a distance of little over one mile. Still, there is a good stalker's path to ease the pain. The last time The Manager and I tramped this way, just before the track breaks out onto the soggy summit plateau, we heard voices coming from a rocky bastion off to our right. A young man and a woman were exchanging a fond embrace. We tiptoed by, leaving them to their pleasure in one of the most romantic settings in all of Scotland.

Messrs Johnson and Boswell tiptoed past Loch Cluanie along the military road to Glen Shiel in 1773, during their well-recorded tour of the Highlands. The beauty of Glen Shiel and the surrounding area, and in particular the mountain ridge of the Five Sisters of Kintail, is said to have prompted Dr Johnson to write his classic book, *Journey to the Western Isles*. A huge roadside boulder where he and Boswell rested is known to this day as Clach Johnson. Close by, at Bridge of Shiel, is the site where, in 1719, Spanish troops supporting the second abortive Jacobite uprising were defeated.

Rise from the summit of Carn Ghluasaid and carefully edge the lip of the steep-sided corrie northwest. Ahead lies the magnificent, sharp crown of Sgurr nan Conbhairean (1109m) at Grid Ref: 131139; reached after an exhilarating journey of one-and-a-half miles. It is here that the true heart and soul of these mountains is fully revealed. And they are magnificent; sheer cliffs falling into dark corries; smooth green swards, sparkling with tiny blue lochans; the overwhelming panorama of peaks crowding the southern horizon; the view northwards into the calm serenity of Glen Affric.

There is also a comfortable love-nest on the top of Sgurr nan Conbhairean; a fine, sheltered, rock-built cairn which includes a spacious sitting-room. Granted, there is neither roof overhead nor glass in the window, but for me it is captivating, offering fond glances over the skirts of An Reithe (846m) into Glearin Fada. This is the perfect place to drag out the rose you have secreted in your rucksack and offer it to the object of your delight. A far better gesture than breakfast in bed or a long weekend in Paris. Well, at least I think so!

Descend southwest from Sgurr nan Conbhairean to find a narrow ridge overlooking the blue mystery of Gorm Lochan, then climb again to reach the summit of Drochaid an Tuill Easaich (1,000m) at Grid Ref: 123135, unnamed on the OS map. The way home is south, down the soft shoulder of Meall Breac (650m, Grid Ref: 121117) to cross busy Allt Coire Lair burn at Grid Ref: 128115. A convenient track will lead you to the line of the old military road. On reaching it, hang a left and march back to the car park.

During the day wind and weather may buffet you, but neither you nor your partner will be much bothered by demonic, thong-wielding priests.

42. CREAG MEAGAIDH

As you may remember, I have little regard for Charles Edward Stuart. His ill-fated rebellion of 1745 gave the Lowland and London authorities exactly the excuse they needed to ruthlessly root out, once and for all, 'the barbarity of Gaelic'. Or at least try to do so. Nevertheless, I can't help but admire Bonnie Prince Charlie's stamina as a hillwalker. I suppose he was mightily encouraged, being the object of one of the biggest man-hunts in history, but he certainly covered a lot of difficult ground in frequently horrendous circumstances.

Standing on Stob Poite Coire Ardair above The Window, a deep, jagged cleft in the Creag Meagaidh ridge in Glen Spean, I think of BPC scrambling down to Lochan a'Choire on his way south on 28 August 1746. Sixteen days later he was toiling back up, heading for Loch nam Uamh and the ship that was to carry him safely to France. Once through The Window, BPC skirted the lochans on the north side of Creag Meagaidh and descended into Glen Roy; following the headwaters of Uisge nam Fichead burn and the track leading to Annat and the River Roy.

Most visitors to Creag Meagaidh follow the path from Aberarder Farm out to Lochan a'Choire, where the dramatic cliffs of Coire Ardair offer challenging winter climbs. For the less experienced, the high tops are challenge enough. The route from Carn Liath (1,006m) to An Cearcallach via Creag Meagaidh (1,130m) is one of Scotland's finest ridge walks. Much of this area is a carefully managed National Nature Reserve, as is evidenced by the range of wildflowers growing amidst the rocks and corries; cow-wheat, with milky-coloured pods, cloudberry and bilberry, bog asphodel and bell-heather.

So, today, leave your claymore in the loft and join me on a wonderful walk through this magical land. Park at Aberarder, Grid Ref: 482874 on OS Map 34, second series, Scale 1: 50,000, then follow the track north, behind Aberarder House. As the path climbs and bears left, near a small stand of silver birch trees (Grid Ref: 483884), strike north directly uphill to reach the summit of Carn Liath (Grid Ref: 472903). Ancient iron fence posts, wireless and forlorn, mark the way ahead.

The route west from the tumbled cairn on Carn Liath is obvious on a clear day. In bad weather, however, great care must be taken. The track lies perilously close to the sheer sides of Coire a'Chriochairein (Grid Ref: 450894). During snow-filled winter months, stay off the hill unless you are thoroughly competent, fit and prepared. However, on a fine day the views from all along the ridge are magnificent, north, south, east and west. Loch Spey, the source of Scotland's fastest flowing river, lies like a silver shilling on golden moorlands, backed by the blue mountains of Culachy and Corrieyairack.

Across Glen Spean, the Lochaber peaks and Ben Nevis crowd the horizon; Stob Coire Easain, Aonach Beag, Aonach Mor and Carn Dearg. The River Spean glides through the Braes of Lochaber, collecting in cold waters from a hundred streams, hurrying them to their meeting with the river Lochy by Mucomir Power Station. This is ptarmigan country, the quintessential bird of the high tops, pure white in winter apart from a black, white-tipped tail. In summer and autumn, ptarmigan retain white wings and white underparts, with grey-and-black breast and flanks.

It is also the country of *Monarch of the Glen*, the much-admired television programme about life on a Highland Estate. The series is filmed at Ardvrekie, a wilderness landscape to the south of blue Loch Laggan. The waters of the loch have been harnessed as part of a hydro-electric generating scheme and consequently levels fluctuate greatly; leaving an unsightly shoreside tidemark. The impact of the scheme, and other factors, have destroyed the River Spean as a salmon stream.

After negotiating The Window (Grid Ref: 426885), climb steeply to the summit of Creag Meagaidh – a paradise moment. From the summit, descend south over a carpet of grassland to visit Meall Coire Choillerais (Grid Ref: 434861) and peer into the vast corrie that cups a tiny lochan. A further mile southeast brings you to An Cearcallach (Grid Ref: 422854) where there is welcome shelter amongst the boulder-strewn crest. Carefully descend from An Cearcallach to pick up the line of the Moy burn that leads to the A86 road at Moy. Tramp happily roadside to Aberarder at the end of a rewarding 15-mile day.

43. LITTLE LEGS ABOVE LOCH RUTHVEN

You always remember the first time, even in hillwalking. When the youngest member of Clan Sandison, Jean, was five years old, we introduced her to some serious tramping and she has never forgotten the. experience. It wasn't too arduous for little legs, four miles there and back, but the going was rough to rocky. She managed the hike just fine and I have a photograph to prove it: of Jean, her elder brother Charles and The Manager, shivering one sharp April afternoon in weak sunlight on the summit of Craig Ruthven (420m), to the south of Loch Ness.

Find Craig Ruthven on OS Map 26, Inverness, second series, Scale 1:50,000 at Grid Ref: 622270 in Strathnairn. This gentle strath is rarely busy. Motorists thunder up and down the A9 Edinburgh–Inverness road in search of more famous places to visit and higher hills to climb, and seldom head west along the B851 into Strathnairn. Dour Loch Ness knifes the Great Glen to the north, whilst the blue Monadliath mountains guard the skirts of the strath to the south. Linger here awhile. There is a multitude of reasons for doing so. Anglers will find a series of splendid trout lochs, including Loch Ruthven (Grid Ref: 620275) itself and its smaller neighbour, Loch a'Choire (Grid Ref: 626292) which contains Arctic char, descendants of fish that have survived in these waters since the end of the last Ice Age. There is a famous garden centre, also the excellent 'Grouse and Trout' restaurant and one of the oldest fishing hotels in Scotland, The Whitebridge Inn near Loch Mhor.

More famous visitors to Strathnairn were less anxious to linger. After his defeat at the Battle of Culloden in 1746, Bonnie Prince Charlie fled this way at the start of his enforced tour of the Highlands. He stopped briefly at Gorthleck House by the shores of Loch Mhor, hoping for help, but the shutters were drawn. News travels fast in these airts. The present road through Strathnairn largely follows the line of one of the roads built between 1728 and 1837 to keep the Highlanders subdued and peaceable. So, nae luck there, then.

Park peaceably today at the east end of Loch Ruthven in the Royal Society for the Protection of Birds (RSPB) car park at Grid Ref: 638280.

The loch is the most important breeding site in Britain for rare Slavonian grebe; an ornithological showman of a bird, magnificently plumaged in chestnut, black, brown and white with a spectacular tuft of yellow feathers projecting like horns from the head. Look out also for Mr Osprey, Scotland's most consistently successful fisherman. In the woodlands you may see siskins and redpolls and on the hill, black grouse, peregrines, hen harriers and coal-black ravens.

Climb southwest from the car park onto the lower slopes of Stac Gorm (430m). An easy 20 minutes brings you to the summit. From there, continue along the ridge to Craig Ruthven. Make a longer day out of the expedition by descending from Craig Ruthven to the flat wildflower-decked marshland and meadows by Ruthven Farm (Grid Ref: 603274). Ahead, you will see a notch in the ridge of Tom na Croich (380m). Head for this point and turn northeast to stride on to reach Creag nan Clag (391m) at Grid Ref: 599287.

Time for lunch, and to visually map out the forward route. You will see the minor road below you, and the way northeast past Dalcrombie (Grid Ref: 609288) to Creag Dhearg (308m). Here, the ragged horseshoe cliffs enfold Loch a'Choire in a fond embrace. Follow this ridge east and then descend gently to the east shore of the ice-blue loch. Circle round the loch to the boat-mooring bay at the south end and pick up the forest track leading south. The way through the woods quickly brings you to a stile and back to civilisation.

It also brings you to an Aladdin's cave of a shop at Balavoulin (Grid Ref: 631288), which is full of irresistible goodies, from paintings and woollies to splendid locally produced craftwork. On reaching the minor road, hang a right and march back to the car park. If you still haven't seen Slavonian grebe, now is the time to stop off at the RSPB hide to do some serious birdwatching. The round trip covers approximately eight miles and, unlike BPC, believe me, you can afford to linger along the way. This is an easy option in Strathnairn.

44. ELGIN

James Ramsay MacDonald found that the First World War seriously interfered with his golf. MacDonald, then the leader of the Independent Labour Party, along with Keir Hardie and others advocated a policy of peace by pacifism, rather than by recourse to arms. MacDonald had seen for himself the nightmare of trench warfare and was sickened by the senseless slaughter.

Not so his fellow members of the Moray Golf Club near Lossiemouth. MacDonald was branded as a 'traitor and coward' and expelled from the club in 1916. When MacDonald became Britain's first Labour Prime Minister in 1924, an attempt to have him reinstated failed. The club relented in 1929, when MacDonald was again Prime Minister, but he did not even bother to reply to their invitation.

Angst has a long provenance amidst the fertile lands of the Laich of Moray. The most famous example happened in 1390; the burning of Elgin Cathedral, Elgin town, Pluscarden Priory, Forres and anything else that happened to get in the way of the anger of Alasdair Mor Mac an Righ, known to history as the Wolf of Badenoch, Big Al to his cronies. Alasdair was the illegitimate child of King Robert II and he had married the Countess of Ross for her lands, rather than for her looks. When Big Al discovered the marriage contract excluded said lands, he deserted his wife for a mistress. The countess complained to Bishop Burr of Moray, who eventually excommunicated the Wolf. This 'insult' prompted the Wolf's less-than-friendly visitation upon Elgin Cathedral.

I suppose that even in those days it paid to read the small print on contracts. King Robert forced his son to beg forgiveness, on his knees, on the front stoup of the Blackfriar's Priory in Perth before the assembled Scottish Court. Unrepentant, Alasdair returned to the pleasures of his mistress and finally shuffled off this mortal coil, allegedly as a forfeit for losing a game of chess to the Devil at Ruthven Castle, near Kingussie.

Elgin and the surrounding area are perfect walking country; undemanding physically but rich in wildlife flora and fauna, and evidence of Scotland's turbulent past. The ruined cathedral dominates Elgin, but the first significant religious building was constructed at Spyne, to the north of Elgin. When Ramsay MacDonald checked in his final life-score card in 1937, he was laid to rest at Spyne.

The cathedral at Elgin, known as the 'Lantern of the North', was extended over several centuries from 1224 onwards. It fell into disrepair following the Reformation; the quaint title given to that period in Scottish history when so many wondrous works of art and architecture were 'reformed' by Protestant zealots. Witness the Elgin minister who, in 1640, aided and abetted by the lairds Innes and Brodie, boasted that they had 'broke up the rood screen for firewood'. The central tower of Elgin Cathedral collapsed in 1711 and from then until 1807, when preservation work commenced, the site was used as a quarry; old stones were carted off during the hours of darkness and built into nearby dwellings. However, much of the thirteenth-century work can still be seen, notably the choir, and the fifteenth-century chapterhouse. Look out also for the grave of that arch-villain of the nineteenth-century Highland Clearances, Patrick Sellar, who so callously carried out the eviction of the people of Strathnaver in Sutherland.

The town itself has a number of fine buildings and monuments: the seventeenth-century Little Cross, fifteenth-century Grey Friar's Chapel; the 1694 house of Duff of Braco; the memorial on Lady Hill to George, 5th Duke of Gordon (1770–1836) who raised the Gordon Highlanders, famous for their part in the Battle of Waterloo when they hitched a lift into the fight by grasping hold of the stirrups of the horses of the Scots Greys. They ran at the enemy, yelling 'Scotland for Ever!'.

A short distance south from Elgin is Millbuies Country Park complete with well laid-out, informative woodland walks, including a 'Tree Trail' and a 'Plant Trail'. There is also an excellent artificial loch, created in the early years of the twentieth century when a melt-water channel was dammed. This loch is regularly stocked with brown trout for the fishing enjoyment of both visitor and local alike.

Time spent in reconnaissance is seldom wasted and the best way to begin your adventure in Elgin is to obtain a copy of Richard Gordon's excellent guide, *The Complete Moray Rambler*. Further information can be obtained from: Moray Tourist Board, 17 High Street, Elgin, Morayshire. Tel: 01343 543388, Fax: 01343 552982. I suppose, also, if you intend to play golf or visit the cathedral, you should perhaps check over your moral armoury as well, just in case.

45. KNOCK FARRIL

Although the town of Strathpeffer is of recent origin, the surrounding area has been home to man since Mesolithic times. Consequently, after Ann and I had enjoyed the delights of the spa's Victorian architecture, we set off in search of a older dwelling probably built 2,000 years ago.

The Iron Age hill fort on Knock Farril sits on the highest point of the long ridge which shelters Strathpeffer from southeast winds. It is one of the most dramatic in the north of Scotland. We turned right at the Ben Wyvis Hotel and followed the signpost to Knock Farril. Our dogs did likewise, panting in the heat, ready for anything, particularly rabbits.

At the end of the tarmac road from town, a track leads up the side of a neat field where there are iron seats strategically placed to calm the heaving lungs of passers-by. As we gained height, the town shrank to model-like proportions. Blackmuir Wood wraps itself around the western end of the hill and we entered through a binder twine-secured gate. Where would our farmers be without binder twine, a mainstay of every agricultural repair?

The way through the woods winds uphill, along a forest track marked by colour-tipped posts. As we neared the top, the trees thinned. The Firth Lands of Ross and Cromarty lay before us: a patchwork of woodlands and fields splashed with the yellow of oilseed rape. The hill ahead was covered in bracken and the dogs dashed off into the undergrowth. Castle Leod, ancient home of the Mackenzies of Kintail, thrust aggressively from the grasslands of Blairinich to the north. The Mackenzies, astute operators in the politics of Scotland's Middle Ages, assisted King James VI in quelling disturbances in the Outer Isles. As their strength and importance grew, so also did the strength and importance of their magnificent five-storey tower.

A more modest, yet none the less dramatic, monument rests on the crest, a few hundred yards east of the forest: the Friendship Stone, a head-and-shoulders bronze sculpture of a woman holding two children. After the dreadful Yerevan earthquake in Armenia, pupils of Dingwall Academy raised money for the children who had suffered and subsequently a party from Dingwall Academy visited Ycharents School in Yerevan.

When the visit was returned, the Armenian children brought with them the Friendship Stone, which they had made. At a moving ceremony on Knock Farril on Saturday, 15 September 1990, attended by more than 150 pupils and parents, the sculpture was unveiled.

Relics of more ancient politics may be found at the end of the crest overlooking Dingwall and the Dornoch Firth: the vitrified hill fort of Knock Farril, a massive array of remains of walls and ditches on the grassy summit. The principal part of the fort measures 130m by 38m, but it is the extent of the subsidiary structures which make Knock Farril notable, and there is clear evidence of the process of vitrification.

These structures were invariably built in exposed, windy places, providing maximum all-round visibility and maximum defensive capabilities. Walls were constructed of interwoven timbers bonded together in order to support considerable weight. If the structure were set on fire, either deliberately or by accident, the heat generated by the conflagration could melt the lower stones; as is evidenced at Knock Farril by the remnants of a vitrified wall.

Ann and I lunched in the fort surrounded by a feeling of contentment; of people busy with the small tasks of living, bringing up their families, hunting, fishing and tending their sparse crops. The people may have gone, but at Knock Farril their spirit lingers.

Barking from Breac and Heathcliff roused us and we called the dogs to heel. They arrived, rabbitless and exhausted by their exertions. We gathered our bits and pieces together, left the ridge and continued down the crest of the hill towards the line of the old railway at Fodderty Lodge. At the bottom we turned left and walked to the end of a field before climbing a broken stile to join the arrow-straight track back to Strathpeffer.

A neat cottage marks the end of the line, and the entrance to the station. It has been converted into shops and there is an excellent tearoom. Stripping off my dripping shirt I ordered a bowl of water, two cups of coffee and scones. A tiny, dark-eyed robin bobbed onto the back of a chair, looking for crumbs. He would have to be patient. Ann arrived with Heathcliff and we ordered more water. More lapping.

When Ann finished her coffee, we tethered the dogs, and, wearily, hauled them back to the square where the car was parked. Heathcliff jumped aboard. Breac had to have a lift. They settled and, almost instantly, were fast asleep. I looked south to Knock Farril, the Friendship Stone and the fort on the hill and smiled my thanks for a wonderful day.

OS Map 26, Inverness, second series, Scale 1:50,000. Strathpeffer Grid Ref: 483583; Gate into Blackmuir Wood Grid Ref: 490577; Exit from Blackmuir Wood Grid Ref: 496577; The Friendship Stone Grid Ref: 499580; Knock Farril Hill Fort Grid Ref: 506583; Fodderty Lodge Railway Bridge Grid Ref: 514591; Strathpeffer Station Grid Ref: 486585.

46. BLACK ISLE FOSSIL BEDS

The phrase 'Quos deus vult perdere, prius dementat', 'Those whom God wishes to destroy, he first makes mad', is true. After all, this is exactly what happened to the last Tory Government. You must have noticed their increasingly staring eyes, the flowing hair, beware, beware, the chopping hands, flailing arms and cries of despair. I pondered these matters as I paused at Eathie Glen on the shores of the Moray Firth in the Black Isle. It is the sort of place that makes you ponder thus. Hugh Miller, stonemason, geologist, author, accountant and fossil-gatherer supreme, worked here during the early years of the nineteenth century and recalled seeing fairies in the glen.

I believe him. Eathie Glen is exactly the sort of place one would expect to see ethereal beings. It is a wild tangle of bramble, bracken and birch trees, patched yellow with pools of fallen sand, centred by a tiny crystal stream hurrying seawards. Just the spot for fairies and a bit of god-like plotting.

The rock formations along the shore are known to this day as Hugh Miller's fossil beds. He discovered them and the fossil fish they contain, coccosteus and peterichthys. The rocks are of the Old Red Sandstone period, 350–400 million years young, weathered into fantastic shapes and patterns, red, blue, black, white, and grey, described by Miller as 'calcareous shales containing hard limey nodules with occasional fragments of primitive armour-plated fish'.

A tenement-sized oil tanker throbbed by, carefully negotiating the narrows between Fort George on the south shore and the long finger of Chanonry Point near Fortrose to the north. Fort George was built after the 1745 rebellion to help suppress Highland Jacobite unrest. Chanonry Point is famous because two tragic women, found guilty of 'diabolical practices of magic, enchantment, murder, homicide, and other offences', were burned to death there in the year 1578.

I think Miller went mad. He must have done so, because he committed suicide in 1856. He shot himself. He was a deeply religious man and had become embroiled in the ecclesiastical ructions that led to the Disruption of the Church of Scotland in 1843. Miller disagreed with Darwin's Theory of Evolution and said so in his book, *Footprints of the Creator*. But he is best remembered for his definitive work, *The Old Red Sandstone*.

The walk along the foreshore to Hugh Miller's fossil beds begins near Eathie Mains Farm on the minor road that links Newton and Janefield on the A832 Cromarty–Rosemarkie road to the north. Park at the farm, after first asking permission to do so, and walk west to the edge of the forestry plantation. A stile here helps you over the red-painted gate and on to the muddy track that leads to the top of the cliff overlooking Eathie Fishing Station.

Descend steeply to the rocky beach and hang a left. The fossil beds and Eathie Glen are reached after a walk of three-quarters of a mile. A further mile, round the next headland, brings you to another magical glen, dominated by steep-sided gorse and bracken-covered slopes. An old hut, full of dust and fishing nets, crouches by the shore and close by is St Bennet's Well, a secret, overgrown emerald-green pool that should be approached with caution, otherwise you could give yourself a second baptism.

The round trip there and back is only about four miles, but this is a walk to cherish, particularly on a warm, sunny day. wildflowers abound: foxgloves, primroses, bluebells, tormentil, rose-bay willow-herb, heather, ragwort, and wild roses. The seashore is busy with pied wagtails, wheatears, dunlins, and oystercatchers. Wrens pipe from the troglodyte-like undergrowth. Sea gulls join you for lunch. Black-humped dolphins porpoise off shore.

An understanding of geology and some knowledge of Hugh Miller will greatly enhance the pleasure of your day. You will find this information at Miller's birthplace, in the attractive village of Cromarty. His whitewashed thatched cottage is now owned and cared for by the National Trust for Scotland. It hosts a well-ordered museum, complete with artefacts of Miller's life and work, and basic information about the geology of the area and the fossil fish of the Black Isle syncline.

An old calotype photograph of Miller, dated 1843, taken 13 years before he died, shows him in his work clothes; rolled-up sleeves, chisel in one hand, hammer in the other; leaning against an intricately carved monumental stone slab. His head is covered in a shock of dark hair and his eyes stare at us from above a firm, no-nonsense mouth and Romanesque nose. What is he thinking, what troubles this soul who brought us so much knowledge and so much beauty? Why did the gods destroy such a man?

Use OS Map 27, Nairn, second series, Scale 1:50,000. Cromarty Grid Ref: 787675; Eathie Mains Farm Grid Ref: 771639; Eathie Wood Grid Ref: 769636; Eathie Fishing Bothy Grid Ref: 776635; Fossil Beds Grid Ref: 784641; St Bennet's Well Grid Ref: 792651.

47. FINDHORN WALK

Jonathan Edwards, Britain's world-beating triple jump champion, is an inspiration to us all. With a mighty leap of historic proportions, he went straight into the record books and our collective national pride. And he wasn't being chased, either. I thought of this as I looked at 'Randolph's Leap', near Relugas on the river Findhorn. The great leaper here was Alastair Ban Comyn of Dunphail. Randolph, the Earl of Moray, was pursuing him. The angry Earl was intent upon Alastair's murder, which must have added greatly to the spring in Alastair's step. He escaped from his pursuers by jumping the river. It is remarkable what the prospect of an imminent interview with St Peter can do for a man's confidence. We find within ourselves previously unknown reserves of strength – as happened to a government soldier, fleeing after the Battle of Killiecrankie. He hurled himself to safety over the River Garry.

The River Findhorn in Morayshire is one of Scotland's most dramatic and attractive streams, from its source in the grey Monadhliath mountains to the cold waters of the Moray Firth by Culbin Forest near Kinloss. The most spectacular aspect of the river is a 20-mile long, deep gorge that begins at Dulsie Bridge, on the line of the old military road between Lochindorb and Cawdor, and then continues downstream to the famous Sluie salmon pool east of the town of Forres.

The lower levels of the river are known as 'The Meads of St John', after the Victorian writer and naturalist, Charles St John. St John, who was born in 1809 at Chailey in Sussex, lived most of his short life in Moray. In 1834, whilst visiting Rosehall in Easter Ross, St John met and married Miss Ann Gibson, the daughter of a rich Newcastle banker. Which thereafter gave him plenty of time to indulge his passion for field sports.

St John's most famous book, *Wild Sports of the Highlands,* is often referred to as *101 Ways to Shoot an Osprey*. Nothing furred, finned or feathered that ever flew, swam or stalked the moors and rivers of Moravia was safe from his ungentle administrations. St John's stories first appeared in the *Edinburgh Quarterly Review*, edited by John Lockhart, the son-in-law of Sir Walter Scott, who himself was a keen sportsman.

There are a variety of pleasant and undemanding walks along the banks of the Findhorn Gorge, the sides of which are 61m high in places. The scenery is spectacular: woodlands of larch, pine, birch, oak and beech; heather tussocks, juniper, forget-me-nots, primroses, wood sorrel, wood vetch and violets; wrens, thrushes, blackbirds, blue tits, great tits, tree creepers, chaffinches and best-bib-and-tuckered dippers abound.

One of the most easily accessible Findhorn walks starts at Sluie (OS Map 27, Nairn, second series, Scale 1:50,000, Grid Ref: 013524), four miles south of Forres along the A940 Grantown to Forres road. Look out for a sign on the left of the road marked 'Sluie Walk'. Turn right here and drive past Sluie Lodge to reach a car park and picnic area. Walk back to the lodge and follow the track downhill. Take the right-hand fork at the first junction. Within a few minutes, at the Mains of Sluie, you reach a long row of five deserted cottages. This leads to a path along the edge of the gorge, which gives magnificent views of the rushing river below. The track is well marked, but great care is required on this section. After a mile, there is a notice warning you to go no further. Follow the path left, back through the woods to the car park. Randolph's Leap is three miles south from Sluie. Turn right at Logie (Grid Ref: 010504) and park on the B9007 at Grid Ref: 001497.

A short step from the car, through a magnificent wood of ancient beech, oak and Scots pine, brings you to the site of Alastair Ban's extreme effort. Looking at the gap, I am amazed that anyone would contemplate, even for a moment, trying to make such a jump. But I suppose, with certain death behind and a watery grave below as reward for failure, maybe I would have given it a go.

Thankful not to be put to such a test, I tramped back up the hill to the car. On the way, watch for a stone marking the level that the River Findhorn rose to during the great flood of 1829. According to one story, a gardener at Relugas caught a salmon using his umbrella, the water level at the time being an amazing 15m higher than normal.

48. MR AND MRS BROWN COUNTRY

Put a spring in your step this morning, beside the royal River Dee. Grab OS Map 43, Braemar, Landranger Series, Scale 1:50,000 and head for the car park at Linn of Dee (Grid Ref: 061897), where Billy Connolly famously routed press reporters in the film *Mrs Brown*. From here, our way leads west along the north bank of the infant stream to White Bridge (Grid Ref: 020885). At White Bridge, we turn north up Glen Dee to climb to the boulder-strewn summit of Sgor Mor (818m) at Grid Ref: 006914.

From the summit, a fine broad shoulder links Sgor Mor to Sgor Dubh (741m, Grid Ref: 035921), which is reached after an exhilarating high-level hike of two miles east–northeast. Our homeward route descends gently to Carn an 'Ic Duibhe (630m) at Grid Ref: 052908, and then steeply down through ancient Caledonian pinewoods back to the start point. This is a glorious, memorable round trip of ten miles amidst some of Scotland's most dramatic scenery.

Before setting off, pay your respects to the Linn, which is a famous salmon-watching spot. Well, it used to be in the days when there were plenty of salmon to watch. Now, however, with salmon numbers in freefall, it is very much a matter of luck whether or not you see one of these magnificent creatures. A path leads to the edge of the Linn, where the river is gripped between high black rocks for a distance of 55m. A plaque here commemorates the fate of two 1927 visitors to the Linn, who took a step too far and drowned in the turbulent waters. Take care.

The land in this neck of 'Jock Tamson's Bairns' woods is on Mar Estate. Queen Victoria built Mar Lodge, a couple of miles downstream from the Linn, as a wedding present for the Duke of Fife and her daughter, Princess Louise. For centuries, Kings and Queens of Scotland have come to Mar to hunt and stalk and fish. In 1563 Mary, Queen of Scots was entertained in nearby Glen Tilt, when she enjoyed the 'tinchal', a great deer-hunt. Contemporary reports tell us that the Queen was much delighted: 'The Queen's stag-hounds were loosed and a successful chase ensued. Three hundred and sixty deer were killed, five wolves and some roes.' 'Tinchals' continued until recent times. George V (1865–1936), staying at Balmoral when Prince of Wales, used to trot over to join in the fun. Donald MacDonald, whose father was head keeper on Mar, told me: 'I've heard my father say that often 20 or 30 stags would be shot in a day, and I myself have seen as many as 20 ponies going up the hill to collect them.' The world's most famous angler, the Queen Mum, loved the River Dee. The story is told of another woman angler, fishing in the river, being greeted by the Queen Mum. Instinctively she curtsied, earning two bootfuls of icy water for her trouble!

The riverside track from the Linn borders the narrow stream and reaches White Bridge after three miles. This is an important junction for hillwalkers. The track heading south leads down through Glen Tilt to Blair Atholl in Perthshire. This route was greatly admired by Queen Vic and her husband Bertie, who traversed it by coach; as well as by the Welshman, Thomas Pennant (1726–1798), that most caustic observer of all things Scottish, who minced that way in 1765. The route north from White Bridge, up Glen Dee, joins the Larigh Ghru path which links Coylumbridge in Strathspey with Royal Deeside.

Hang a right at White Bridge and trek up the west bank of the Dee. Within half a mile, you will meet the Chest of Dee (Grid Ref: 013886). The Chest of Dee is a long 'staircase' of broken rocks and pools where waters boil in fury, sending an incandescent spray shimmering above the torrent. After heavy rain, or when the snow melts from the high tops of the Cairngorm mountains, the river here is a spectacular sight. At Grid Ref: 002896, where a streamlet tumbles down the hill, leave the track and climb north to find the summit of Sgor Mor. As is so often the case in the Scottish hills, the lesser peaks are generally people-free. The more famous mountains, such as Ben Macdui, Cairn Toul and Braeriach to the north, have more than their share of visitors. But if you limit your altitudinous ambition you will find peace and quiet aplenty amongst 'the large religion' of Sgor Mor and Sgor Dubh.

49. THE TOP OF BENNACHIE

Aberdeen takes a fair bashing in the 'mean city' joke stakes. For instance, in Glasgow, if you want extra sugar in your tea, invariably you will be invited to help yourself. In Edinburgh the hostess is more likely to enquire, politely of course, 'One lump, or two?' Whereas, allegedly, in the Granite City you will be asked: 'Are you sure you've stirred it?' This does not conform to my dealings in Aberdeenshire. The people I know there are amongst the most generous and friendly I have ever met. On the hill, by the river and on the loch, up and down Union Street, throughout all the airts, I have always been made welcome. Though to be honest, I have never asked for more sugar in my tea.

The most notable peak in Aberdeen's immediate vicinity is Bennachie; 528m tall at its highest point, Oxen Craig, on OS Map 38, Aberdeen, Landranger Series, Scale 1:50,000 at Grid Ref: 664226. Bennachie consists of a smooth range of forested hills to the north of the River Don. Aberdeenshire's two mighty rivers, the Don and the Dee, embrace the county. Both are famous for their salmon fishing, and yet are entirely different in character. The Dee is a spate stream, wild and fierce when the Grampian snow melts and after heavy rain, and it tumbles for much of its course through rugged, heather-clumped moorlands. The Don is a more gentle affair, wandering with unhurried calm by fertile farmlands, through deep pools where huge brown trout hide. In land-value terms, Aberdeenshire farmers say: 'A mile of Don's worth twa o' Dee.'

The village of Monymusk (Grid Ref: 685154) and the Grant Arms Hotel is a good base for doing most things in rural Aberdeenshire. Malcolm Canmore, in 1078, certainly thought so. He camped there before sorting out a local rebellion mounted against his kingly authority. Before going into battle, Malcolm traced on the ground with the point of his spear the outline of a church he promised to build there if he was victorious.

One of Scotland's most treasured relics, the Monymusk Reliquary, a seventeenth-century casket reputed to hold a bone of St Columba, was filched from the House of Monymusk and now lurks in the museum at Queen Street in Edinburgh. The Reliquary was carried to Bannockburn in 1314 to encourage the troops, which it did, mightily. In modern terms, however, to my 94-year-old mother, 'Monymusk' means but one thing: the

Scottish country dance of that name. Eight people together, as far as my Aged Parent is concerned, is an irresistible invitation to the dance.

A step north from Monymusk, on the way to Bennachie, is another special place, Paradise Wood (Grid Ref: 675185). I am taking Paradise Wood with me when I finally snuff it. The wood borders the Don and it is supremely lovely, dappled with sunlight and shadow and loud with birdsong. Lord Cullen planted the original trees in 1719 and they are his everlasting memorial.

The hike to the top of Bennachie is best begun from the parking area (Grid Ref: 691245), close to Maiden Castle (Grid Ref: 691245). Bennachie walks are signposted from the car park. Although often busy, the hill is splendidly cared for by the Bennachie Rangers, who are on hand to offer advice and any assistance. To get the most out of your visit, before tramping off purchase a copy of the guidebook at Don View.

At Pittordie (Grid Ref: 692244), on the east slope of the hill, there are the remains of a Pictish Fort. Mither Tap (Grid Ref: 683224) also has the remains of a hill fort. There is a pillar on Mither Tap, and direction lines have been engraved on a brass plate on top. On a clear day the dramatic mountain of Morven in Caithness is visible, 128 miles north. Ben Macdui, Braeriach and Cairn Gorm pierce western clouds. The glory of Aberdeenshire's fields, rivers and forests lie clustered round your feet.

There and back takes as long as you want. It is easy to plan a full day out and just as easy to indulge in a quick canter to the summit. The going is comfortable on Bennachie and this makes the expedition perfect for legs little and large. Nowadays, my Aged Parent would probably beg to be excused from trotting to the top of Bennachie. But I suspect that if I promised to partner her there in a set for Monymusk she would be off like a shot. Aberdeenshire has that effect, with or without sugar.

50. OLD ABERDEEN

The civic toast of the City of Aberdeen, 'Happy to meet you, sorry to part, happy to meet you again,' gives the lie to the scurrilous stories of financial caution spread about by those who know no better. Aberdeen is one of Scotland's most welcoming cities and one of the loveliest. I first arrived there in 1952, aboard the MV *St Ninian* from Leith, with the North of Scotland and Orkney and Shetland Steam Navigation Company, now less glamorously known as P&O Ferries. Not the same, P&O. Then, the company had seven vessels: *St Clair*, *St Magnus*, *St Clement*, *Rora Head*, *St Ola*, *Earl of Zetland* and the *St Ninian*. Breakfast for our family, two adults and three boys, cost 18 shillings (90p). The return fare was one pound eight shillings and sixpence (£1.42); children half-price and meals extra. First-class value, and still the best way to arrive in the Granite City.

Norsemen also arrived by sea, but with less kindly intent and they harried the residents into submissiveness. However, the town by the twin rivers of Dee and Don flourished, mainly as an important port trading with Scandinavia and Europe. The Aberdonian dialect is founded on this 'internationalism', epitomised by Aberdeen's great comedian, Harry Gordon, creator of the hilarious character, the Laird of Inversnecky. Gordon, who died in 1957, frequently performed at His Majesty's Theatre; a white granite building adjacent to the renaissance-style Central Library and near St Mark's Church with its imposing Corinthian portico. These three buildings are irreverently referred to, collectively, by Aberdonians as: 'Education, Salvation, and Damnation.'

The Silver City is best appreciated on foot. Start with a visit to the Tourist Information Office on Broad Street. It is opposite one of the biggest granite buildings in the world, the magnificent Marischal College, second only in size to Escorial in Madrid. It was designed by A. Marshall Mackenzie in 1891 and built on the site of the original college, which was founded in 1593.

Aberdeen's first university, King's College, was established in 1495 by Bishop William Elphinstone to attend to the educational needs of Scots in an area 'separated from the rest . . . in which dwell men rude and ignorant of letters and almost barbarous'. The foundation of Marischal College 100 years later was an expression of Protestant opposition to the Episcopalianism of King's. Until 1860, when the universities amalgamated, violent feuding between their students was commonplace and frequently ugly.

The Tourist Information Office in Broad Street is well organised and contains an excellent range of books and pamphlets describing what to do and see in Aberdeen and the surrounding area. The staff are highly knowledgeable on local history and places of interest and this is supported by a series of information sheets presented in the form of Aberdeen walks. These cover Old Aberdeen, the West End, the Harbour and City Centre. W.A. Brogriden's illustrated architectural guide to the city is also an invaluable companion along the way, as is the Tourist Board's *Easy Guide to the City*. Time spent in reconnaissance is seldom wasted. Spend it at the Tourist Board and your understanding and enjoyment of the city will be greatly enhanced.

I love the sea and harbours and invariably end up wandering around the docks, including visiting the early morning fish market by the P&0 Ferry terminal. Although much depleted in numbers, the fishing fleet still makes an impressive sight in Albert Basin and there is always something of interest going on. But for me, above all, Old Aberdeen is a source of constant delight; a wonderful mixture of ancient and modern, busy with students hurrying along Bishop Elphinstone's cobbled streets, hopefully in hot pursuit of learning. The chapel contains a superb oak-carved screen and choir stalls and the building is surmounted by a glorious stone crown.

Near the chapel, where St Machar Drive and High Street meet, stands Old Aberdeen Town House, a graceful Georgian building now housing a library. Opposite King's College, on High Street, are the old houses of university professors and the landed gentry, interspersed with bookshops, student cafes and inviting watering holes.

Old Aberdeen embraces the soul and engenders trust in the past and faith in the future, as indeed does the rest of the city. Few Scottish towns have managed to preserve so much of their historical identity, intricately interwoven into the hustle and bustle of modern-day living. 'Education, Salvation, and Damnation' have been kind to the Granite City. Sprinkled no doubt with a modicum of monetary probity as well? Bon Accord to you all.

51. WALK TO DUNNOTTAR CASTLE

When I was a child we lived at Muchalls, a tiny Kincardineshire fishing village near Stonehaven. Our house, Stanathro, was perched on high cliffs, the nesting site of seabirds, with precarious access to irresistible sea-fishing from the rocks far below. I revisited the area last month to pay my respects and to explore one of Scotland's most dramatic castles, grey Dunnottar, which crowns a grim, 49 metre-high windy promontory one and a half miles south from the calm of Stonehaven Harbour.

Use OS Map 45, Stonehaven, second series, Scale 1:50,000 to find your way round. Leaving my car at Shorehead (Grid Ref: 877853), I trekked up Common Brae to the start of the clifftop footpath (Grid Ref: 877851) to Dunnottar. Foul weather accompanied me: a biting northeast gale howling over a white-capped, leaden-silver, boatless sea. I pulled my collar up and my hat down, cringing before a sudden snowstorm. Pain before pleasure, the old Scots way.

A Doric War Memorial (Grid Ref: 878845) dominates the track, and I paused to leave a poppy amid the dark columns: a red winter speck of inadequate remembrance. Ahead, Dunnottar beckoned, glimpsed fleetingly through the gloom, surrounded by whirling sheets of gale-driven flakes. The old castle glared: 'Wha dar meddle wi' me?' Some did, including William Wallace, who captured Dunnottar from the English in 1297 during the Scottish Wars of Independence. The defenders took refuge in the chapel, but to celebrate his victory, and presumably to encourage the rest, Wallace set fire to the church and burned them alive. St Ninian, the Apostle of Pictland, who established a church on the rock in AD 500, must have turned in his grave. However, Wallace paid a fearful price. Edward I devised the execution: '. . to be drawn, chained prostrate on a hurdle, by the Strand to Smithfield, and there half-hanged, disemboweled, castrated, beheaded, and quartered.' Edward was, if nothing else, at least thorough.

I climbed to the castle, shuddering at the prospect of having to assail such an imposing fortress. Wallace apart, Dunnottar was never taken by direct assault. In 1652, that 'great, bad man', Oliver Cromwell, well-known for knocking things about, took the castle only after a cannon-battering siege that lasted for eight months, supervised by the military genius of General Overton. I had taken a bit of a battering myself along the windy cliff and was grateful for the respite afforded by the dank shelter of the Gate House.

Outside, the wind raged and the sea roared and I was immediately aware of the presence of a thousand ghosts bidding me, I hoped, friendly welcome. The joy of calling on Scotland's monuments off-season is that invariably you have the place to yourself. That morning was no exception. Not a living soul stirred. Deep in thought by Wallace's Door, I almost jumped over the battlement in fright when a startled thrush shrieked from the undergrowth.

Above me loomed the gaunt Great Tower, 12m by 11m, 18m in height, where the Crown Jewels of Scotland, along with the maces of St Andrews University, were hidden after Cromwell defeated King Charles II at the Battle of Worcester on 3 September 1651. When Overton's Roundheads came knocking unceremoniously at Dunnottar's door, these precious emblems were lowered from the castle wall where a woman, feigning collecting seaweed, spirited them off to safety at Kinneff Church six miles south. There they awaited the return of King Charles in 1660 and the restoration of legal mirth and jollity. Less jolly is the infamous Wings Vault. A total of 122 men and 45 women were incarcerated here during Argyll's futile rebellion in May 1685. I stood by the single window, trying to imagine the cruel suffering of those sad people crammed into a stinking, insanitary hole measuring barely 16m long by 4.5m wide. Later, I muttered a prayer for them in Dunnottar's silent, roofless chapel, now freshly carpeted with pristine snow; watched by a black-eyed, red-bibbed robin and, no doubt, shades of St Ninian and countless other seriously religious gentlemen. Better, however, to be safe in these matters. One never knows who may be watching, or listening.

Leaving Dunnottar to its dreams and nightmares, I walked back to Stonehaven. In the harbour, the *Susan*, *Khina*, *White Rose* and *Orion* lay beached, waiting for the tide. I followed suit in the warmth of the Ship Inn. Visiting November castles can be cold, demanding work.

52. UIG SANDS

When my son Blair was nine I taught him how to play chess. Which was a bad move. Within a few years he was beating me, regularly. I blame the Outer Hebrides for this state of affairs. My set is a replica of the famous twelfth-century Lewis Chessmen, dislodged by the back-end of an itchy cow from some Uig sand dunes in 1831. The intricately carved pieces fascinated Blair and he loved playing with them. Whenever I walk Uig sands, I plot revenge. But it is hard to be malicious in such magnificent surroundings. The whitewashed bulk of Uig Lodge dominates the impressive view. The Rev. W. Macleod, minister of Uig and Timsgarry parish, nurtures the spiritual quality of the area. Timsgarry church bell is tolled from the outside, by a rope dangling from the belfry, reminding all and sundry that on Lewis you are never more than six days distant from the Sabbath.

Miavaig, where Uig Parish Church and the Free Presbytery Church glower in uneasy harmony, is the start of a happy ramble round the shores of Loch Roag, once renowned for the quality of its shellfish, whelks, oysters, scallops and mussels, but now little better than an open sewer, polluted by untreated waste from unsightly fish farms where upwards of 5 million fake salmon are reared.

The township of Cliff bounds this little peninsula in the north, with Valtos to the west. The hinterland is classic Lewis: sparse, rock-strewn, acid soil and peat hags, scattered with tiny lochans, but the shore fronting Kyles Pabay and Traigh na Berie is machair-fringed, fertile, and backed by gentle dunes. There is evidence that there has been human habitation here for more than 4,000 years: Neolithic man, Celts, Picts, Norsemen and rapacious lairds of more modern times. The Egyptian, Ptolemy, called the island 'Hebules' and the Vikings christened it 'Ljot's House'; the Gaelic word for Lewis is 'Leodhas'.

The island of Great Bernera divides east and west Loch Roag and has the distinction of being one of the few Highland communities to successfully oppose its ruthless factor, Donald Munro, who was sacked by his laird during the nineteenth-century clearances because of his brutality. Munro was one of the most influential men in Lewis and he considered himself above the law. With little thought for his tenants, he ordered them off their most valuable grazing lands. When he proposed to restrict their access even to the poor lands he had allocated them, his tenants marched on Stornoway to protest. In the ensuing rumpus several were imprisoned. As a magistrate, Munro tried to use his influence to have the unfortunate crofters found guilty of attacking him. He lost the case and was dismissed from his high position in disgrace.

The sands of Traigh na Berie are an ideal picnic spot and during summer months they offer safe, if somewhat invigorating, bathing in waters warmed by the Gulf Stream. At Berie, by Loch na Berie, is the site of a broch, built between 100 BC and AD 200, also used in later years as a Pictish home. An equally important broch site is a few hundred yards northwest from Berie at Loch Barabhat, on a small island joined to the shore by a causeway. Apart from the broch sites, there are the remains of four Norse grain mills along the line of a small stream that slips into Kyles Pabay at the north end of the dunes. Traigh na Berie is also an important bird reserve and the dune habitat hosts a fine array of wildflowers and plants. Indeed, the Miavaig Peninsula has something for everyone, offering a splendid family day out amid the special magic of the 'Heather Isle'.

Park at Miavaig and take the road to Reef. At the end of the road, follow the cliff north to reach Traigh na Berie and its brochs. Return to the coast, to the sites of the old Norse grain mills. Walk north through Kneep and Valtos to reach Eala Sheadha headland, then west round Toa Mor to Camas na Clibhe beach (no swimming due to dangerous currents). At Cliff, climb southeast to Loch Trailavat. Return to Miavaig over Nisa Mhor (136m).

Use OS Map No.13, West Lewis and North Harris, second series, Scale 1:50,000. Uig Lodge Grid Ref: 055332; Timsgarry Church Grid Ref: 053344; Miavaig Grid Ref: 084345; Loch na Berie Grid Ref: 104352; Loch Barabhat Grid Ref: 099354; Traigh na Berie Grid Ref: 105359; Grain Mills Grid Ref: 101360; Valtos Grid Ref: 092370; Eala Sheadha Grid Ref: 090381; Camas na Clibhe Grid Ref: 084365; Cliff Grid Ref: 083360; Nisa Mhor Grid Ref: 090353.

53. WALK GROSEBAY

I was in Harris recently, courtesy of Calmac, sailing from Uig in Skye to Tarbert at the 'waist' of the Long Island. The sea was millpond calm, splashed with graceful porpoises busy earning their keep in the deep blue waters of the Little Minch. As the ferry approached the rocky, broken shoreline, tiny, dun-coloured, storm petrels fluttered above the surface in the wake of our vessel. Looking out over the innocent ocean, it was sad to think that every inch of the water I surveyed was contaminated by the world's biggest-ever outbreak of amnesiac shellfish poisoning. I wondered how much this disaster, which has so damaged the business of Hebridean shellfish fishermen, would affect the business of the other creatures, animals and birds, that rely upon shellfish for sustenance?

We edged past Scalpay with its proud new bridge until, with the ship's engines churning the water into white foam, we bumped against the pier at Tarbert, bustling with people waving welcome to relatives and visitors, as others waited to leave after their Harris holiday. Calum Mackinnon from Grosebay was there to meet us. You get nowhere fast on Harris. The route from Tarbert south to Grosebay follows a narrow, tortuous, coast-hugging minor track known as the 'Golden Road', so called because when the civil servant that authorised its construction was presented with the final bill, he is reputed to have exclaimed in horror: 'For goodness sake, what is this road made of – gold?' Half an hour later we were in Calum's sitting-room, looking at one of the most spectacular seascapes in Europe.

Clan Macleod ruled the island for centuries and it has been said of them that 'They are like pikes in water; the oldest of them, if larger, eats the younger.' This comment is attributed to their erstwhile arch-enemies, Clan Mackenzie, no sluggards either in the rapacious pursuit of self-interest. The Mackenzies eventually managed to wrest control of Harris from the Macleods in 1779. Today, a different breed of self-interest controls this magical isle. Absentee southern gents own virtually the whole of Harris. They use it as their private sporting plaything, buying and selling their land on the open market to any Tom, Dick or Rupert who has the cash to pay, once they themselves have tired of aping the Highland Laird.

Calum Mackinnon's cottage above Grosebay (Tel: 01859 530356) is a comfortable B&B establishment and the perfect base for exploring Harris.

You will need OS Map 14, Tarbert and Loch Seaforth, second series, Scale 1:50,000 to guide you round. Grosebay is at Grid Ref: 155930. An excellent preliminary hike is from Bayhead in the east, over the hills to the Atlantic and the yellow sands of Traigh Luskentyre in the west. The walk, eight miles there and back, is fully described in an excellent brochure written by Ian Stephen and Bill Lawson, available from the Tarbert Tourist Office (Tel: 01859 502011). Park at the Stockinish road junction on the Golden Road (Grid Ref: 127930), then follow a track which leads northeast to Loch Glumra Beg. After quarter of a mile, at a T-junction, hang a left towards Bayhead. From Bayhead, the track climbs over the *bealach* between Maoladh Mhicearraig (340m) to the south and West Stocklett (218m) to the north.

The paths you tramp have carried many feet in days past. This is a 'coffin' road, the route taken by the people who lived on the east coast when they laid their loved ones to rest. The depth of soil in the east is so sparse that it is impossible to dig a proper grave. Hence, the dead were carried to the more fertile machair lands on the west coast, where they were buried in the old graveyard at Seilebost. Cairns of stones by the side of the path mark the places where they rested during the journey. As the route passes little Loch Carran (Grid Ref: 088961), bear right to reach the A859 Tarbert–Leverburgh road.

Walk towards Tarbert for half a mile, to where the River Laxford crosses under the road at Grid Ref: 102969. Find the old track again, on the south side of the main road, and follow it back to the start point past Loch Laxdale, via the Golden Road. The contrast between the jagged lands of the east and the gentle, supreme beauty of the west is stunning. Indeed, this is true of the whole of the island. There is an ethereal beauty here which captivates the soul. Even today, this is a wild, untamed land – matched only in time and space by the enduring courtesy and kindliness of the people who call Harris home.

54. VALLEY AND THE SUNKEN CAVES OF HOSTA

'Nae man can tether time or tide.' But you can learn to live with them. As an exciseman, Scotland's national bard, Robert Burns, was well aware of this fact, as were the smugglers he hunted. Therefore, before enjoying one of North Uist's loveliest walks, carefully check time and tide. Otherwise, be prepared for a long wait on Valley Island until the seas recede and you can return safely to the mainland.

At low tide, Valley Island is separated from North Uist by two miles of golden sand. Then it is safe to walk out and explore this summer primrose-covered paradise. An hour will take you round the coast and on the north shore you will find the finest beaches in Britain, backed by golden dunes, solitary and remote. Like Tam o' Shanter, it is easy to forget time and tide on Valley and succumb to the 'songs and sweet airs' of this magical isle. Nor will you be the first visitor to fall under Valley's spell. The ruined house that dominates the island was once the home of the Granville family, cousins of the queen, who still own much of Uist. Four thousand years ago, Stone Age man grazed cattle on Valley and even today Uist crofters from the villages of Sollas, Malaclete and Middlequarter take their sheep over the shining sands to crop summer grass.

The 'Children of Colla' were evicted from their homes in 1849 to make way for the 'Great Cheviot'. Godfrey William Wentworth MacDonald, fourth Baron of the Isles, was £200,000 in debt and hard pressed by creditors. Sheep were to be his financial salvation. The only problem was his people. At the first attempt to issue writs of eviction, sheriff officers were sent scuttling from Malaclete in a shower of stones, thrown by angry, fearful tenants. A force of 33 constables, armed with truncheons and led by William Colquhoun, sheriff substitute, and Superintendent MacBean, sailed from Oban to beat the men of Sollas into submission. Ever anxious to please his superiors, an island minister, Macrae, accompanied the force: God's Law as well as man's would be used to bring the villagers to heel. Alexander Mackenzie, in his *History of the Highland Clearances*, described the scene:

> There was no discussion, no argument, no appeals. The police formed two lines down the street of the township. Sheriff-officers asked one question only at the doors of the cottages, whether those within were prepared to emigrate on the terms offered. If the answer was no, and it invariably was, then bedding, bed-frames, spinning-wheels, barrels, benches, tables and clothing were all dragged out and left at the door. Divots were torn from the roof and house timbers pulled down ready for burning.

The villagers, grouped into a small army, began to hurl rocks and stones at the constables. MacBean put his men into two divisions and sent them forward against the crowd with their batons. One took the villagers in the rear, the other in the flank, and drove them over barley rigs and dykes, along the shore. The end was never in doubt. Three years later, on Christmas 1852, the villagers of Sollas, Malaclete and Middlequarter, everyone other than the old, the sick and the lame, left their Uist lands forever. The smallpox-ridden frigate *Hercules* sailed for Australia, taking with it the tormented souls of an abandoned people. As you drive past the empty shells of their ruined homes, spare them a thought.

Westwards along the quiet road that circles North Uist is a Victorian folly, an incongruous tower on the south shore of Loch Scolpaig. From behind the croft, at the end of the track that divides the two 'wings' of the loch, a path leads north along a cliff to the Sunken Caves of Hosta. Natural arches, carved by thousand-year-old waves, throw up endless Atlantic breakers in sheets of white spray. Caves probe deep into the rocks, and near Sloc Roe the land has given up the battle, tumbling into a great, gaping hole. On wild days, storm-driven waters howl at the foot of the pit.

The remains of a Pictish fort lie on the heights above Bagh Blaaskie: Caisteal Odair, 'castle of the dappled hill'. A long wall protects southern approaches to the promontory, pierced by an entrance 15ft long and 5ft wide. The site of the fort must have made it almost impregnable and inside the fortifications are outlines of circular stone foundations, home and hearth to generations of early Gaels.

The walk over to Valley Island takes about 40 minutes and an hour will see you round its shores. Return to the car and drive south for a few miles to begin the hike to the Sunken Caves of Hosta. You can't miss the Victorian tower, and you should park nearby. Walk down to the shore, where you will find yet another glorious beach. Hang a right here and follow the cliff path north to the caves and Caisteal Odair. Return to base by retracing your steps.

As the long Hebridean day drifts towards its close over Valley Island, and the late sun dips into western seas, there comes a stillness, a moment of timeless beauty when curlews call down the hill and lapwings dip and twist in the gloaming. Then, there is no lovelier place in all of Scotland to say goodnight to the world.

You need OS Map 18, Sound of Harris, second series, Scale 1:50,000 to follow the routes described above. For Valley Island, park at Grid Ref: 781736; Valley Island Grid Ref: 775765; Loch Scolpaig Grid Ref: 733751; Sunken Caves Grid Ref: 726765; Caisteal Odair Grid Ref: 731769.

55. MARKET STANCE TO SCARILODE

Benbecula, Beinn a'faodhia, 'the hill of the fords', is a flat, moorland landscape dominated by Rueval, the highest hill on the island. Here, in a shallow cave on the nights of 25 and 26 June 1746, Bonnie Prince Charlie anxiously awaited Flora Macdonald. Flora's stepfather, Captain Hugh Macdonald, had supplied the travel documents that allowed the prince, disguised as Flora Macdonald's maid Betty Burke, to escape. And not a moment too soon. Word was out that the fugitive was hiding on Benbecula and General Campbell had arrived to hunt him down, commanding a force of more than 2,000 men. The following month, that relentless pursuer of the Prince, Captain Ferguson of HMS *Furnace*, arrested Flora. She was imprisoned in the Tower of London. Flora was released in 1747 under the Act of Indemnity and three years later married Alan Macdonald of Kingsburgh. Dr Johnson met her there in 1773, by which time Flora Macdonald was 50 years old, but still a considerable presence. The doctor reported: 'We were entertained at Kingsburgh with the usual hospitality by Mr Macdonald and his lady Flora Macdonald, a name that will be mentioned in history and if courage and fidelity are virtues, mentioned with honour.'

Until recent times, Benbecula was isolated from its near neighbours North and South Uist by the North and South Fords, when passage over the shifting sands was dangerous and difficult. In 1943 a causeway was built over South Ford, still known as O'Regan's Bridge in honour of the priest most active in advocating its construction. Seventeen years passed before Benbecula was linked to North Uist. In 1960 the Queen Mother opened the route, thus completing the link.

Ann and I first visited Benbecula in 1977. With four children, ranging from two to 16 years, we stayed in a caravan near Balivanich. One fine bright morning the family set off to Market Stance, a few miles south of Gramsdale, intent on a picnic, fishing and walking. In days gone by Market Stance was where cattle were bought and sold. Mainland dealers would gather there to haggle with the locals and buy their black cattle.

We parked by the shores of Loch Ba Una where Ann, our daughter

Lewis-Ann, young Charles and infant Jean disembarked to splash and play in shallow waters. My elder son, Blair, and I set off eastwards along Clanranald's Kelp Road to find the ruined village of Scarilode. During the Great War, kelp was the major industry of Benbecula. Potash, produced by burning kelp, was essential to armaments factories and more than 600 tons were exported each year.

The old track winds round the south side of Rueval through a wilderness of heather-covered moorlands, blue and silver with shining lochs and tiny lochans. Northeast, behind Rueval, lies one of the most notorious of these waters: Loch na Beire. Two small islands grace the loch, Mheribh Mhor and Mheribh Bheag. On Mhor there is said to be a circular hole, now hidden beneath heather and bluebells, carved from ancient rock and once used as a place of execution. Condemned men were bound, thrust into the hole and left to die. At a convenient time, the corpse was removed and buried on Mheribh Bheag, presumably to make way for further miscreant occupants of that infamous pit.

Apart from the section between Scarilode and the north arm of the Kelp Road, this is an easy walk, a round trip of about eight miles. On the way home, climb Rueval and search for Prince Charlie's cave. This eastern area of Benbecula was once part of a large farm known as Nunton, owned in the 1920s by Lady Gordon Cathcart, resident of Bournemouth. The islanders who survived the carnage of the First World War returned expecting to find, as promised, a 'land fit for heroes to live in'. Instead, they found the same entrenched divisions they had been told they were fighting to end: landlords protecting hereditary legal rights and their near-destitute tenants expected to be humbly thankful for the smallest morsel of approbation.

The Crofting Acts of the late nineteenth century ended the monstrous iniquity of summary eviction and gave tenants security to work and improve their lands. However, what it didn't do was return the land so brutally sequestered to its previous occupants. Benbecula ex-servicemen took the law into their own hands and seized their land by force, defying the law and anyone else to remove them. The many marks of shielings on Benbecula's map show the results of their desperate efforts to live and work on the land they loved and had fought so hard to defend.

Seven years before my first visit the crofts at Scarilode were still occupied, bright with the sound of laughter and smiling faces, in spite of the constant battle against the elements to wrest a meagre living from the sparse soils. How much would world-weary businessmen in City 'trenches' pay today for the privilege of living amidst the magnificent, isolated, god-like splendour of Scarilode? Eternity was born here, amongst the surging foam and singing gulls. Priceless.

Use OS Map 22, Benbecula, second series, Scale 1:50,000. Market Stance Grid Ref: 805535; Start point Grid Ref: 801535; Scarilode shielings Grid Ref: 846520; Rueval Grid Ref: 826535.

56. THE HECLA RIDGE

I saw them far below me, running across the moor. Four matchstick figures, brightly dressed, eating up the ground with frightening rapidity. Good Lord, I thought, they must be fit. At the pace they were going they would be upsides with me in about half an hour. I turned back to the broken crags of Beinn na h-Aire and climbed on towards the final, smooth shoulder of Hecla. June sunlight sparkled over the hill. The golden machair lands of South Uist mingled with the green-and-white of Atlantic waves. In the distance I saw the gentle Monach Isles and glimpsed the sentinel stacks of St Kilda on the horizon. The silver-and-blue maze of Benbecula and North Uist lochs and lochans spread northwards like a wondrous geological map, crowned by hazy Harris hills.

I rested for coffee on the subsidiary top of Ben Scalavat. Moments later my pursuers appeared, hardly out of breath; they were soldiers from the army base at Balivanich on Benbecula, enjoying a gentle trot to break the monotony of military discipline and the calm of a Hebridean weekend. They passed by with a cheery wave: 'Sorry for disturbing you,' called the back-marker. 'Have a nice day!' Then they disappeared in good order towards the summit of Hecla.

My wife, Ann, and I fell in love with the Outer Hebrides many years ago and of all the 'long islands' South Uist is our favourite. Hecla (606m) lies at the north end of the island, the last in a spine of dramatic peaks extending from Loch Eynort in the south, over Beinn Mhor (620m) and Ben Corodale (527m) to Loch Skipport. I lunched on the summit of Hecla, looking towards Loch Corodale and the site of the Prince's Cave above Corodale Bay. Over 100 people lived there at the time of Bonnie Prince Charlie; a thriving, vibrant community which courteously received their unwelcome, notorious guest. His escape was planned there. Descending from my rocky bastion, I picked my way carefully down to the saddle ridge that links Hecla to its lesser, western crests: Coire Rudale and Maoladh Creag nan Druidean.

I scrambled down the steep-sided glen and followed the course of the tiny stream flowing from Loch a'Choire. As it grew in stature, I stopped to bathe in a crystal pool, wearing the water like an all-embracing dream. A mile further brought me to one of the most glorious and beautiful lochs in the world, Loch Spotal, dimpled and ringed with rising trout. As I paused by the edge, a small, brown, whiskered head broke the surface. The otter watched me curiously, secure and unafraid. We chatted a while, about this and that, before he excused himself to attend to supper.

A graceful yacht, sails neatly stowed, sheltered in Caolas Mor bay as I reached the coast. The smell of cooking drifted over the water and quickened my step homewards. A track lead round the shore past a solitary cottage to the roadside at Lochskipport, where I had parked my car. I looked back to Hecla, now shadowed in evening sunlight, and said 'thank you'.

Find the route round the Hecla ridge by using OS Map 22, Benbecula, second series, Scale 1:50,000. Park at Grid Ref: 828385. From the parking place, follow the obvious track south. This leads round the coast, ending just past a neat cottage on the hill. Now, head in the general direction of the clearly visible north end of the Hecla ridge, picking up a high sheep track that leads along the north shore of Loch Bein. Cross the stream at the end of the loch and follow this inlet burn up onto the ridge. From there, walk south, climbing across Maol Martaig, Beinn na h-Aire and Ben Scalavat to reach the summit of Hecla. Come down from Hecla via the western spur, onto Coire Rudale. Midway along the crest, descend to Loch a'Choire. Follow the outlet burn north, bearing quarter-right after half a mile to reach Loch Spotal. Cross between Spotal and its neighbour, Loch Fada, and walk northeast back to the coastline track. Follow the track to the car parking place.

You will cover a distance of approximately nine miles across rough country and should allow six hours for this expedition. Unless, of course, you choose to run. A compass and map are essential, particularly for the return to the car should the weather deteriorate. Key points are: start of ridge Grid Ref: 847373; Beinn na h-Aire Grid Ref: 844357; Ben Scalavat Grid Ref: 838348; Hecla Grid Ref: 825345; Coire Rudale Grid Ref: 815355; Loch Spotal Grid Ref: 833366.

57. SOUTH UIST AND HOWBEG

It is high summer, in spite of the prevailing mix of bitter weather blessed by the occasional bright day. Therefore, I think a trip to downtown

Howbeg on the island of South Uist is appropriate; to pay respects to Neil MacEachen who was born there and who helped Bonnie Prince Charlie escape from the Hebrides in June 1746. MacEachen chummed BPC to France, where his illustrious patron promptly dumped him. Eventually he settled at Sedan, where he married. His son, Jacques Etienne Joseph Alexandre Macdonald, became mega-famous during Bonaparte's European wars. Napoleon appointed him governor of Rome in 1798, and Duke of Taranto and a Marshall of France in 1809. But Macdonald never forgot his ancestral home. He visited Howbeg in 1826 and gathered stones and earth from his father's birthplace. When he died, these mementos were buried with him.

Our expedition today starts at Howmore, where there is a thatched-roof Youth Hostel. Close by are the ruins of a twelfth-century church. Pause in this grassy sanctuary, and I promise that you will be overwhelmed by a sense of utter peace. Leave the church and head west to the mouth of the Howmore River. A golden tramp follows, along a deserted beach cascaded clean by white-washed waves, eventually returning you to the start point over wildflower-rich machair lands; an easy, uninhibited, nine miles. You don't really need a map, or indeed a swimming costume if you decide to chance a bracing dip in the surf en route, but OS Map No 22, Benbecula, second series, Scale 1:50,000 is useful.

The Youth Hostel is at Grid Ref: 757364; the mouth of the Howmore River, Grid Ref: 754363; Howbeg is at Grid Ref: 755356. Return from Howbeg to the beach and hike south past rocky Verran Island (Grid Ref: 729349) to find the Neolithic standing stone at Grid Ref: 735337. Enjoy the next two-and-a-half miles listening to the singing sound of 3,000-mile-old Atlantic breakers and the cry of seagulls. Lunch lies ahead on the little peninsula of Rubha Ardvule, by Dun Vulan Broch (Grid Ref: 712297). The broch was built some 2,000 years ago and an archaeological team from Sheffield University have been uncovering its secrets during the past decade; supported by South Uist Estates, Bornish township Grazing Committee, the local History Society, Historic Scotland, Royal Archaeological Institute, Scottish Natural Heritage and South Uist Builders. Brochs are unique to Scotland and were built to a similar pattern: walls were 4.8m thick and 9–12m in height, tapering towards the top, which was covered by a thatched roof. Within the walls was a stairway with galleries and windows to the inside. A small, easily defended door in the base gave access to the central area which enclosed a space approximately 15m in diameter. A museum at Kildonan (Grid Ref: 745275), to the east of the A865 Lochboisdale to Benbecula road, contains finds from Dun Vulan as well as a reconstructed Iron Age wheelhouse. Wheel-house villages, around which our ancestors grew crops on the fertile machair land, tended their sheep and cattle and fished in the rough seas, were numerous in South Uist.

Leave Dun Vulan and walk east towards Loch Bornish. At Grid Ref: 730299, turn north onto the machair and head for the ruins of Ormiclate Castle at Grid Ref: 749318. This is an old Clanranald home, mysteriously burnt down on 13 November 1715, the day Clanranald himself was killed during the Battle of Sheriffmuir where the Earl of Mar and the Duke of Argyll fought an indecisive action which gave rise to the rhyme:

There's some say that we wan
And some say that they wan
And some say that nane wan at a' man.

Nearly 200 years later, Lady Clanranald's jewellery, which had been lost in the blaze, was rediscovered by a visitor probing about in the ruins.

Jewels of another kind adorn the machair, an amazing profusion and variety of wildflowers; cranesbill, tufted vetch, lady's bedstraw, machair pansies, scarlet pimpernels, spotted orchids, butterfly orchids, wild thyme, clover, buttercups, daisies, selfheal and lesser meadow rue. The machair is also home to rare species of birds such as corncrakes, corn buntings, twites, dunlins, redshanks, snipe, oystercatchers, lapwings and ringed plovers.

The track now skirts the west shore of Loch West Ollay, famous for the size and quality of its wild brown trout, and returns to the standing stone visited on the way out. Follow the route above the beach to the mouth of the Howmore River and back to the Youth Hostel. Say 'thank you' nicely for a glorious day.

58. BEINN MHOR

The bar at the Lochboisdale Hotel on South Uist is the longest I have ever seen. In whaling days, thirsty crews, fresh from South Atlantic storms, disembarked in dry-throated droves demanding instant service and plenty of space to raise and lower elbows. When it comes to elbow raising I'm no slouch myself, but some occupants that night seemed intent upon breaking the world record for the greatest volume of whisky consumed during the course of a single evening. They would have had to go some to beat the current holders, though – Creagorry Hotel, just up the road on the neighbouring Island of Benbecula. There, the back of the bar used to be lined with prepackaged takeaways, each containing half a bottle of whisky and a couple of cans of export to round off the evening, discreetly wrapped in plain brown paper bags.

Pride of place in the Lochboisdale public bar is given over to a huge photograph of the island's patron saint, Saint SS *Politician*, immortalized in Compton Mackenzie's book *Whisky Galore*. Thousands of cases of *uisge beatha*, 'water of life', were 'rescued' when the vessel ran aground between Eriskay and South Uist during the Second World War. I think the islanders have been praying for similar heavenly munificence ever since.

A single road runs the length of the west coast of the island. The rest of South Uist is a desolate, trackless, moorland wilderness rising to majestic mountains fringed by spectacular cliff scenery. There are three peaks: Hecla (606m) to the north and Beinn Mhor (620m) to the south. Sandwiched between them is Ben Corodale (529m). Because these mountains rise suddenly almost from sea level, the South Uist mountains look dramatic and daunting. But they are easy to climb, provided you choose the right route and the right day.

The approach to Beinn Mhor starts from the coastal road north of Market Stance, near three lochs called Ollay: West, Mid and East. I fished there fruitlessly a few years back and renamed them respectively Damn, Bugger and Sweet Fanny. Nevertheless, they do contain some excellent fish, particularly West Ollay, which holds glass-case-sized wild brown trout. This is a compass-and-map country; stout walking boots and full wet weather gear are required. Uist weather is fickle: one moment clear and fine, the next a storm racing in from the Atlantic. Should mist come down, you must be prepared. There are dangerous crags on Beinn Mhor and great care must be exercised. In spite of its modest height, treat Beinn Mhor with the utmost respect.

Park at Grid Ref: 768341 (OS Map 22, Benbecula, second series, Scale 1:50,000). A comforting peat track leads eastwards from the A865, egging you on, then deserts you for rough, soggy, heather-covered moors. However, the going is not too tough and your reference point should be the north shoulder of Beinn Mhor. Aim for Maola Breac (Grid Ref: 796333). Once there, the walking becomes easier. As you climb, the coastal machair plain spreads below, a springtime wildflower-covered masterpiece edged by a golden carpet of miraculous empty beaches.

A ragged, narrow ridge leads southeast from Maola Breac, rising towards the summit. Pick your way cautiously upward. The hardest part is the final scramble, threading carefully over and round jagged boulders. Once on the summit (Grid Ref: 809311) the reward is everything and more than you could ever wish. North across Ben Corodale and Hecla blush South Harris hills, the 'heather isles'. Over the silver seas in Skye rear the mighty Cuillin hills: Sgurr Alasdair, Sgurr nan Eag and Sgurr Dearg. Beyond, on mainland Scotland are the Assynt and Fisherfield peaks, an Teallach, Ben More and Quinag. Southwards is Heaval, on Barra, its attendant small isles shadowed in shimmering seas.

At the foot of Beinn Mhor, locked in an eastern mountain prison, nestles little Loch Hellisdale (Grid Ref: 828310). Close by, on cliffs guarding Corodale Bay, is Prince's Cave (Grid Ref: 834313). The luckless Young Pretender, Bonnie Prince Charlie, hid there after the flight from Drummossie Moor in 1746, tattered and bedraggled and not so bonnie by all accounts. I suppose after months running for his life, living wild, that was only to be expected. But I have damn-all sympathy for that vagabond prince. He carried with him nothing other than disaster wherever he went and hammered the last nail into the coffin of a way of life that had survived for centuries.

This is the land of the golden eagle. Once, one clear sunny autumn day, Ann and I watched from the shores of Loch Druidibeg as an eagle circled in the thermals above Hecla. Even from such distance its huge dark shape dominated the skies. As we watched, a second bird thrust itself from the purple crags to join its mate. If you dream of seeing the 'lord of the skies', then amidst gracious Uist mountains that dream will come true.

59. NORTH GLENDALE

Brighten up in glorious South Uist. The Manager and I pilgrimaged there a couple of weeks back. We were stunned by the quality of light; an ethereal, mystic glow, banding the Hebridean horizon in silver and gold. No other place in Scotland has such soft air. No other place in Scotland has such an overwhelming, all-embracing presence.

We paid our respects to the SS *Politician* of *Whisky Galore* fame. Not by diving on the wreck, you understand, but in the public bar of the Lochboisdale Hotel (Tel: 01878 700332). Pride of place is given over to a photograph of the famous vessel that brought so much happiness to the islands when it ran aground off Eriskay during the Second World War. Its cargo contained thousands of cases of whisky, an unspecified number of which were 'liberated' by drouthy, *uisge beatha*-starved natives. At the time, a customs officer spoke to the crew of a boat tied up at Lochboisdale pier. He asked them why they were not up in the pub having their drams, as they usually did when in Lochboisdale? They invited the official aboard. After three hours the man was seen walking unsteadily homewards whistling happily, clutching a large, bulky, brown paper bag to his chest.

Whistle with me today on a hike to the south of Lochboisdale. Clutch OS Map 31, Barra, second series, Scale 1:50,000 to your chest whilst doing so. Our objective is a walk of eight miles along marginal tracks and over broken hill ground to climb Maraval (162m) at Grid Ref: 796157. There are higher peaks in South Uist, Hecla (606m), Ben Corodale (527m) and Beinn Mhor (620m), but modest Maraval has a grace and charm of its own which cannot be denied.

Approach the start point from the B888 road that runs south from Daliburgh. Hang an east at Grid Ref: 755180 and park after three miles at North Glendale (Grid Ref: 791178). Walk along a bit, and on your right you will see a very inviting grassy slope leading up the hill. Climb here to reach a gate and the moorland track. For some distance it is difficult to discern the path, but the walking is easy, so press on ahead. You will soon come to a more obvious track heading southwest. You will see a path leading down towards Loch Kearsinish over 'duck-boards'. Don't be tempted, it will only take you to a fake-fish farm site.

Once past the loch, the route contours along the side of Beinn Bheag (Grid Ref: 810167) above Loch Marulaig, eventually dropping down to the ruins of a village at the head of Loch Hartabreck, a sea loch, and Eilean Dubh (Grid Ref: 818153). Have your lunch watching seals and seagulls. As you chomp, spare a thought for the people who lived here until the settlement was deserted in 1927. Children walked to a school each day through these wild hills, winter and summer, regardless of the weather.

From Hartabreck, look out for a line of broken fence posts pointing the way forward over steeply rising ground. Head for a break in the crags on the east side of Hartabreck (150m, Grid Ref: 822149). Admire the splendid view, then make for the ridge of Cruachan, with its tiny unnamed lochans on the summit (Grid Ref: 807149). Continue now to the top of Maraval, half a mile northwest from Cruachan. Although these hills are modest in height, there is a fair bit of hands and knees work in places, so take care, particularly in wet weather. Better safe than sorry.

Look out from Maraval over a wondrous vista. Eriskay lies before you, the new causeway being built between South Uist and Eriskay fingering its way across the blue and azure waters where the SS *Polly* lies asleep. To the south, beyond the islands of Gighay and Hellisay, Heaval (383m) on Barra dominates the horizon. To the east, amidst white-capped waves, rears the dark shape of the Cuillin on Skye. Northwards, the mountains of North Uist and Harris crowd the view.

Head home by descending the western slopes of Maraval. Find the track at the foot of the hill (Grid Ref: 791158). It will guide you comfortably past Loch Kearinish to the start point at North Glendale. Back at the Lochboisdale Hotel, ready for well-earned refreshment, you will be assured of space at the bar. The counter in the public bar is the longest in Scotland, much needed when whole crews from whaling ships arrived home from the south Atlantic, demanding prompt service. Join them. Toast these magical isles, and the SS *Politician* on the wall behind you.

60. HEAVAL

Not many people are aware of the fact that Noah knew The Macneill of Barra. He did, because prior to the Great Flood Noah sent The Macneill a message telling him that there was a place reserved in the Ark for him and for his wife. The Macneill replied, with typical Highland courtesy, saying thank you, but no, he already had a perfectly good boat of his own.

Barra is the largest of the southern isles of the Outer Hebrides. The other, smaller, islands are Vatersay, Muldoanich, Sandray, Flodday, Lingay, Pabbay, Mingulay and Berneray. Apart from Vatersay, which is now joined to Barra by a grand new causeway, these islands are uninhabited. Climb to the top of Barra's highest peak, Heaval (383m), past the Carrara marble statue of the Madonna and Child to enjoy a heart-stopping view of this southern seascape. Looking down from the top of Heaval, the dark speck of Kisimul Castle grandly guards the town: a squat, black tower set in a silver-blue sea, ageless and all-enduring. In times past, the Macneill piper would proudly proclaim from the battlements: 'Hear, Ye People, and listen, Ye Nations! The Macneill of Barra having finished his dinner, all the princes of the earth are at liberty to dine!'

In 1839, when the last of the main line of Macneill chiefs, General Roderick Macneill, was declared bankrupt, the infamous Colonel Gordon of Cluny bought Barra. The new laird presided over years of brutal eviction and the enforced emigration of his tenants. Against their will, the people were shipped to Canada and their lands given over to sheep farmers. Robert Lister MacNeil, a Canadian architect and the descendant of a dispossessed Barra man, successfully proved his claim to the chieftainship and became the 45th Chief in 1915, restoring and living in Kisimul Castle in Castle Bay. Robert Lister is buried in Kisimul Castle and his son, the 46th Chief, now cares for the ancient clan home of Clan Macneill.

If ever there was a place to introduce little legs to the joy of hillwalking, then Barra is that place. From the single, circular island road there are numerous jumping-off points which offer a variety of less-than-taxing expeditions admirably suited to all degrees of fitness. Barra hills are almost devoid of heather and, at least in dry weather, the walking is easy. Also, because the island is only eight miles long by up to six miles wide, you are never far from civilisation. Use OS Map 31, Barra, second series, Scale 1:50,000 to help you choose your route.

Another famous Barra resident was Compton Mackenzie, author of *Whisky Galore*. The film of the book was shot on Barra, with Compton Mackenzie himself playing a part. Mackenzie, who came to live on Barra in 1928, was a founder member of the Scottish Nationalist Party, and built himself a fine house on the north coast of the island overlooking the white sands of Traigh Mhor; cockle strand, where Loganair land their aeroplanes, weather and tide permitting. Compton Mackenzie lies at rest in the graveyard of Cille Bharra, one of the oldest places of Christian worship in Scotland, perhaps dating back as far as the early years of the seventh century. The chapel was founded, tradition has it, by St Finnbarr, patron saint of Barra, whose dramatic statue dominates an outcrop in the sea at Northbay. The 'Aberdeen Breviary', from the sixteenth century, tells us that Finnbarr was born in Caithness, ordained a priest in Rome and then returned to Scotland, where he 'converted many to the faith of Christ'.

Cille Bharra is the start point for a super Barra walk. Park near the chapel (OS Map 31, Barra, second series, Scale 1:50,000, Grid Ref: 30407) and climb south to the top of Ben Eoligarry (102m). Look northeast to the island of Eriskay and the Prince's Strand where Bonnie Prince Charlie first set foot on Scottish soil in 1745. In fact, BPC had made a prior call at Kisimul Castle, but the Macneill, diplomatically and happily, given the horrendous aftermath of the uprising, was 'not at home'.

Descend south onto the white sand and golden-green marram grass-spiked dunes of Traigh Eais. Three thousand-mile-old blue foam-crested Atlantic waves crowd the shore and dash in fury against the black crags of Ben Erival (200m). The landscape lies essentially unchanged, as awe-inspiring today as it must have been in the days when Finnbarr's monks trembled and prayed before their mysterious maker. At the end of the beach, cross the narrow neck east to reach the road near the cement-block factory. The offices are Compton Mackenzie's old house (Grid Ref: 695056). Walk north now over Traigh Mhor, keeping a weather eye open for incoming Loganair flights, to regain the eternal peace and calm of Cille Bharra.

61. VATERSAY

Walk the world's edge with me this morning, over golden sands, heather-tussocked hills and wildflower-sprinkled machair lands on the Hebridean Island of Vatersay. The island is now linked by a causeway to Barra, but on my first visit an open-decked boat chugged me there across the sea-green shallows from Castlebay. That morning, apart from the district nurse, three homeward bound youths and the local vet, the most vital cargo we carried was six cases of whisky; stacked in the stern and about a bottle per skull of the island's population.

Vatersay is noted for a land raid which occurred in 1908. Eleven Barra men took possession of the island and began farming. Lady Cathcart owned Vatersay at that time. She had inherited the island from the monstrous Colonel Gordon of Cluny, who had brutally cleared 2,000 people from their homes. He packed them off, destitute, to Upper Canada, so that he could rent the ground to lowland sheep farmers. Lady Cathcart, who had never set foot on Vatersay, followed her ancestor's example. She brought legal proceedings against the raiders which led to their incarceration in dank Calton Jail in Edinburgh. Public outrage because of the incident secured their release. In 1909, the Scottish Office bought Vatersay from Lady Cathcart and turned the island over to crofting.

South from Vatersay lie ten other islands, three of which recently hit the headlines: Mingulay, Berneray and Pabbay, up for sale to the highest bidder and expected to command a price of £1m. Any Tom, Dick or Harry with cash to spare and an inclination to play the laird could have snapped them up. Happily, after some dithering, the National Trust for Scotland made an acceptable offer to the crofter-owners and these islands are now in their capable hands. And, if you are an angler, ponder upon what fishing opportunities might await on Vatersay's closest neighbour, Sandray. I have read that about 50 years ago, Loch na Cuilce, the only freshwater loch on the island, was full of huge trout. For piscatorial adventure, arrange to be dropped off there by boat from Castlebay. Remember, however, to go fully prepared. Should the weather decide to turn nasty, you could be marooned for days.

The largest islands were once populated, but were cleared over the years by their landlords, fate and changing fortune. Sandray, which rises 195m from the surrounding sea, was worked until about 1934. In the same year, the population of Mingulay gave up the struggle against the elements and left their towering 244-metre-high cliff-girt domain to the cry of the gulls, which had provided them with an essential source of food. Since 1855, crofters have grazed sheep on Pabbay, Mingulay and Berneray, but the increasing cost involved in doing so forced the sale of these magical isles.

Clutching OS Map 31, Barra, second series, Scale 1:50,000, cross the causeway to Vatersay and park at Grid Ref: 632945, the metropolis of Vatersay; a few houses, a church, burial ground, shop and playing field. Walk south to the beach at Bagh a Deas. From there, continue east to Eorisdale and climb Am Meall (90m, Grid Ref: 650946), which guards the rocky islet of Muldoanich.

Now tramp the north shore of Vatersay Bay over Ben Cuier (60m), to find one of the most magnificent yellow strands in Scotland. At the end of this beach, you will see a white-painted schoolhouse. Climb north and northwest from behind the schoolhouse to gain Vatersay's highest hills, Heishival Beag (169m) and Heishival Mor (190m, Grid Ref: 626964). Coming down, avoid the crags on your right by following the line of the little stream. At Grid Ref: 628957, head for the beach fringing the west side of the narrow isthmus which separates the north and south parts of Vatersay. Overlooking the bay is a monument commemorating a vessel that foundered there in a huge storm on 20 September 1863:

> The ship *Annie Jane*, with emigrants from Liverpool to Quebec was totally wrecked in this bay. Three-fourths of the crew and passengers, numbering about 350 men, women and children were drowned and their bodies are interred here. 'And the sea gave up its dead who were in it.' (Revelations: 5: 133.)

Vibrant life has revitalised this lovely island, thanks to the advent of the causeway and, no doubt, because of more accommodating access to liberal quantities of the 'water of life'.

62. ARDNAMURCHAN

South from Loch Shiel, the A861 touches Loch Sunart at Salen before swinging east towards the village of Strontian at the head of the loch. Strontian is famous as the place where, in 1791, Charles Hope discovered the element strontian, isolated in 1806 by Sir Humphrey Davis. The Strontian mines, closed since 1871, were reopened in 1983 to supply the North Sea oil industry with barytes. Less well known is the story of the only floating church in Scotland, built in Glasgow and paid for with money raised in Sunart. After the Disruption of 1841 and the formation of the Free Church of Scotland, the local laird refused to allow the new church to be built on his land. Hence the floating church, which served the community faithfully for many years.

At Salen a minor road, the B8007, wends westwards along the north shore of the loch, past Glenborrodale Castle and St Columba's Well to Ardslignish. Ardslignish Point dominates the immediate view and below the headland, where the waters of Allt Tor na Moine flow into Camas nan Geall Bay, is the slender column of Cladh Chiarain, dedicated by St Columba and marking the grave of St Ciaran, who died in AD 548. The stone is inscribed with a cross and a dog.

The west of Ardnamurchan is a hillwalker's delight. There are miles of empty moorlands, scattered with tiny blue lochs and lochans, surrounded by craggy peaks and dark cliffs. Much of the coastline, particularly in the north, may only be visited by means of man's oldest method of locomotion, his feet. The landscape is dominated by a series of modest hills, the highest of which is Ben Hiant (528m), 'the holy mountain'. Few roads intersect this wilderness and those that do are tortuous, narrow and single-tracked. The unique geological feature of Ardnamurchan is the great Tertiary Ring at the western end, formed 58 million years ago by a vast volcano, one of the many which gave birth to much of northwest Scotland and the Inner and Outer Hebrides. Massive explosions showered the surrounding area with molten rocks, the most notable example of which is known as Maclean's Nose, the jagged cliffs below Ben Hiant and Stallachan Dubh overlooking the Sound of Mull.

The best way to appreciate the character of these superb crags is from the sea. The circular core of the Ardnamurchan volcano covers an area six by nine miles, the centre being midway between Achnaha and Glendrian, north of the village of Kilchoan; the principal, indeed the only source of supplies and comforts in the west of Ardnamurchan. A more ancient and uncertain source of comfort was Mingary Castle, a clifftop eyrie between Maclean's Nose and Rubha Aird an Iasgaich. After the Battle of Bannockburn in 1314, King Robert the Bruce consolidated his power and control over his barons by grants of land to those who had supported him during the war with England. The Coymns, implacable enemies, were banished and their lands given to Angus Og of Islay, including a charter to Morvern and Ardnamurchan.

Future Scottish kings also experienced difficulty in controlling their wild western subjects, who often acted as though the Lordship of the Isles was a kingdom in its own right. The young King James IV settled the problem by taking the lands back into his personal ownership, much to the dismay of Maclean of Ardnamurchan. The king and his court arrived in force at Mingary Castle in May 1495 and there received the submission of the unruly lairds where, it was claimed, 'the pepill ar almaist gane wilde'.

Portuairk is a small hamlet at the end of the B8007 and a good starting place for an easy walk northwards to Lochan an Dobhrain and a traverse of the rim of the extinct volcano. Sanna Bay is a popular picnic spot because of its delightful sandy beaches. In summer, the warm shallow waters make it perfect for a family outing.

The old crofting community at Sanna suffered the same fate as so many of the other settlements in the area when, during the middle years of the nineteenth century, the people were evicted to make way for more profitable sheep. Alisdair Maclean graphically describes these sad events in his book *Night Falls on Ardnamurchan*. Allt Sanna burn flows gently by the ruined remains of a once bustling, happy village.

After crossing the Allt Sanna burn, I walked east over the floor of the extinct volcano to the ridge of Meall an Fhireoin. From the top, the edge of the volcano circles south and west enclosing a broken landscape ringed by hard, dark hills. Once on the summit of Meall nan Con (437m), I was rewarded with a magnificent view encompassing Ardnamurchan, Mull, Sunart, Moidart and Ardgour. The islands of Tiree and Coll shimmered in a blue haze and, on the horizon, I glimpsed a distant prospect of the Outer Hebrides, the magical 'heather isles'. I was filled with a deep awareness of my small presence in these silent places where eagles soar and otters play. Where the only enemy was my own restless spirit and my greatest friend, the calm hills.

You will need OS Map No 47, Tobermory, second series, Scale 1:50,000 to find your way round. Portuairk Grid Ref: 440680; Sanna Grid Ref: 446696; Glendrian Caves Grid Ref: 464708; Lochan an Dobhrain Grid Ref: 479701; Meall an Fhireoin Grid Ref: 490698; Meall nan Con Grid Ref: 505681; Meall an Tarmachain Grid Ref: 493664; Creag an Airgid Grid Ref: 477669; Nbeinn na h-Imeilte Grid Ref: 459671.

63. TABLE OF LORN

Dogs can be difficult on holiday. Which is why Ann and I were impressed with the Ardtornish Estate in Morvern. There are excellent, virtually dog-proof fences at all the important places. Ardtornish is a welcoming estate where the emphasis is on providing everything for a relaxing holiday for every member of the family, including dogs. Bicycles with baby seats on the back are available for hire, there are good laundry facilities, and even a lending library for fireside evenings. During our visit we stayed in Kinlochaline Cottage, a comfortable house near the black tower of Lochaline Castle. In spite of variable west coast weather, we managed to spend most of our time out-of-doors exploring the wilds of Morvern, walking and fishing along the way, including a visit to the famous Ardtornish Gardens, 28 acres of superb parkland, shrubs and trees.

The woodlands are magnificent: native birch, larch, firs and pines, dark green against the pink sandstone of Ardtornish House, bought by Owen and Emmeline Hugh-Smith in 1930. Each year they received presents of named and unnamed hybrid rhododendrons from Sir John Stirling Maxwell of Pollock House in Glasgow. Consequently, the Ardtornish plants are renowned throughout Scotland for their colour and variety.

Most of the ancient Morvern woodlands were destroyed in 1745 during the Jacobite Rebellion. General Campbell ordered the 'wasting of Morvern' because of local support for the Young Pretender, Prince Charles Edward Stuart. Captain Robert Duff, RN carried out the work on 10 March, with marines and sailors from the sloops *Terror* and *Princess Anne*. Forests were set alight from Drimnin in the west to Ardtornish, a distance of eleven miles.

To the east of the gardens an estate road leads past Achranich by the banks of the River Rannoch out onto the hill. It climbs steeply through old woodlands, as the river charges down a spectacular series of falls and white-churned pools. At the top of the hill, trees give way to a wide moorland strath, enclosed southwards by Glais Bheinn and the Table of Lorn, a dramatic ridge guarding Coire Slabhaig.

The going is easy along a well-defined track that cuts through the mountains of Morvern and Kingairloch, reaching the sea by the ruined castle of Glensanda on the shores of Loch Linnhe. A number of fine streams flood into the River Rannoch from the Table of Lorn, Allt na Socaich, Allt Strath Shuardail and Allt na Feinne, flowing over a fertile plain, scattered with ruined croft cottages.

Spring in Morvern is a contrary affair; one moment sunlight, the next storm. As we reached the confluence of Allt Dubh Doire Thearnait Burn with the River Rannoch, a storm whistled down from Meall a'Chaorunn, bringing with it huge flakes of snow. Seconds later we were white-fronted and gasping for shelter. We found relief at a mountain bothy overlooking Loch Tearnait. Warmed by hot soup, sandwiches and coffee, we relaxed, closely guarded by two dripping dogs, alert for anything that might come their way. We had brought our fishing rods in the hope of an early season trout. Miraculously, the storm passed, the sun shone, and we noted a few dimples on the surface of Loch Tearnait. Quickly putting up our rods we marched purposefully lochwards, the light of battle shining in our eyes.

After half an hour's fruitless effort we abandoned all hope of supper and decided to walk on, our objective being Meall a'Chaorunn and the traverse of the long ridge westwards over An Sleaghach, Mam a'Chullaich to Glais Bheinn, including the summit of An Dunan, the Table of Lorn, a modest 480m in height. But height is of little relevance, at least to Ann and me; more important is the simple pleasure of being part and parcel of the joy that is Scotland. We walked happily along the tops, dipping down into secret glens, climbing grassy slopes to reach our evening table. The Blue Mountains of Mull beckoned from across the narrow waters of the sound: Sgurr Dearg, Beinn Talaidh and the Mull's solitary Munro, Ben More (966m).

Lengthening shadows fingering the sides of Coire Slabhaig hurried us down the smooth slope to Bealach a'Ghoirtein Deirg and the banks of the River Rannoch. Loch Aline shone like well-used pewter as we nodded to the stately pines by the Tam O'Shanter bridge across the River Aline. 'What's for supper, Ann?' I mused. 'Not trout, dear, that's for certain,' replied my better half.

This walk is 13 miles. There are no problems along the way and the going is easy. Pack OS Map No 49, Oban and East Mull, second series, Scale 1:50,000. Ardtornish House Grid Ref: 703475; start of track Grid Ref: 708474; Leacraithnaich bothy Grid Ref: 742471; Loch Tearnait Grid Ref: 750470; Meall a'Chaorunn Grid Ref: 769445; Mam a'Chullaich Grid Ref: 741432; the Table of Lorn Grid Ref: 722438; Bealach a'Ghoirtein Deirg Grid Ref: 710457.

64. ARDTORNISH CASTLE

Morvern and Ardtornish are one of Scotland's least visited areas, and retain a sense of peace all too often lacking in many of Caledonia's more famous airts. There is no easy way in to Morvern. The best route is by the short ferry crossing over Loch Linnhe at Corran Narrows, eight miles south of Fort William. Even then, for most of the way, you will find yourself in the grip of a tortuous single-track road climbing through Glen Tarbert down to the sea at the head of Loch Sunart. Then the A884 south, winding up the long hill from the shore between Beinn nam Beathrach and Taobh Dubh into Gleann Geal, the White Glen of Morvern.

I became interested in the area after reading Philip Gaskell's book *Morvern Transformed*, a wonderfully researched social history. I was also interested in Morvern because of my interest in the exploits of Patrick Sellar. He is still one of the most hated men in the north, infamous for the part he played in the brutal Strathnaver clearances in Sutherland during the early years of the nineteenth century.

After the clearances, two men owned most of the land round Ardtornish: Octavius Smith, who bought Achranich Estate in 1845, building what is now known as Ardtornish House, and Patrick Sellar. Using the fortune he had amassed from his acquisition of the lands he helped to clear, Sellar bought Ardtornish Estate and built himself a grand house overlooking the Sound of Mull. Smith, who was born in 1796, made his fortune out of a gin distillery at Pimlico Lane in London. Sellar's holdings, to the east and west of Achranich, were divided by Smith's property. With two such strong-willed personalities, dispute was inevitable and it eventually centred upon salmon fishing rights in the River Aline, a classic Highland spate stream.

Smith owned one bank of the river, but he discovered to his horror that Sellar owned the whole of the fishing rights, and so he could not fish the river. Smith retaliated by denying Sellar right of way across Achranich to tend to his business at Loch Arienas in the west. The matter was placed in the hands of their respective lawyers and the young families of the stubborn men were ordered to ignore each other on pain of severe retribution. The disagreement was settled before the matter came to court. In 1850 a binding document was signed giving Sellar legal right of way across Achranich, in return for which Sellar sold half of his fishing rights on the River Aline to Smith for the sum of £400. Thereafter, the two families lived happily and Eleanor Sellar later recalled:

> 'I remember Gertrude, Mr Smith's youngest daughter, telling me how the new peace was inaugurated by her mother and herself, then a child of eight, lunching at Ardtornish. Mr Sellar set her beside himself and called her his little lady. The goings to and fro between the two places were as perpetual as they had been strictly forbidden the year before.'

In time, the families were united in marriage and the estates merged into what is the present Ardtornish Estate. As was the custom in Victorian England, many great and famous people travelled north to enjoy Ardtornish hospitality. Alfred, Lord Tennyson, the then poet laureate, accompanied by Francis Turner Palgrave of *Golden Treasury* fame, visited

William Sellar, Patrick's heir. William was Professor of Humanities at Edinburgh University and the two poets stayed with him in 1853 whilst on their way to Loch Coruisk in Skye. They never reached Skye and Tennyson later wrote:

> For though he missed a day in Skye,
> He spent a day in heaven.

John Buchan, statesman, soldier, author, poet and angler, met Gerard Craig Sellar, Patrick's grandson in South Africa in 1902 and he and his wife stayed regularly at Ardtornish. Indeed, Buchan probably conceived the idea for his book *John Macnab* from the earlier dispute between Smith and Sellar and used Ardtornish as the setting for his wonderful tale, which he dedicated to Rosalind Maitland, Craig Sellar's sister.

Ann and I set off one morning on a journey through these once-disputed lands, crossing the little River Rannoch by Ardtornish House and making our way southwards along the track by the shore of Loch Aline. It was a happy morning, sun-bright and gull-wheeling, with both of our dogs busy with whatever dogs are busy with amidst thick fern and bracken.

A thin ribbon of woodland edges the track as it leaves the shore and winds up the slow hill towards Ardtornish Point and the ruins of Sellar's once-grand mansion, now a grey cluster of semi-derelict buildings, old flagged courts and moss-covered roofs. A low wall borders the ruins, tangled with bramble thickets and tumbled trees. As we poked and pried, few birds sang. We walked out to the dramatic remains of Ardtornish Castle, glowering towards Mull from its lofty perch above the waves. Had Tennyson stood amidst these old stones, searching for inspiration? A chill wind slid down the Sound of Mull, slipping through the empty castle to engulf us. Time for home.

Use OS Map 49, Oban and East Mull, second series, Scale 1:50,000. Ardtornish House Grid Ref: 703457; site of Patrick Sellar's house Grid Ref: 693433; Ardtornish Castle Grid Ref: 692426.

Sandwood Bay, looking north towards Cape Wrath

Quinag and Little Assynt

Peanmeanach Beach

Whaligoe Steps

Dunkeld Cathedral

Hugh Miller's fossil beds

The burial place of the heart of Robert the Bruce, Melrose Abbey

Hermitage Castle

Buchan Burn, Glen Trool

Vatersay Strand
and Barra

Torrisdale Beach

The descent from Canisp

MacG

Hecla from East Loch Bee, South Uist

The Ptarmigan
Ridge, Killin

Borgie Forest

Ben Hope

Assynt

Skerray, Sutherland

65. LARACHBEG

When the government vessel HMS *Harebell* arrived at Lochaline on the evening of Friday, 29 August 1930, on board were the people of St Kilda, evacuated from their distant island home on 'the edge of the world'. The Scottish Office had arranged for 27 of the islanders to be resettled at Larachbeg in Ardtornish, Morvern. As Ann and I wandered by Larachbeg where the River Aline flows to the sea, we paused and remembered the St Kildans. From 1925 until 1930 the islanders had cost the government £2,388. Officials were 'concerned'. Evacuation was the obvious solution. Twenty-five years later, the government spent more than £500,000 to establish a missile tracking station on Hirta, the main island. If only the St Kildans had been able to hold on until then. The arrival of the St Kildans in Morvern reversed the trend of depopulation that had been in progress since 1813, when 2,000 people lived on the peninsula. Until then, no lowlander owned a single Morvern acre. But between 1813 and 1838, every property changed hands, due largely to the profligate lifestyle of Morvern's owner, the sixth Duke of Argyll. He reduced his family fortune by about £2 million. Selling up was his only option.

Clearances and evictions soon followed. In 1838, Patrick Sellar acquired 6,816 acres of land around Loch Arienas. He brought sheep down from his Sutherland holdings. To make room for them, 44 families amounting to 230 people were immediately evicted. Sellar, a former agent of the Duke of Sutherland, was well practised in the art of eviction. John Macdonald was one casualty and he was appointed spokesman when, in 1883, the Napier Commission came north to hear evidence of these events. At a meeting in the Free Church Hall the old man, when asked by the Commission what he wanted, replied: 'I would like to be the way I was before, if it were possible, that is. I should like to have a croft and my cows back again, as before.'

There is nothing at Larachbeg to mark the passing of the St Kildans, nor any other monument in Morvern in remembrance of the suffering the clearances brought to these glens. A mile beyond Larachbeg, at Claggan school, where the River Aline tumbles through a ragged gorge, Ann and I crossed the A884 and walked north to Acharn. Here the Black Water, flowing south down Gleann Dubh, the Black Glen, from Loch Clachaig, meets the White Water, which rises from the moorlands at the head of Gleann Geal, the White Glen. When either or both of these streams flood, such is the force of the flow that rather than sweeping into the River Aline, they swing westwards into Loch Arienas.

At the bridge over the Black Water we turned north along the path by the stream, enfolded between the firm slopes of Braigh Uladail to the east and Meall Achadh a'Chuirn to the west, on the edge of the John Raven Wildlife Reserve. John Raven, a previous owner of the Ardtornish Estate, was an eminent botanist and an expert on the mountain flowers in the area. The reserve covers 4,200 acres encompassing Beinn Iadain, Beinn na h-Uamha and the long arm of Loch Teacuis. This land is particularly noted for species such as purple saxifrage, yellow rose-root, red campion, white campion and alpine lady's mantle. Red deer also abound and may often be viewed at the end of the little road that twists out past Loch Arienas and Loch Doire nam Mart to Kinlochteacuis, grand bucket-and-spade country for little ones. More than 136 different species of birds have been recorded in the reserve, and as we tramped up the Black Glen a solitary golden eagle soared over the moors. A dam has been built across the pool below the falls in the Black Glen gorge. A magnificent oak wood, full of the song of finches, wrens and warblers, surrounds it. The trunks of trees are lichen-covered and are home to a wide variety of insects, the most spectacular of which is the golden-ringed dragonfly.

Our most convenient track crossed the silver river beyond the gorge and gently led us round the slopes of Monadh Meadhoin to Crosben. From there, we contoured the hill to Loch Clachaig and paused for coffee in the morning sun. A brief struggle with the slopes of Beinn Chlaonleud gave us the grassy plateau of a gentle ridge and we strolled happily south to the third summit, a mile distant and 465m above Gleann Geal. We lazed at the top and watched the world go by.

After lunch we began our descent to the road and a small bridge across the river at Alltachonaich, following the busy stream down to the waterfall at Eas na Mucaireachd, then on to our last top, the rounded summit of Meall Damh (342m). Loch Tearnait and Leacraithnaich bothy lay to the south, with the cluster of lochans by Meall nan Clach glinting in the distance.

The peak of Beinn Mheadhoin (740m), the highest mountain in Morvern, reared west. A raven eyed us curiously, then flew off purposefully in the direction of craggy Meall a'Chaorunn. A long moorland tramp past the pool on Braigh na Glaice Moire and the woods of Braigh Dubh Dhoire brought us back to Larachbeg and the River Aline. Evening chummed us home by the river.

Use OS Map 49, Oban and East Mull, second series, Scale 1:50,000. Ardtornish Grid Ref: 704475; Larachbeg Grid Ref: 696485; Claggan School Grid Ref: 700498; Acharn Grid Ref: 703504; Crosben Grid Ref: 720542; Loch Clachaig Grid Ref: 744563; Bridge at Alltachonaich Grid Ref: 747508; Meall Damh Grid Ref: 740485; Braigh na Glaice Moire Grid Ref: 725486; Braigh Dubh Dhoire Grid Ref: 715485.

66. BEN MORE MULL

I went up in the world recently, to the summit of Ben More (966m) on the Island of Mull. In fact, 26 of us arrived safely on the top that day to cheer my cousin, Bruce Reynolds from Ardmore in northwest Sutherland, to the peak of his last Munro; the 284 Scottish mountains over 3,000ft in height. Ben More is unique in that the climb starts from sea level. To get the full effect, we dampened the soles of our boots in Loch na Keal before setting off. After 726m we were enveloped in cloud, but small stone cairns ahead marked the way. We celebrated Bruce's achievement in style in the summit cairn with champagne and cake. It was an unforgettable day.

Just as unforgettable was our experience the following evening, when eight of us decided to visit the 'flesh-pots' of Tobermory in search of a bar meal. The harbourside establishment we chose had been given a good write-up by others in our party, who had eaten there when they arrived on the island. The staff were welcoming, polite and friendly, and as we settled over pre-dinner drinks, we chatted happily about this and that; hills climbed and our plans for future adventures. The dining area was situated in the large lounge that was substantially empty of other pleasure-seekers. Because the obligatory piped muzac was overtly loud, we asked for the volume to be turned down. No problem.

However, other problems began with the arrival of the live music, provided by a guitar-playing singer and his keyboard partner. Once plugged in and amplified, the noise was utterly deafening. It was impossible to make conversation, other than by shouting directly into the ear of the nearest neighbour. Rather than spoil my supper, I took my meal and ate outside. My companions suggested, urgently, that the band be deamplifed. Given that our group had already spent a considerable amount of money in the establishment and were in the process of spending more, this seemed to me to be an entirely reasonable request. But the lead singer was incensed and instead, he turned up the volume. Further requests for some peace and quiet were similarly ignored and eventually, the singer stamped off stage and marched over to our table. He was cross.

'You are just a bunch of old snobs!' he roared. 'You lot would be better off listening to a string quartet in a corner.' Reason could not prevail. One of the women in our party asked if he would play and sing alternative songs, perhaps some Scottish numbers? We were told that we wouldn't be able to recognise good music even if we lived to be a hundred. He returned to the stage, followed by rousing cheers from the three or four people sitting there drinking half pints of beer, and began roaring out yet another slab of nasal-twang twaddle. For an island that substantially depends upon tourist business for its survival, this exhibition of unbridled rudeness was simply not acceptable.

The crunch came when we were presented with the bill. We did not refuse to pay, but suggested, because of the din and the insulting behaviour of the lead singer, that the manager review the total. When this seemed to present the staff with a problem, we asked to speak to the manager personally. We left the bar and waited for her outside by the harbour. Half an hour later, the manager appeared and quickly established the facts, speaking to her staff and to the 'live music' man. She apologised courteously and reduced the bill by 50 per cent. I only hope that the guitar-wielding desperado who had so discomfited us was made to fork out the other 50 per cent and summarily sent packing.

I suppose the moral of the story is to make sure, before sitting down to eat, that if there is to be live entertainment, it will not destroy your meal or your sanity. We ended our evening in another, much more user-friendly harbour bar. There we found three men playing to a packed house. And yes, the noise was deafening, but the difference was that they were, quite simply, amongst the best musicians I have heard in years. I could have listened to them for hours – they were brilliant. During a pause, the pianist announced, looking directly at us, 'Is this loud enough for you?' News travels fast in Tobermory.

67. MORAR

The White Sands of Morar are one of the most photographed views in Scotland. But it is easy to escape the crowds and all you need in order to do so is OS Map 40, Loch Shiel, second series, Scale 1:50,000, a compass and map, stout walking boots and a willing heart. The hinterland of this area is a hillwalker's joy, wild and desolate.

One of the best ways to appreciate it is to make a circular walk of North Morar. Follow the north shore of Loch Morar, the deepest freshwater loch in Europe, to Swordland and then north to Tarbet, returning via the south shore of Loch Nevis by Stoul and Lochan Stole. The depth of Loch Morar is recorded at just over 305m. However, recent soundings show that the loch is in fact closer to 335m in depth. Like Loch Ness, its more famous neighbour to the north, Loch Morar is also reputed to be the home of a 'monster' affectionately named Morag.

Simon Fraser, 12th Lord Lovat, one of Prince Charles Edward Stuart's most controversial supporters, was apprehended hiding in a tree trunk on one of the islands at the west end of the loch. Lovat, who had fought on the Hanoverian side during the 1715 uprising, capturing Inverness on behalf of the government, felt that he had not been sufficiently rewarded for his trouble and so joined Bonnie Prince Charlie during the '45. Lovat has the distinction of being the last person publicly beheaded in Britain, cheerfully mounting the scaffold on 9 April 1747, in his 80th year.

More recently, I parked the car by Bracorina and set off eastwards along the shores of Loch Morar, accompanied by my faithful (most of the time) hound, Breac. Loch Morar was formed some 60 million years ago, during the Tertiary period, when massive land movements and upheavals gave birth to many of our most dramatic mountains and to the Hebridean islands. To the east, rocky moorland hummocks mount unrelentingly to the high tops: Sgurr na h-Aide, Carn Mor and the shapely pinnacle of An Stac.

Loch Morar is 12 miles long and is estimated to contain some 81,000 million cubic ft of water, impounded behind a rock shelf just below the surface at the shallow western end of the loch. The River Morar, exiting from the loch, is the shortest river in Scotland, being only 274 metres or so in length. Loch Morar is deeper than the neighbouring Atlantic until that ocean plunges over the continental shelf, 430 miles west.

Past Brinacroy, the track wends tortuously along crags overlooking the loch, eventually reaching the Victorian splendour of Swordland Lodge. The margins of the loch shelve very steeply, but even so, in some of the bays water lobelia grows profusely, its pink stems carrying slender, lilac flowers, and often, close by, the non-flowering quiliwort.

So much of Scotland is now owned by non-Scots and absentee landlords that it is very hard not to be somewhat resentful of the grand, private shooting lodges scattered across our glens. It is hard to forget that not so long ago these lands were busy with people who inhabited them by right of ancestry, and who were removed from them by laws designed for the benefit of their alleged superiors.

I left Swordland and swung north, tramping through the dark narrow pass between the sides of Cnoc a'Bhac Fhalaichte to the east and Eun-tuim to the west, down to the shore of Loch Nevis and the pier at Tarbet. Knoydart beckoned, bathed in bright sunlight, its mountains shining jewels against a blue-white, cloud-scattered sky: Meall Buidhe, Beinn Bhuidhe and Sgurr Coire Gobhar.

My way west from Tarbet followed the south shore of Loch Nevis: trackless, wild, stumbling country, by the ruin of Ardintigh, hugging the contours of the steep hill down to the tiny wood by the shore at Torr nan Gamhainn and the scattered buildings at Stoul. I heaved myself south over Bealach nan Sac, Breac plodding dolefully at my heels, to the stepping stones across Lochan Stole. As I wandered down the moor to Bracorina, Loch Morar glistened in early evening sunlight. In the west, Rum, Eigg and Canna settled to sleep on their Atlantic pillow. Beyond the Sound of Sleat, the Cuillin was fringed with the fire of the setting sun. A proud, noble land, where 'the blood is strong'.

OS Map 40, Loch Shiel, second series, Scale 1:50,000. Morar Grid Ref: 678930; Bracorina Grid Ref: 725928; Brinacroy Grid Ref: 754914; Swordland Lodge Grid Ref: 789914; Tarbet Grid Ref: 793924; Ardintigh Grid Ref: 778931; Stoul Grid Ref: 757943; Lochan Stole Grid Ref: 745935.

68. THE SINGING SANDS

I asked the yellow strand, 'Give us a tune, then?' and it did. The Singing Sands of Gortenfern struck up good-style. As my wife and I walked on, our feet, breaking the wind-compacted crust of the beach, created ethereal music; a high-pitched, continuous flow of sound which reminded me of 'Neptune, the Mystic', from Gustav Holst's haunting suite *The Planets*.

Our concert hall was a wide, empty expanse of beach, busy with small white-tipped waves from the Sound of Arisaig brushing the pebble-black shore. Golden marram grass dunes, overlooked by a green forest, backed the sands. To the west, listening, lay the Island of Eigg, dominated by the jagged ear of An Sgurr (393m). In the distance, other Small Isles, Rum and Muck, nodded appreciation. We stealthed forward, enveloped in the magical sound.

Find the Singing Sands on OS Map 40, Loch Shiel, second series, Scale 1:50,000 at Grid Ref: 613690, where the burns from Leac Shoilleir (440m) tumble into Camas an Lighe Bay. There are a series of five small coves here. Each one leads northwest to ever-more-dreamlike settings; past Sgeir nam Meann (Grid Ref: 620696) and Creag nam Fitheach (Grid Ref: 624698) to the headland at Sgeir a Chaolais (Grid Ref: 625702), looking over to Ardtoe on the north shore of shallow Kentra Bay.

Even today this corner of the Highlands is difficult to access. It was less so before the 1960s. Until then, a steamer from Glenfinnan plied the 18 miles of Loch Shiel to a pier where the River Polloch enters at Ceanna Garbh (Grid Ref: 780695). Now, getting to the start point of this walk involves a tortuous drive along the A861 from Lochailort, through Glen Uig past the head of Loch Moidart, then over the Cruach an Bhlair (155m) to the village of Acharacle (Grid Ref: 675680), where the River Shiel begins its short journey to the sea.

After crossing the bridge over the River Shiel, turn right on the B8044, signposted to Ardtoe. Take the first left, a minor road that ends where the Allt Beithe burn enters Kentra Bay at Torran Lamhair (Grid Ref: 650677). Park here, the start of the walk to the Singing Sands. This is not an arduous hike and it is ideal for little legs unused to more rugged terrain. There is a well-made path all the way, with no serious ups and downs. Out and back, including exploring the bays, is approximately eight miles. But it is a marvellous eight miles through myriad contrasting environments; the muddy flats of Kentra Bay, where red-billed oystercatchers poke and probe and statuesque herons gloomily ponder life over the prospect of lunch. The first few miles, to the ford at Gortenfern (Grid Ref: 635679), lead through 'proper' woods; ancient, moss-decked oak and beech trees, delicate, drooping silver birch and red-proud rowans. The forest floor is carpeted with wildflowers; milk-white wood anemone, yellow primrose and bluebell, speedwell and forget-me-not. Tiny wrens and tits note your passing.

A step on from Gortenfern returns you to reality as you enter a more modern forest; regimented, blanket rows of closely packed conifers which stifle the growth of virtually everything other than their own uppermost branches. A signpost at Grid Ref: 612687 brings relief and directs you through the thinning woodlands to the first of the Singing Sands beaches. This is the most popular beach. If you are going to have human company, this is where you will find it, although more often than not even this first beach is deserted.

My favourite bay is the last one, a mile or so further on. The sand dunes are steep here and between them and the forest there is a wide, sandy plateau, dotted with comfortable trees which provide welcome shade on hot summer days. If you relish an all-over tan, this is the place to bronze. You will not be disturbed. Butterflies flit by in the haze and sleep comes easy. Lazing here is reminiscent of the Atlantic coast of southwest France. Pack a loaf of bread and a flask of wine to complete the illusion.

However, one word of warning. Don't try to continue north round the coastline to rejoin the track home. Even the sheep give it a miss. It doesn't work and, because of the nature of the terrain, it is downright dangerous to attempt to do so. The shore is littered with rocky, hidden, gorse-covered, ankle-breaking potholes. Amble safely back to the first bay and seek an encore from the Singing Sands.

69. PEANMEANACH AND ARDNISH

Bring a bucket and spade. We are heading this morning for the deserted settlement at Peanmeanach and one of Scotland's most splendid beaches; eight easy miles there and back, ideal for little legs unused to arduous hikes. The route begins near Polnish on the Road to the Isles. Check it out on OS Map 40, Loch Shiel, second series, Scale 1:50,000. Park on the right-hand side of the A830 Fort William/Mallaig road at Grid Ref: 743834. Look right, look left, and right again, then march smartly across to the other side. You will find the track out to Peanmeanach just before the lane leading down to Polnish House.

Bonnie Prince Charlie did a lot of looking out for danger here. He arrived in mainland Scotland, in August 1745, a few miles further up the road at Loch nan Uamh. Thirteen months later, after deserting his ragged Highland army after their defeat at Culloden, BPC arrived back at Loch nan Uamh where, with never a backward glance, he fled to France. Neat that, in and out by the same door and nothing worse than sore feet. At least, it was for BPC. For those who supported him and many who did not, there was no escape. Butcher Cumberland cared for them with unforgiving savagery.

Before the Highland Clearances of the nineteenth century, upwards of 80 people lived around Peanmeanach, tending black cattle and sturdy sheep and cultivating, in the acid soil by the shore, sparse crops of barley and vital potato plots. There are other ruined houses to the north of the bay at Glasnacardoch (Grid Ref: 707806) but the largest settlement was at Peanmeanach (Grid Ref: 711805). Those who should have protected them, their own lairds, evicted the population. The ruins of their homes stand on a raised plateau overlooking the beach close to the outlet stream from Loch Doir a'Ghearrain (Grid Ref: 725818). One dwelling has been renovated and is used as a bothy. Whitewashed stones line the path to the green door. Red-painted window-surrounds watch for weary bodies.

It has been known to rain, heavily, in these airts, and the track out to Peanmeanach can be a wet plod after a storm. But the sun soon returns and sets silver droplets sparkling on drooping birch branches and summer-green ferns. The path crosses the line of the West Highland railway where further left-and-right looking is required, but it quickly leaves civilisation behind as it begins to climb out of the railway gully. Well, not really, because every step of the way reminds you of the feet that must have tramped here in days past. The track is marvellously constructed, more a motorway than a hill track, and it is obviously the result of years of hard labour by the men who built and tended the route. The flat rocks they positioned to step the track over the hill are now overgrown with lichen. Wildflowers: milkwort, primrose, sundew and St John's wort, blush shyly in sunny corners. But the road builders have gone.

The track reaches its high-point at Cruach an Fhearainn Duibh (212m). From here there is a mind-stunning vista out to the Small Isles, Rum, Eigg and Muck; a glorious watercolour landscape painted by the hand of God. On the horizon lies a distant prospect of the blue Cuillin on the misty island of Skye, dominated by mighty Sgurr Alasdair (993m). The path descends through native woodland peopled with oaks busy regenerating themselves, their vibrant offspring spiking skyward from the forest floor. Black-eyed wrens peek from tangled tree-roots. Chaffinches and tits chatter crossly at the intrusion as you pass by. Sea-green moss-covered boulders guard the way down the hill to the level plain where Peanmeanach rests.

Time to start digging, if you are blessed with tender years. Otherwise, let youth have its way whilst you lunch on the sands. Oystercatchers will wait on you, decorously best bib-and-tuckered in black-and-white, red beaks probing busily amongst the rocks. The seagull-souls of sailors soar overhead as you dine, anxious for leftover crumbs and crusts. The sound of the endless breakers of the broken waters of the Minch beating on the beach comfort your siesta. Dreams of the Highlanders who once made Peanmeanach their home will fill your slumber. Listen to the laughter of their children as they play the same games and toss the same pebbles into the same azure-white waves.

70. STREAP

I came late to Glenfinnan. My first glimpse of 'Concrete Bob' McAlpine's famous 380m long railway viaduct was in the 1970s, and very impressive it was too. But my first visit to the area could have ended up being a family disaster. I had loaded Clan Sandison into a boat for a fishing trip down lonely Loch Shiel and it was only when I cut the outboard engine that I realised, to my horror, that I had forgotten to pack the oars. Fortunately, the engine started first-pull and we beat a hasty retreat back up the loch to safety. As I passed the monument which commemorates the raising of Prince Charles Edward Stuart's standard at the commencement of the 1745 rebellion, I swear I heard the Highlander perched on top mutter: 'Damned fool, let that be a lesson to you.' BPC landed at Glenfinnan on the morning of 19 August at 11 a.m. By close of play, approximately 1,500 men had rallied to his cause. When I think of the waste of human life and the devastation which followed, I curse the chiefs who so thoughtlessly led their kinsmen to disaster.

Glenfinnan is still a busy place today, busy with tourists and visitors eager to gape at the memorial to one of the saddest events in Scotland's story. But it is also a convenient jumping off point for more user-friendly adventures into the surrounding hills. Two fine glens, Glen Finnan and Gleann Dubh Lighe, lead north into Lochaber and the wilderness lands which separate Loch Shiel from glorious Glen Pean and deep Loch Arkaig. Drag on the boots, pack OS Map 40, Loch Shiel, second series, Scale 1:50,000 and let's get started.

There are two Munros here, Sgurr Thuilm (963m) and Sgurr nan Coireachan (956m). But our objective this morning is their lesser near-neighbour, graceful Streap (909m), a Corbett; a mountain of between 2500ft and 3000ft in height. John Rooke Corbett didn't hang about during his climbing days. Not only had he 'bagged' all of the Munros and tops by 1930, but he then went on to climb all the hills in Scotland of over 2000 feet as well. J.R. Corbett was no slouch.

Park at Grid Ref: 906809 just off the A830 Fort William–Mallaig road, 'The Road to the Isles'. Whistle the tune as you tramp north up the west bank of the River Finnan under the damp arch of Bob McAlpine's dramatic bridge. There is a good track all the way to Corryhully Bothy (Grid Ref: 913844), but once you cross the stream here you are on your own. Time to pant, now, rather than whistle, on the unrelenting ascent up the line of the burn to reach Grid Ref: 927840. Hang a left there and continue to the col (844m) immediately ahead.

The summit of Streap lies one-and-a-half miles due north (Grid Ref: 946863) along a roller coaster of a ridge walk via the Bealach Coire nan Cearc to Stob Coire nan Cearc (887m) at Grid Ref: 937851. The last few hundred yards to the top of Streap require care and a reasonable head for heights. The final ridge narrows considerably with precipitous drops on either side. Hasten slowly and you will come to no harm, but, if in doubt, don't. Better safe than sorry.

In the process of watching where you put your feet, keep an eye open for one of Britain's most special wildflowers, Diapensia lapponica. It was discovered 2,500ft up on an exposed plateau in the Glenfinnan hills on 5 July 1951 by ornithologist and naturalist C.F. Tebbutt. The flowers, which appear in May, are 'rather waxy and creamy-white, borne on a shiny-red stalk'. How this tiny Arctic gem came to be growing in Glenfinnan remains a mystery, but it is thought a vagrant Arctic bird must have dropped the initial seeds.

Beat a retreat to the start point by retracing your steps. The total distance covered during the day is about ten miles. Post-hike rest and recuperation may be obtained at the Stage House Hotel, a comfortable and welcoming hostelry just up the road from the Glenfinnan Monument.

As you relish suitable refreshment, ponder the fate of BPC. After the rout at Culloden, he returned to Glenfinnan where he shivered amidst the broken crags of Sgurr Thuilm while government forces searched for his royal personage. One cannot help but think: 'Damned fool, let that be a lesson to you.' Which reminds me, if you happen to stumble across a pair of oars during your travels, I'm your man. I know I left them somewhere.

71. CASTLE TIORAM

Afternoon sunlight sparkled. So did the dogs, sensing a walk. With Heathcliff on the lead, sheep-proof, and Breac bounding ahead to the first muddy stream, we left the car and walked north along the shore by Castle Tioram and Loch Moidart. The tide was out, leaving golden sands splashed dark green with seaweed.

Walk first, castle later. We followed a well-made trail into a woodland wonderland. Oak, wych-elm, silver birch and ash shaded our way. Sunbeams dappled the forest floor. Wildflowers blinked from rocky crevices. The gentle path led us on through a rust-covered wrought-iron fence and gate and across the hill. This shoreside track is known as the 'Silver Path' and in places it is very rocky, with plenty of scrambling up and down over lichen-covered rocks. Perfectly safe, but as always, caution is required. Who needs a sprained ankle? The dogs seemed impervious to danger, dashing around, sniffing and snuffling under every boulder and fallen log.

Entirely content, we ambled by the sea, stopping frequently to enjoy the sheer beauty of our surroundings, dropping down to a small rocky bay where a stream tumbles in from the shoulder of Beinn Bhreac (241m). The path continues eastwards, but a small cairn here marks the route south, up the line of the stream. Tall green ferns brushed our sides as we tramped the damp track, awash with recent showers. A wren chattered noisily from the undergrowth. Droplets of water clung to silver spider webs and sparkled on delicate birch leaves. A heron flapped lazily by, shoreward to fish. Insects buzzed and hummed. Brilliant butterflies fluttered in the light breeze. Peace was tangible.

Clearing the trees, the path led us onto a verdant plateau clustered with the ruins of a crofting settlement, perhaps half-a-dozen buildings, grey stones tumbled over thick turf. Foxgloves nodded from derelict hearths. The smokeless chimney stacks and broken walls filled the scene with a sense of sadness. A startled hind gazed at us inquisitively before bounding off through the bracken. It must have been a good place to live. A hard life, yes, but complete and self-contained, a place where children could grow up and grow old in safety. A few cattle, sheep, hens, a patch of barley and a firm belief in the awesome power of the Almighty. What did they feel, those Highland people, when they were evicted from their homes so many years ago? Whatever it was, they left behind them a kind legacy in their glen, a song of happiness.

Beyond the crofts the track climbs easily round the west shoulder of Beinn Bhreac, through a narrow pass where we turned east to scramble to the ragged summit. At the top a magnificent vista greeted us; wild mountains, rearing north, east and south: shapely Rois Bheinn in Moidart, Beinn Odhar Bheag by Loch Shiel, Sgurr Dhomhnuill in Ardgour and Beinn Resipol in Sunart. Westwards was the endless charm of Ardnamurchan.

With typical west-coast wickedness, the weather turned nasty. A knife-like storm rushed in, sending us scurrying in search of shelter. We found cover in a wood by the side of Loch Blain and huddled beneath the trees sipping hot coffee. A pair of red-throated divers eyed us suspiciously from the middle of the loch. We retraced our steps to regain the track. It climbed from the glen to a crest, and then downhill past a deep lochan full of rising trout. Breac plunged in and swam parallel to our path high above the shore, to the far end where the waters had been impounded by concrete dam.

Wet, but happy, we trooped through the dripping trees back to the little road by Eilean Uaine and, turning north, returned to the car park and Castle Tioram. As we arrived at the narrow causeway leading to the castle, the sun broke through from behind dark clouds, bathing the majestic ruin in brilliant light.

Castle Tioram was built in the fourteenth century and for generations was the principal mainland residence of Clanranald. We explored the old rooms and staircases, peering through broken windows, expecting at any moment to be confronted by a claymore-wielding custodian demanding to know what right we had to be there.

Castle Tioram was never taken by force. The end came in 1715 when the last occupant, Allan Clanranald, ordered it to be burnt, lest it should fall into the hands of government troops during the Jacobite Rebellion. Clanranald was said to have had a vision of death before he left to join the fray, and his 'second sight' proved all too accurate: he was killed a few weeks later at the Battle of Sheriffmuir near Dunblane, fighting for his 'king across the water'.

We paused and pondered the sad fate of warlike Clanranald, and on the even sadder fate that was to befall his people in the aftermath of the war. But leaving the castle and walking back across the sands, dogs scampering ahead, it was hard to remain sombre on such a glorious evening.

OS Map 40, Loch Shiel, second series, Scale 1:50,000. Car Park Grid Ref: 685721; Castle Tioram Grid Ref: 663725; shoreside Cairn Grid Ref: 679724; ruined Crofts Grid Ref: 677720; Beinn Bhreac Grid Ref: 684715; Loch Blain Grid Ref: 674707; Dam Loch Grid Ref: 672711; Eilean Uaine Grid Ref: 664714.

72. LOCH CORUISK

The British Army is the finest training school in the world, and I never regretted my decision to accept the Queen's Shilling. Boats had a lot to do with it. I have always loved boats and the Royal Army Service Corps, which I joined, had a Water Transport Regiment, based on the Isle of Wight, responsible for providing service and support by sea. I graduated Seaman B4 and spent much of my time afloat on the Solent or messing about in boats after work in the evening on the reed-fringed River Yar. Consequently, when my brother recently invited me to join him on a Hebridean cruise, I accepted readily. The vessel was an Oyster Class 39-foot yacht, crewed, happily, by several strong young men and a competent skipper. The weather was splendid, with decent winds and fair sailing. It was an exhilarating and prosperous voyage.

Also, it was a most convenient way of arriving at Loch Coruisk on Skye in the heart of the Cuillins. We had sailed through the night from a marina to the south of Oban, inching between Luing and Scarba, past the remote Garvellachs Islands and the Ross of Mull, lunching in Hynish Bay off Tiree and over-nighting by Arinagour on the Island of Coll.

The next morning we scudded north past Muck, between the blue mountains of Rum and rocky Eigg. In front of us, the glory of the Cuillins beckoned: Gars-bheinn (926m), Sgurr nan Eag (3,037ft) and mighty Sgurr Alasdair (1,009m). At about 4 p.m. we slipped quietly past the Island of Soay and into the calm shelter of Loch na Cuilce. Abandoning ship, we rowed ashore to find our land legs, hiking by the river Scavaig to climb the lower slopes of Meall na Cuilce. Loch Coruisk sparkled in evening sunlight, surrounded by some of the most dramatic peaks in all of Scotland, a climbers' and hillwalkers' paradise.

But a paradise not easily attained. Unless you arrive by sea, the walk in from either Sligachan in the north or Kilmarie to the east is long and arduous – even before you begin the serious business of scaling the peak of your choice. But the wild journey is a splendid adventure and worth every step of the way. For less experienced hillwalkers, the northern approach from Sligachan, although longer, is safest. Follow a good path which rises steeply southwest across the hills near little Lochan Dubha, crossing between Sgurr Ham and Druim Ham and descending by a'Choire Riabhaich Burn to reach the shores of Loch Coruisk.

The more exciting route is from Kilmarie on the A881, via Camasunary, fording the river which flows into Camas Fhionnairigh Bay, thence across the infamous 'Bad Step' on the south shoulder of Sgurr na Stri (the Peak of Strife) and down to the Memorial Hut by Loch na Cuilce. 'The Bad Step' is reached about two miles west from Camasunary. The way ahead seems impossible because of apparently inaccessible crags. However, the track exposes a narrow crack in the cliff rising across the rocks. This is 'The Bad Step' and it may be safely negotiated with care and an appropriate head for heights.

Loch Coruisk and Camasunary are not only a magnet for hillwalkers, but also attract hardy anglers in search of sea trout. Both systems offer excellent sport and because of their remoteness are infrequently fished. The most complete account of these waters is contained in a marvellous book, *Fishing from Afar*, by Stephen Johnson. Johnson's family rented the sporting rights on Camasunary Estate prior to the last war and he wrote his account of fishing there in a German prison camp to while away the dangerous hours preceding peace. The best night's fishing he can remember saw 15 sea trout caught, weighing a total of 73lb, five over 8lb and one of 9lb.

Such sport is unlikely today, given the sad decline in sea trout stocks that has taken place during the last 12 years. But anglers are ever-hopeful creatures and, who knows, the glory days might eventually return. I scoured the water carefully when I was there and saw little evidence that such an event was imminent.

As we weighed anchor the following morning and nosed out through Loch na Cuilce to Loch Scavaig, seals basked on green, weed-covered rocks and seagulls cried. The Cuillin Hills rose behind us, a majestic curtain enfolding a distant wonderland. An enduring memorial to all that is best about my native land.

Find Loch Coruisk on OS Map 32, South Skye, second series, Scale 1:50,000. Kilmarie Grid Ref: 546174; Camasunary Grid Ref: 516188; The Bad Step Grid Ref: 495192; Loch Coruisk Grid Ref:485205; Lochan Dubha Grid Ref: 497243; Sligachan Grid Ref: 487299; Loch na Creitheach Grid Ref: 5113205.

73. KILMELFORD

Everyone needs pampering from time to time and when the Melfort Club at Kilmelford near Oban suggested a visit, I agreed with alacrity. We would have a few days of walking, fishing and being pampered. The club buildings were originally used for the manufacture of gunpowder until the invention of dynamite ended that dangerous occupation. The restaurant is called The Shower of Herring, named after the following occurrence: 'On a small eminence above Melfort House, a shower of herring fell in 1821, in every respect so large and good that the tenants by whom they were found were reduced to sending some to their landlord, then residing in Edinburgh.' (*Edinburgh New Philosophical Journal*, October 1826.)

Mesolithic man left reminders of his passing at Melfort, near a cave on An Sithean, 'the hill of the fairies'. Before Hydro Board blasting operations covered the site in 1956, hundreds of flint and quartz artifacts were discovered, including scraps of teeth and charcoal fragments dating back more than 7,000 years.

Melfort is Clan Campbell country, the ownership of which was hotly disputed by the neighbouring Clan Macdonald. In one incident Alexander Macdonald descended on Melfort, intent upon wreaking havoc while the laird, John Campbell, was absent. The laird's wife, with great perspicacity, in order to minimize damage to her husband's property, laid out a magnificent banquet for the invaders and then retreated with her family to hide in the woods nearby. Delighted with this reception, Macdonald gave orders that Melfort should be spared; but as he stopped to rest on the pass north of Kilninver and looked back, he was horrified to see the Campbell home going up in flames. Three Irishmen were found guilty of starting the blaze and they were hanged on the spot, known to this day as Tom a'Chrochaidh, 'the mound of the hanging'.

I first travelled that way on a family holiday when we spent a night on the lovely Island of Eriska, overlooking the Lynn of Lorn. Whilst Mother, Father and my younger brother Fergus stayed in style in the Eriska House Hotel, my brother Ian and I were given permission to camp out on the west shore of the island. When we awoke, Ian and I washed ourselves in the sea, surrounded by seals and the cry of gulls. Across Loch Linnhe the mountains of Kingairloch shimmered in morning mist and I realized then that I had found something very special.

Fearnach Bay, close to Melfort House, was crowded with sailing boats when Ann and I arrived. The Melfort Club offers guests a wide range of water sports, including boat hire, windsurfing, canoes, water skiing and scuba diving. These activities are directed from the old pier which used to service gunpowder-packed vessels as they edged their way carefully out of the rock-strewn confines of Loch Melfort.

A perfect little track twists west from Melfort, hugging the shoreline, then winds uphill through delightfully wooded crags past the small hamlet of Kilchoan to the end of the road at Degnish. Just before Degnish, on the right, a track leads north into the lands of Kilbrandon and Kilchattan, heading steeply up the southern slopes of Dun Crutagain. Ignoring the track, Ann and I, and the inevitable dogs, tramped straight up the shoulder of the hill to the summit, 273m above sea level.

From the top a magnificent panorama of scattered islands greeted us: Seil, Easdale, Torsa, Luing, Shuna, Lunga, Scarba and the Garvellachs. There are the remains of a fort on Dun Chonnuill, the most northerly

Garvellach isle, and the ruins of a monastery on Eileach an Naoimh to the south. Swinging northeast, we angled down Dun Crutagain towards the track, joining it where an old drystane wall divides moorland from cultivated pastures to the north. We crossed the top of Bealach Gaoithe, 'the pass of the wind', and walked down to the gnarled hawthorn tree, known as the Lucky Tree, by the side of the track. The lower trunk of the tree is covered with coins, hammered into the bark; a custom reputed to bring good luck. I produced a coin to leave our mark. After all, who needs bad luck?

Then, blessed with the prospect of good fortune, we returned to the top of the pass and struck off eastwards over the hill towards the Kilchoan Loch in search of supper. There are two lovely little lochans, nestling between high crags, and we spent a happy hour exploring their delights.

As the sun sank beyond the misty islands, we walked back to the track and down the hill to the car. In the distance, over Luing, the crags of Scarba sparkled whilst, beyond, the Garvellachs settled to sleep under the dark-blue blanket of night.

This is an easy walk of about eight miles, there and back from Degnish. Use OS Map 55, Lochgilphead, second series, Scale 1:50,000 to find your way round. Melfort Grid Ref: 834142; Kilchoan Grid Ref: 795135; Degnish Grid Ref: 782126; start of the track Grid Ref: 786126; Dun Crutagain Grid Ref: 785137; Bealach Gaoithe Grid Ref: 789151; Lucky Tree Grid Ref: 788152; Kilchoan Lochs Grid Ref: 798143.

74. BEN TEE

On reaching Glengarry the first place we came to was Greenfield, possessed by Mr McDonald. The house was really a curiosity. It was built of earth and the walls were all covered with a fine verdure, but on calling, we were conducted into a clean and neat-looking room. The ladies, Mrs McDonald and her sister, were handsome and genteelly dressed, although unapprised of our arrival, unless by the second sight. They were very easy and agreeable in their manners, and very unlike the outside of their habitation.

James Hogg, the Ettrick shepherd, thus described his arrival in Glengarry during his tour of the Highlands in 1803. His friend, Sir Walter Scott, had persuaded Hogg to send him a series of letters along the way, recounting his adventures, and Scott arranged to have them published in *The Scots Magazine*, probably the oldest magazine in the world.

An equally hospitable welcome awaits travellers in Glengarry today, at the Tomdoun Hotel. There has been a coaching inn at Tomdoun for more than a hundred years. *Murray's Handbook* notes in 1894 that 'carriages may be hired there' for the journey through Glen Shiel, past the Five Sisters to Kyle of Lochalsh and Skye. The road beyond Tomdoun is the longest dead-end route in Britain, following the gloomy shores of Loch Quoich to finally reach the sea at the head of Loch Hourn, 'the loch of hell', in Knoydart.

The dark ruins of Invergarry Castle are all that remain of the ancient home of the Macdonnell Lairds of Glengarry. Charles Edward Stuart rested there briefly during his flight west after the Battle of Culloden. Two years later Butcher Cumberland's troops arrived at Craig an Fhithich, 'the rock of the raven', ravaging the people and their lands and burning Glengarry's ancestral home in the process.

South from Loch Garry, the view is dominated by the graceful shape of Ben Tee (901m) 'the hill of the fairies'. From the summit, walkers are rewarded by one of the grandest views in all of Scotland. The lower slopes are thickly forested with the commercial plantations, but once clear of the dark trees a moorland wonderland opens. Ben Tee is also known as Glengarry's Bowling Green. Stones from the mountain were used to build the old castle by the shores of Loch Oich. Getting the stones down from Ben Tee was achieved by forming what is probably the longest chain-gang in history, a line of men passing the stones, hand to hand, from the slopes of Ben Tee to Loch Oich, a distance of more than five miles.

In times past Glengarry was a wildlife paradise. But Victorian sporting gentlemen wreaked havoc here, conscientiously recording their deeds. One note gives gamebook shooting details in Glengarry between 1837 and 1840: 198 wild cats, 246 pine martens, 67 badgers, 48 otters, 27 sea eagles, 15 golden eagles, 18 osprey, 275 kites, 63 goshawks, 656 buzzards, 462 kestrels, 63 hen harriers, 6 gyrfalcon and 106 assorted owls.

Ben Tee can be climbed from two directions: from the shores of Loch Lochy in the Great Glen, and from Glengarry. The Lochy access is from Laggan Locks and Kilfinnan and involves a very sharp ascent by the north bank of the Kilfinnan Burn via dramatic falls, along a narrow and often muddy track. The Glengarry access, from Greenfield, although somewhat longer, offers a less daunting approach. A drove road used to run south from the edge of the forestry plantations, but walkers now keep to the hill beyond the forestry, along the delightful track that borders the little Allt Ladaidh Burn. The real fun begins a mile further on, where the track branches left, heading up Allt Bealach Easain,'the pass of the little falls'. From there on it is teeth-gritting time and a hard haul to the summit.

Few Scottish views can match the splendour of the vista from the top of Ben Tee. Half of Scotland is displayed for your pleasure. The mountains of Glen Affric and Kintail, the blues and greys of the Monadhliath, Corrieyairack and Creag Meagaidh. The mighty bulk of Ben Nevis, the Grey Corries and Glencoe. Westwards, the crags and peaks of Knoydart.

James Hogg never climbed Ben Tee – at least, if he did, he left no record of having done so, but I thought of the Ettrick Shepherd as I surveyed the stunning view. There is a memorial to Hogg near his border home at the south end of St Mary's Loch. The stone statue is inscribed with the line: 'He taught the wandering winds to sing.' An appropriate sentiment on the summit of Ben Tee. My heart sang with joy at the marvellous beauty of my native land.

OS Map 34, Fort Augustus, second series, Scale 1:50,000. Tomdoun Grid Ref: 157011; Greenfield Grid Ref: 202005; Allt Ladaidh Grid Ref: 230003; Allt Bealach Easain Grid Ref: 226984; Ben Tee Grid Ref: 241972.

75. LOCH AN EILEIN

A gentle canter this morning round the shore of Loch an Eilein in the Rothiemurchus Forest near Aviemore. The town itself is best avoided. It is a classic example of tourism gone mad; which is probably why they now propose to knock it down and start again. At present, the whole place exudes the smell of a vast 'milking parlour', where unsuspecting visitors are separated from their hard-earned cash. Tourists play the part of tightly tethered cows whose only purpose is to be ruthlessly milked dry. I think that Aviemore is a disgrace to those who built it and to those who have encouraged its squalid expansion.

Loch an Eilein is a small space of sanity amidst rampant materialism. During the summer months and at weekends it can be busy, but off-season and mid-week, you will be assured of peace and quiet. Find Loch an Eilein on OS Map 36, Grantown and Cairngorm, second series, Scale 1:50,000. The car park is at Grid Ref: 898086. Allow three hours for the tramp round the loch. Mug up on your wildlife knowledge before setting out, because this is the principal attraction of this walk. It is ideal for little legs, easy going and interest-packed all the way. The estate offers guided walks led by experienced rangers. Further information about them and what they offer may be obtained from the Rothiemurchus Visitor Centre at Inverdruie (Tel: 01479 812345).

Have a look at the Visitor Centre at Loch an Eilein first, then follow the path down the west shore of the loch. This is the line of the 'thieves road', the route used by clansmen from the west when they descended upon the fertile lands of Moray to rob, pillage and generally remove anything not firmly nailed down. The beauty of the woodlands here is almost overwhelming, a physical presence, particularly the tangled branches of mature Scots Pines (*Pinus sylvestris scotica*). These are remnants of the Old Wood of Caledonia that used to cover most of Scotland. Rothiemurchus trees have travelled far and wide. After the great fire of London in 1666, Scots Firs from the estate were cut into lengths and bored hollow to make pipes for the water system in the rebuilt city. The work was carried out where the Milton Burn joins the River Spey (Grid Ref: 896105). The pipes were then floated downstream to Gartmouth for onward transportation to London.

The castle on the island in Loch an Eilein is often referred to as being a 'lair' of the infamous Wolf of Badenoch, who burned Elgin Cathedral in 1390. In fact, very little is known of its history other than that it was last occupied in 1690. The castle was one of the final places of refuge for ospreys in Scotland. They survived there until 1899, in spite of constant persecution. Today, it is the haunt of coal-black jackdaws and visiting black-headed gulls. A few hundred yards south from the castle are some spectacular Scots Pines, 300 years old. The forest floor and fallen trees provide shelter for a wide variety of creatures. Woodpeckers and tits dig their nest sites in the boughs. Look out for coal tits, great tits, blue tits and long-tailed tits, and also one of my favourite birds, the graceful little crested tit. As a youth, I proudly wore the tie of the Scottish Ornithological Society, whose motif was a crested tit.

As you round the head of the loch and drop down to a bridge across the Milton Burn, an adjacent water, Loch Gamhna, 'the loch of the stirks', lies to the right. There are fine views from here up to the steep summit of Creag Dhubh (848m) where you will be spied upon from the hillside by circumspect red deer. There is also an excellent chance of seeing the UK's only endemic bird, the Scottish crossbill, and the 'horse of the forest', the capercaillie, which is about the size and shape of a small turkey. Goldcrest wrens, our smallest native bird, also flit and feed amidst the trees.

Red squirrels are common, eviscerating pine cones, and the wildflowers which border the path are a constant pleasure: Cross-leaved heath, ling and bell heather, primroses, chickweed wintergreen, violets and spotted orchid. Bell heather is best loved by me. The late Norman MacCaig immortalised the plant:

> A modest immodesty is a good thing,
> Little blaze of blue on a rock face.
> I'll try it myself.
> Will the bees come.
> The wild bees, with their white noses?

76. MEALL NAN TARMACHAN

Time for Meall nan Tarmachan (1,043m) and a hike along the mountain ridge which guards Killin at the west end of Loch Tay. Whilst walking her dog, The Manager had checked out the weather report on a board in the window of the outdoor centre, although Hareton is not really a dog, more of a Yorkshire terrier. According to the report, conditions looked good for three cautious hillwalkers: clear skies, no snow and a temperature above freezing point on the high tops. A fine morning to say hello to 'the hill of the ptarmigan'.

Killin is an ideal base for exploring the area. There is enough easy and not-so-easy walking nearby to last several lifetimes, let alone the sparse week which we had managed to steal from the hubbub of routine. Our base was a warm cottage linked to the Killin Hotel; very comfortable and conveniently close to the bar for apres-tramp refreshment. Hareton particularly appreciated the hairdrier, which was perfect for unmatting his brown, tangled strands after a hard day in the hills. Usually, he just can't do a thing with it.

We set off, clutching OS Map 51, Loch Tay, second series, Scale 1:50,000, past the Ben Lawers visitor centre to the car park at Grid Ref: 599389 south of the bleak dam which impounds the waters Lochan na Lairige. Why do these dams always look so threatening, as though they had been designed by a manic-depressive failed architect recovering from a bad night out in Barlinnie? Still, the sun was shining and the sight of the Tarmachan ridge ahead was far too inviting to harbour dark thoughts.

The Tarmachan ridge, although highly user-friendly, is narrow in places and you must be able to cope with the prospect of a sheer drop a couple of yards to the left of your route. There is a well-marked track most of the way, but the descent from some of the peaks, particularly from Meall Garbh (Grid Ref: 577383), unnamed on the OS map, requires caution in misty conditions. You should be experienced in these matters. In bad weather, stay away. Remember the golden rule: if in doubt, don't.

A step along the Land-rover track from the car park brings you to a pile of stones on your right: the way up. On our May morning the air was full of bird-song, larks and meadow pipits, twittering loudly as though there wasn't a nasty songbird-slaughtering raptor for miles. Strange, I mused; Scotland's lairds would have us believe these little birds had been all but wiped out by cruel, hook-beaked, grouse-eating buzzards and hen harriers. Surely they can't be mistaken?

After rain the going is soggy, but once on the shoulder of Meal nan Tarmachan, the ground becomes firmer. My partner and her faithful hound soon disappeared over the first ridge. From the top of the second knowe, I paused for breath and a peer back down to Loch Tay. A speedboat trailed a long white wake. Sailing boats had come out to play from Milton Morenish and looked like tiny swans on the surface of the loch. Killin was a toy town of neat buildings, smoke drifting lazily from a hundred lums.

I caught up with the advance party on the plateau before the final ascent. She was admiring the delicate flowers of purple saxifrage. He was sniffing deer dung. The last 30m is steep, up the line of a stream, but we reached the cairn at the top (Grid Ref: 585389) by coffee time. The way ahead is obvious, by a group of small lochans that were still ice-covered when we passed. Victorian relics, phallic-symbol fence posts, black-border the track, tapering and five-ringed, with a knob on top. The path now steepens and climbs to the narrow ridge on Meall Garbh, the most dramatic part of the walk.

We lunched on Meall Garbh. 'If this is supposed to be the 'hill of the ptarmigan', then where are they?' I demanded of my wife. On cue, a bird coughed, discreetly, nearby, as though to say, 'You called?' It was a ptarmigan, resplendent in winter-white apparel. Before rocketing off, he watched us negotiate the narrow ridge and begin a careful descent. We tramped on, over Beinn nan Eachan (Grid Ref: 572383) to the last peak, Creag na Caillich (Grid Ref: 563376); dropping down Coire Fionn Lairige (Grid Ref: 565378) to the concrete ruin and the start of the Land-rover track leading back home (Grid Ref: 574372). The larks were still singing.

77. DOWN BY THE RIVERSIDE

I am irresistibly attracted by water. Not just to enhance a decent dram with aqua, but also by the scent and sound of a busy stream bustling about its lawful business. As a youth I trekked miles up tiny burns, following them through heather-banked moorlands to discover the secret of their birth. I have made lifelong friends by the water's edge; mute swans, ring ouzels, best bib-and-tuckered dippers, coots, statuesque herons, red-speckled Tammy Troot, Greenland fresh Atlantic salmon and marvellously silvered sea-trout. I have also fallen in a lot. Into the South Tyne in Northumberland, the Tweed, Lyne Water, Manor Water and the Whiteadder; into the rivers Tay, Findhorn, Borgie, and Dionard, the Kirkaig and the fast-flowing Spey. However, advancing years have brought with them greater caution and during the past decade I have managed to remain relatively dry, apart from continuing to regularly explore the depths of 'the water of life'.

I renewed my acquaintance with the Spey recently when, accompanied by The Manager and her allegedly faithful hound Hareton, we walked the riverbank on a warm spring day. Well, it was warm after it had stopped snowing, but a flake or three of the white stuff was not going to put us off. OS Map 36, Grantown and Cairngorm, second series, Scale 1:50,000 will guide you round this eight-mile excursion. Be well shod, because the last part of the journey can be very wet and soggy.

Park the car at Grid Ref: 035268 near the new bridge over the river. A path leads down to the westbank at the top end of the Castle Grant Water. The Spey is one of Scotland's most famous salmon streams and during the walk you may watch various piscators going about their lawful business. Chucking rocks, or dogs, into the river will not be appreciated. A good track leads comfortably north to the Old Bridge at Anagach (Grid Ref: 040274). This three-span structure, built in 1754, is now closed to traffic and is stiffly corseted with iron stays to hold it together.

As we walked on, we were joined by a pair of buoyant goosanders in mid-stream, lunching on salmon smolts, whilst redshanks and snipe whirred overhead. Red-beaked oystercatchers pecked in a ploughed field nearby. A self-important dipper, guarding a water gauge, nodded a curt 'good morning' as we passed. A long-tailed fieldmouse scampered across the track, nervously intent upon avoiding detection. The first of the season's wild violets blushed amidst the tangle of silver birch and hazel. Yellow celandines clustered by the water's edge. Along the way, majestic Scots Pines, remnants of the Caledonian Forest, guard the path. Rampant clumps of huge daffodils bobbed in the light breeze. Black-headed gulls, feeding avariciously, swooped on flies hatching on the surface of the river.

A further easy two miles brought us to the narrow bridge at Cromdale (Grid Ref: 065290). We crossed over to have lunch and pay our respects to the old church. The stump of a severely coppiced beech tree overhangs the graveyard wall. As we entered the confines of the church, a buzzard circled ominously. Some of the tombstones date back to the time of the '45 Rebellion. A plaque on the wall notes details of an earlier battle which took place on the Shaughs of Cromdale (Grid Ref: 100274) in 1690. Some of the gentle sleepers beneath the green turf must have witnessed that fight. On 1 May that year, a government army crossed the river at Cromdale and routed a Jacobite force, killing 400 and capturing 100, forcing the remainder to flee, 'many of whom were near-naked having been compelled to abandon their plaids in the confusing circumstances'. Their defeat emphatically ended the first Jacobite uprising in the Highlands in support of the restoration of King James II.

The return route, up the east bank of the river, is a far less orderly affair than the well-manicured path down the opposite bank. It follows the line of a disused railway. Frequent diversions are required to circumvent the gaps left by bridges that have been removed, and flood ponds. At one point, briefly, it runs adjacent to the main A95 Grantown to Aberlour road, but soon descends again to the serenity of the riverbank.

Stop for coffee on the seat overlooking the dark pool below the Old Bridge. You will be surrounded by splendid beech trees and in excellent company: grey-and-yellow wagtails, mallards, chaffinches and blue tits, the glimpse of the white rump of a roe deer disappearing into the forest, and the sweet scent and sound of the river, hurrying endlessly north to greet the sea.

78. CREAG UCHDAG

I blame Scottish country dancing. And bagpipes. My downfall had nothing whatsoever to do with whisky, that other contiguous component of a guid

New Year. It was 'hornpipes, jigs, strathspeys and reels' that did for me, not *uisge beatha*. I lay on the floor, writhing, unlamented, unnoticed, kilt in a birl, sporran askew. Fifteen minutes later I was trolleyed into Edinburgh Royal Infirmary, ashamed and embarrassed at being yet another unwelcome statistical thorn in the side of an already overworked New Year's Eve hospital staff. Happily, all I sustained was a bruised ankle. My badly bruised ego I kept to myself. Bound, admonished and judge-sober, I limped home with the aid of a stick. The following morning, of sympathy came there none, only complaints that I had spoiled our New Year's Day walk. My better half was as frosty as the white top of Dundreich (622m), the Moorfoot hill which had been our intended destination. I spent the day, subdued, in a little wood on the east shore of Portmore Loch while she tramped off her ire on the lower slopes.

To avoid a recurrence of unstable Highland flings, we decided it would be safer to see in the next New Year away from home. Which is how we found ourselves, along with our friends Tony and Isabelle Sykes from Bridge of Weir, ensconced in a small pub in the border village of Town Yetholm. Including six small children, our ladies' theory being that there is safety in numbers.

It was a riotous New Year. At one stage I am convinced that people were coming down the chimney. The place was packed. About noon on the day we left, I asked the landlord if business had been brisk. He began to list a seemingly endless number of 40-fluid-ounce bottles of varying hue. 'Well,' I opined, 'not a bad New Year, then?' 'What do you mean, New Year?' he exclaimed, 'that was only this morning.'

That New Year's Day Ann and I took the children, ranging in age from two-and-a-half to eleven years old, for a walk. Our fellow revellers of the previous night were resting. It was cold, biting, Borders cold, but we set off in good order, cheerful and expectant. Shotton Hill (230m), east of Yetholm Mains and just in England, is a modest affair but steep going for little legs. They managed, even running the last hundred yards to the top.

Few things more adequately blow away revelry cobwebs than a sharp winter hike and what better place is there to welcome in the New Year than amidst the magnificent wilderness of January snows? All-important, however, is to keep well within the limit of your ability. Be well dressed, pre-pared, and properly equipped, safe rather than sorry.

A splendid walk which meets these requirements is to the south of Loch Tay on Creag Uchdag (879m), 'the crag of the hollows'. There are several routes in, but the one my wife and I prefer is from Ardtalnaig. Park with care near the gate at the end of the road up the hill from Loch Tay. The first mile and a half is unrelentingly up, by the side of a fence, but the ground eases as you reach the shoulder of Tullich Hill (682m).

Thereafter, a convenient fence marks the route ahead towards the first summit, Meall nan Oighreag (818m), where a right swing takes you on over good going to the rounded top of Creag Uchdag. The best way off the hill is south to the headwaters of the River Almond. Follow the stream down the glen to the shelter of the shieling at Dunan.

A track leads north to the start point in four easy miles. If you are feeling particularly fit, return to Loch Tay by climbing Dunan Hill to the east and traversing Creagan na Beinne (887m) north down to Tullichglass. Along the way, look out for mountain hares. There are hundreds in these hills, snow-white, dreamlike creatures, utterly beautiful, at one with their environment. And, even nicer, like me they can never resist the temptation of dancing to the coming spring. After all, what is New Year for, if it is not for dancing and *uisge beatha*?

Find your way round Creag Uchdag using OS Map 51, Loch Tay, second series, Scale 1:50,000. Park at Ardtalnaig at Grid Ref: 704389. Key points on the walk are: Tullich Hill Grid Ref: 703377; Meall nan Oighreag Grid Ref: 703341; Creag Uchdag Grid Ref: 708324; Dunan Grid Ref: 740341; Dunan Hill Grid Ref: 745355; Creagan na Beinne Grid Ref: 745368; Tullichglass Grid Ref: 725386.

79. DRUMMOND HILL

They have a unique way with words in Coshieville. Brief and to the point. Like: 'I'm sorry, the hotel bar is closed.' On a hot Perthshire summer day a few years ago, my hiking party and I, in desperate need of four cooling beers and pretty damned quick if you don't mind, loitered in a deserted reception area ringing various unresponsive bells. Eventually, a flaxen-haired young woman appeared. 'Yes, what can I do for you?' I explained our predicament. 'I'm sorry,' she said, 'but the hotel bar is closed.' I ventured, 'Is there anywhere else nearby where we could possibly get a drink?' 'Yes,' she said, 'in the public bar round the corner. The entrance is at the side of the hotel.'

We found it. The door was locked. We banged and rang more bells. As we were about to give up, we heard the sound of footsteps approaching. The door opened and the same woman appeared. 'Yes,' she said, 'what can I do for you?' Didn't she recognise us? I bit my tongue, hard, and repeated my request. 'Please can we have a drink?' She hesitated and then, smiling, led us into the bar.

This drouth had been acquired during a super forest walk round Drummond Hill (458m), which crouches between Loch Tay to the south and Glen Lyon to the north. The hill is owned by the Forestry Commission – well, to be accurate, the Forest Enterprise, since the 'powers that be' hacked the Commission into two organisations – and it is magnificently planted with mature Scots pine, Norway spruce and Douglas fir. Their scent is an enduring memory of the hike.

There is really no need for a map, but, nevertheless, pack OS Sheet 51, Loch Tay, second series, Scale 1:50,000 because it will help you to identify surrounding features from the view point at The Black Rock (Grid Ref: 763456). There are two routes, signposted by red-and-blue markers. Both begin at the car park at Grid Ref: 771461. Combine them and enjoy a walk of approximately three hours, depending on how long you pause at the Black Rock to ogle the view.

The woods are full of the birdsong of tits, finches and wrens, which alight on the forest floor 'with tiny-eyed caution, jerkily to eat'. But the most famous resident here is the capercaillie, the Gaelic 'great cock of the wood'. This magnificent bird was hunted to extinction by the mid-seventeenth century and then reintroduced to Scotland at Drummond Hill in 1837 by the Campbell Earls of Breadalbane. The chance of seeing a capercaillie is sufficient reason in itself for making this walk.

Another object of great size to be seen along the route is the dark, blue-grey bulk of Taymouth Castle. It was knocked about a bit by the Breadalbane lairds over the years and visited by Queen Victoria in 1842. She was amused by her reception and commented that it was 'princely and romantic'. Hundreds of Breadalbane's tenants were herded into service to delight the diminutive Queen and fires were lit on the surrounding hilltops for her pleasure.

From the Black Rock on Drummond Hill, the view south and west is splendid; over the village of Kenmore and Loch Tay to the gently rounded peaks of Meall nan Eanchainn (850m), Ben Chonzie (929m) and Creag Uchdag (879m). These hills and Loch Tay have comforted Jock Tamson's bairns for centuries. You will see evidence of earlier times by Croft na Caber, where a Crannog has been reconstructed. Looking at the Crannog from the hill, it is as though one has stepped back into pre-history. Crannogs were built on natural islands, or artificially created islands, close to the shore of a loch. They were circular in shape, some 15m in diameter, with a thatched roof and an adjacent harbour to park dugout canoes. A narrow timber causeway joined the crannog to the land. It was designed to be just submerged at normal water levels, thus making it hard for the occupants to be surprised by unwelcome callers. This feature has been omitted at Croft na Caber on the presumption that visitors will be friendly and may therefore be allowed to approach dry-shod. Better for twentieth-century business.

No doubt the builders, given the effort involved in their construction work, also acquired a considerable thirst under the hot summer sun; collecting hunks of rock, floating out and sinking hundreds of tonnes of stone for the foundations of their dwelling. I imagine them at close of play, trooping off to some Early Iron Age pub in search of sustenance, and some flaxen-haired Celtic girl asking them, politely, 'Yes, what can I do for you?'

80. STUCHD AN LOCHAIN

Big boys and girls do them both on the same outing – climb Stuchd an Lochain (958m), 'the peak of the little loch', and Meall Buidhe (931m), 'the yellow hill'. Team Sandison – The Manager, me and her faithful hound Hareton – pondered this matter whilst parked below the dam at the east end of Loch an Daimh. We decided not to be greedy. Discretion was the better part of valour. We would confine our tramp that day to 'the peak of the little loch': Meall Buidhe could wait for another time. After all, it wasn't going anywhere.

I had tramped Meall Buidhe before, but had been forced to cut my visit short. The Yellow Hill is not a demanding Munro, but I had been caught in a snowstorm. After an hour's battering I wimped out and hurried carwards. Whilst recovering, I glanced at the vast, snow-covered bulk of neighbouring Stuchd an Lochain. A black dot, a lone climber, was yomping down the hill, moving quickly and confidently. Clearly a better Gunga Din than me. But I made a mental note then to climb the peak in more clement weather, because it looked incredibly inviting.

These peaks dominate Loch an Daimh at the head of Glen Lyon, Perthshire's gracious glen, to the north of Loch Tay. Find them on OS Map 51, Loch Tay, second series, Scale 1:50,000. Park at Grid Ref: 509463. Stuchd an Lochain is at Grid Ref: 482449, Meall Buidhe lies at Grid Ref: 499499. Having made our executive decision to scale Stuchd an Lochain, we followed the road to the dam and skirted the shore of the loch. A small cairn and rusty iron post mark the start of the way up, a muddy track at an easy angle across the hill. Soon, however, it throws caution to the winds and simply climbs heavenwards.

Within half an hour the vans by the dam offices were dinky-toyed, the corrugated iron shed and grey boats by the shore of the loch scaled down to mere landscape blobs. The stream which tumbles from Coire Ban (Grid Ref: 505454) was crystal-clear and busy. Delicate purple saxifrage blushed in profusion. Clumps of cloudberry, made of less stern stuff, huddled close to the ground awaiting better weather to flower. When it is wet care is required here, going up and coming down; one slip could return you in a dangerous, snake-ladder slide back to Go. As I paused for breath a pair of ominously black ravens, croaking, crossly circled the loch, black against the blue sky.

On Coire Ban, away from the soggy slope, the going becomes easy; perfect walking country with splendid views down Glen Lyon. Route finding is not a problem: a line of old iron fence posts marks the way to Creag an Fheadain (887m) at Grid Ref: 499451. Coffee time, as we peered into the spectacular corrie that cups Lochan nan Cat. We dipped down from Creag an Fheadain along the crest of Coire an Duich to begin the final assault on the summit of Stuchd an Lochain. The sun broke through. Lochan nan Cat sparkled azurine blue. Chunks of cumulus whisked by in the sharp breeze. A snow bunting bobbed greeting.

Lunch was munched on the summit, huddled behind a huge, marble-speckled rock. The watery wilderness of Rannoch Moor lay before us, slashed by the silver strip of Loch Laidon. We noted the bay in which many years ago we had seen a monster trout, a fish of at least 10lb in weight, rise lazily to take a distressed blue-bottle struggling on the surface; and we gazed, awe-struck, at the blue-grey mountains of Mamore and Glencoe and the distant peaks of Knoydart. Turning away, leaving, was hard.

Indeed, harder than I had anticipated. To avoid the steep descent from Coire Ban, I insisted that we followed the fence posts east, intending to circle north on lower ground to reach the start point. The Manager was not best pleased but held her peace, and her little dog, as we ended up negotiating tougher-than-expected going and a couple of unexpected crags.

I did it my way, but it took ages. When we eventually regained the lochside track, I apologised humbly and reasonable communications were restored. As we dragged off our boots at the car I paused and looked back. Four fellow hikers were crossing the dam wall, having 'done' Stuchd an Lochain. Unhesitatingly they strode strongly north and disappeared in full cry towards Meall Buidhe. Obviously the 'big boys and girls'.

81. MACGREGOR'S LEAP AND GLEN LYON

Jocks easily jump vast distances. Our ankles are like coiled springs, the result of centuries of practice avoiding our enemies, and we wear the kilt because it gives our shanks freedom of movement in dangerous situations. Unlike loin-strangling breeches, the free-flowing kilt allows us to hurl ourselves unhindered over cavernous ravines. As we escape from our pursuers by leaping the void, they gape helplessly in awe at the sight of our manly nether regions in full flight.

The most famous 'leaps' are tourist attractions: Randolph's Leap over the River Findhorn near Relugas in Morayshire; the Soldier's Leap across the River Garry at Killiecrankie to the north of Pitlochry; Macgregor's Leap over the River Lyon in Glen Lyon, a mile up the glen from Fortingall. Visiting these chasms, I am astonished that any mortal, let alone a distraught Scot, should have dared to jump them. Amazing what being pursued by a bayonet can make one do.

Ann and I pondered these matters recently as we stood on the edge of Macgregor's Leap, whisped by damp spray from a peat-stained river in spate. 'Listen,' I said, Why don't you have a go? I'll get down to the river's edge, count to three, you jump and I'll take a photograph. It will make a great shot.' Answer came there none, but I clambered down anyway. From below, peering up, the leap looked even more daunting, a huge chunk of empty space arched over the raging torrent, an invitation to disaster.

Find Macgregor's Leap on OS Map 51, Loch Tay, second series, Scale 1:50,000 at Grid Ref: 727476. There is no signpost but the location is obvious. Park off the road on the wide grass verge and follow the sound of the turbulent stream to find the north side of the Leap. Personally, I prefer these places unsignposted. Keeps the hoards away. Otherwise, Glen Lyon is a mass of noticeboards, unfriendly messages from local lairds: no parking; no picnics; no fishing; no canoeing; no fires; no dogs; no camping – no breathing?

Prior to paying homage to the great leaper, we tramped Gleann Da-Eig; a comfortable six miles there and back from Camusvrachan (Grid Ref: 620479). Well, sort of comfortable. Once we left the track to scale the buttress of Creag nan Eildeag (636m) at Grid Ref: 600464, we found ourselves in intimidating, soggy, ankle-breaking country. So rather than hike south to Meall Luaidhe (780m), we came down at Grid Ref: 595455 to regain the stalkers' path. In fairness, I should say it was raining. In fact, it was a positive Noah's flood of a day.

However, on top, the weather cleared for half an hour and rewarded us with a splendid view of Glen Lyon; backed by the bulk of Ben Lawers (1,214m) to the south, with Carn Mairg (1,042m), Meall nan Eun (847m) and Creag Mhor (981m) crowding to the north. Glen Lyon is Clan Gregor country and they were known as 'the children of the mist'; so-called because of their astonishing ability to nip out of the said mist to remove anything not securely nailed down and then disappear back faster than anyone could mutter 'mayhem'. In 1603 James VI, once safe in London and ensconced on the throne of England, decided to sort out his 'misty' children once and for all. An Act was passed authorising: 'the extermination of that wicked, unhappy race of lawless lymmaris, callit the MacGregor.' The clan were hunted like animals; men summarily shot, women branded, their children sold off as slaves to Lowland and Irish farmers. Happily, many survived, including the family whose descendants gave birth to my maternal grandmother, Jean Macgregor. In the fourteenth century the inhabitants of Glen Lyon were less fortunate: the Black Death, bubonic plague, killed them all. They lie buried at Fortingall, where a tall stone in a field marks their resting place. Another, more user-friendly resting place here is the Fortingall Hotel, ideal for drying out after a wet day in the hills. Close by is the famous 3,000-year-old Fortingall Yew, reputed to be the most ancient tree in Europe, alive and kicking when Pontius Pilate was allegedly born at Fortingall, 'the fort of the strangers'.

As we left Macgregor's Leap and the white-foamed river, Ann turned and said: 'If you are so keen to see someone perform that long-jump, why not do it yourself — scared, are you?' 'Not at all,' I replied. 'Under other circumstances I wouldn't hesitate for a moment.' 'So why not today then?' she asked. 'I should have thought that was obvious,' I retorted. 'I am not wearing the kilt.'

82. GHOST WALK BY LOCH TUMMEL

My first sight of Schiehallion (1,083m) came during an early-season visit to Dunalistair Water, a shallow, flooded area between Loch Tummel and Loch Rannoch on the Road to the Isles. With friends, we had booked a cottage overlooking the loch for an Easter walking and fishing holiday. It seemed like a good idea at the time. Rest and relaxation after a long, cold, busy winter. But it turned out to be a near-disaster, because of the state of the cottage we had rented. The water system was non-functional, the back-up being a pipe from a nearby stream. Cooking had to be done in the tiny sitting room on the open fire, which also heated the whole house, or was supposed to. Beds were damp, blankets few. We spent three nights sleeping in our clothes to keep warm.

I wonder why we didn't just leave? Perhaps because the owners, who also had, amazingly, a hotel in Aberfeldy, were sort of friends of relations. So we grinned and stuck it out. However, it is astonishing what a few drams and good company can do. Looking back, we roar with laughter, but I never pass that Aberfeldy hotel without feeling a strong desire to hurl a brick through their dining-room window.

Schiehallion, 'the smooth slope', was marked on the first-known map of Britain by the Egyptian second-century astronomer Claudius Ptolemy, and this is the land of Clan Gregor, 'the children of the mist'. The Privy Council in Edinburgh outlawed the clan in 1603.

The climb to the summit of Schiehallion is one of the most popular walks in Perthshire, a rewarding five-hour-there-and-back tramp from the Forestry Commission car park near Braes of Foss on the B846 Coshieville–Tummel Bridge road. The route is clearly marked 'Schiehallion Path' and although the going is rough in places, most reasonably fit bodies will have little trouble reaching the top in good order.

Just as rewarding, however, is a walk to the south of Loch Tummel through the mountains and glens round Meall Tairneachan (787m), Creagan Loch (700m) and Farragon Hill (783m). Start at the east end of Frenich Wood (OS Map 52, Aberfeldy and Glen Almond, Grid Ref: 826589). Follow a good track south, along the edge of the plantation, up the line of Frenich Burn.

After one-and-a-half miles, at the end of the forest, climb southwest over Doire Leathan (Grid Ref: 808555) to gain the summit of Meall Tairneachan (Grid Ref: 808544). The way east to Creagan Loch (Grid Ref: 823543) is eased by a barytes mine track, but the descent from Creagan Loch requires care, particularly in poor weather. On a fine day the views are splendid, particularly into the dark corrie of Lochan Lairig Laoigh, 'the loch of the pass of the calf', at Grid Ref: 52/829544.

Approach Farragon Hill (Grid Ref: 840553) from the southwest, where there is an easy gully leading to the summit. From the top, descend northwest to find the Frenich Burn and follow it back down the hill to Frenich Wood and the start point on the shores of Loch Tummel.

This walk is very much 'off the beaten track' ' and it is unlikely that you will meet another soul along the way, other than red deer, grouse and golden eagles, one of the great attractions of hiking here. The surrounding vista is stunning: Schiehallion to the west, Ben Alder and the Grampians to the north and east, the blue sweep of Loch Tummel.

The last time my wife, Ann, and I walked this way, on a bright, sunny, heather-scented August morning, as we crossed the floor of a small, enclosed glen, Ann suddenly ran past me, clearly distressed and alarmed. She had felt an overwhelming sense of fear, a strong feeling that women and children were in danger.

I later discovered that during the days when Clan Gregor was being hunted, when danger approached, the men often hid their families in remote glens on the hill; and that sometimes these hiding places were discovered by their tormentors, who then stole the MacGregor women and children. When the present owner of the land heard this story, he contacted me to ask exactly where our experience had occurred. I gave him a map reference and he confirmed that for years, in his family, this same glen was always avoided because it invariably aroused the same feelings when they walked there: a terrible sense of danger, fear and distress.

83. THE BIRKS OF ABERFELDY

I set the camera on a suitable post and hurtled back to Ann. Kicking Heathcliff, her Yorkshire terrier, into an accommodating position, I faced the lens and grinned. The wretched dog, outraged, sank its needle-sharp teeth into my ankle and I yelped. Click – a perfect shot of a 'birk' at Aberfeldy. In spite of the fact that I have been the brute's principal support for more than a decade, his wellspring of canine gratitude is as dry as a two-month-old buried bone. I just have to look at him the wrong way and his teeth bare, hairy face twisting into a hideous, threatening grin.

But it is hard to remain out of sorts for long amidst the Birks of Aberfeldy. It is always exhilarating; tramping the woodland path by the crystal stream with sunlight slanting through May-budded branches, surrounded by the sights and smell of a golden spring day. The walk up the Den of Moness is one of the most beautiful in Scotland, maintained by the Countryside Ranger Service of Perth and Kinross District Council. The glen was formed some 10,000 years ago as the last Ice Age ended, leaving deep, sheltered ravines where a wide variety of trees and plants flourished.

Much of the Great Wood of Caledonia was cleared during the Middle Ages, to make safe the travellers' way and provide timber for domestic purposes, ship-building, and agricultural purposes. However, some survived: in the Black Wood of Rannoch, on Speyside, and among the high banks of the Birks of Aberfeldy which is a noted Site of Special Scientific Interest.

Park in the Square in Aberfeldy. Walk west up Main Street. The route is signposted on the left, just before the bridge over Moness Burn. Cross the A826 road to reach the Nature Trail. At the first junction, go downhill and over the stream. Follow the route in a clockwise direction. The walk is ideal for all ages and all stages of physical fitness. It is just about right for introducing little ones to the wonder of the great outdoors; two and a half miles of sheer delight, climbing 167m to a spectacular view of the high Falls of Moness, the mid-point of the trail.

Stout steps and bridges, complete with handrails, negotiate the most difficult parts of the route. Nevertheless, keep dogs and children under control; accidents happen all too easily and the sides of the glen are steep and dangerous. Wear good walking shoes and warm clothing, and stay on the track.

The Ranger Service has produced a pamphlet describing points of interest along the way. This is essential reading if you are to get the best out of your visit. Nine observation points explain the flora and fauna of the glen: birch, beech, hazel, ash, red campion, bugle, yellow pimpernel, wild garlic, sweet woodruff, bitter vetch and chickweed wintergreen. Birds are less obvious, singing from the tangled branches. Stop and let them come to you: green woodpeckers, grey wagtails, dippers, wrens, willow warblers, treecreepers, siskins, bullfinches and many more. A song of another kind immortalised the Birks of Aberfeldy, composed by Robert Burns when he walked this way on 30 August 1787:

> Now simmer blinks on flowery braes,
> And o'er the crystal streamlet plays;
> Come, let us spread the lightsome days
> In the Birks of Aberfeldy.

The path can be muddy, but presents no difficulty. There are conveniently situated benches along the way for rest and recuperation, as well as the stone ledge where Burns composed his poem. If you use the Ranger Service information pamphlet, the round trip should take around two to three hours.

Scotia's Bard was no doubt dogless when he made his visit. Otherwise, and most probably, the world would have been robbed of several gracious verses. Now, if you will excuse me, I must have a serious word about manners and the necessity not to bite the ankle that feeds you with a certain taciturn Yorkshire terrier – whose mistress just happens to be absent for the moment.

Carry OS Map 52, Aberfeldy and Glen Almond; second series, Scale 1:50,000. Start of walk Grid Ref: 856490; Nature Trail Grid Ref: 855486; Falls of Moness Grid Ref: 852480. Copies of the Birks of Aberfeldy pamphlet may be obtained from the Tourist Information Centre, The Square, Aberfeldy. Tel: (01887) 820276 or from Countryside Ranger Service, Leisure and Recreation Department, Perth and Kinross District Council, 3 High Street, Perth. Tel: (01783) 639911.

84. BRUAR FALLS

I am ambivalent about the Victorians. To me, they epitomise an elitist authoritarian principle that dictates one set of moral standards for those who 'have', and an entirely different set of moral standards for those who 'have not'. Their discriminatory interpretation of morality was, to say the very least, a highly suspect commodity. An obvious example is Patrick Sellar, agent of the first Duke of Sutherland, who made a fortune out of the Sutherland Clearances. By the time it was over, Sellar had the rental of 85,000 acres, mostly acquired from the people he had evicted. Sellar then purchased a grand estate at Ardtornish in Morvern and embraced the lifestyle of laird, after evicting the last 40 families from his new domain.

Scotland, romanticised by Sir Walter Scott and made fashionable by the 'unamused' Queen Victoria, became little other than the sporting plaything of wealthy English industrialists; suitably encouraged by impoverished Highland landowners who cared more for the fullness of their sporrans than for the ancient rights of their unfortunate tenants.

It is easy to blame Victoria. She was, after all, the 'keystane' of their power. But the lady had a deep-rooted love for Scotland. During a pony trek through Glen Tilt she said: 'This was the pleasantest and most enjoyable expedition I ever made and the recollection of it will always be agreeable to me, and increase my wish to make more.'

The Queen and Prince Albert drank from a well to the north of Blair Castle known to this day as 'Queen's Well'. Each morning a jug of water from the well was placed at their bedside. I suspect, knowing my fellow Scots, that on many an occasion, when strapped for time, the long-suffering servants found a more easily accessible source, but it makes a nice story.

Just as nice is the walk round Bruar Falls, a few miles north from the whitewashed grandeur of the castle of Blair Atholl; an easy mile and a half, climbing to 122m along pristine paths through magnificent woodlands bordering the steep banks of the tumbling stream. Queen Victoria enjoyed her visit, as did many of her notable subjects: William Wordsworth (and, of course, his sister Dorothy); Henry, Lord Cockburn; Joseph Mallord William Turner; Sir Charles Tennant; and Sir Robert Puller. But the most famous visitor to the falls at Bruar was Robert Burns, who walked the banks on Sunday, 2 September 1787, during a tour of the Highlands. In his poem 'The Humble Petition of Bruar Water to the Noble Duke of Atholl', Burns plays the part of the river, asking the duke to plant his banks with trees:

> Let lofty firs, and ashes cool,
> My lowly banks o'er spread,
> And view, deep-bending in the pool,
> Their shadow's wat'ry bed;
> Let fragrant birks, in woodbine drest,
> My craggy cliffs adorn;
> And, for the little songster's nest,
> The close embracing thorn.

The Atholl dukes were famous tree-planters. James Murray, the second duke, brought the first larch trees to Scotland from the Alps in 1727 and the fourth duke, 'Planter John', established 10,000 acres of forest during his arboreal reign. Bruar forest was planted in 1790 and 1797. The duke wrote: 'Planting ought to be carried on for Beauty, Effect, and Profit,' a lesson still being learned by modern foresters.

The Bruar River is at its best after heavy rain, when peat-stained water cascades in a white torrent over the Upper, Middle and Lower Falls. The path starts at the car park by Bruar Falls Hotel, close to the Clan Donnachaidh Museum, a shrine to Clan Robertson. Other 'shrines' were built on the route up the hill, to the great distaste of Elizabeth Grant who visited Bruar in 1815 and complained of too many 'summer houses and hermitages and peep-bo places'. The remains of one such edifice may be seen by the Lower Bridge – the others have long since crumbled. But the original path, laid out when the forest was planted, is a sheer delight, edging the stream wherever the view is most spectacular. In September, golden autumn burnishes the trees and rowan branches bend under the weight of red berries; brown-leaved silver birch dances before winter's coming and the woods resound with the call of blackbirds and wrens.

The next time you speed along the A9 Perth to Inverness road, rest and be thankful at Bruar. Pause for thought. The rushing stream and gentle wood will welcome you in, restoring perspective and calming the spirit; refreshing body and mind for the slings and arrows of the long, long road ahead.

The path is well marked. Find it on OS Map 43, Braemar, second series, Scale 1:50,000. Blair Castle Grid Ref: 866659; start of Walk Grid Ref: 822660; Lower Falls Grid Ref: 814664; Upper Falls Grid Ref: 820669.

85. DUNKELD

Private Finance Initiative has a grand sounding ring to it – business interests and government working together selflessly for the good of the nation in general and of local communities in particular. At least, that's the theory. In practice it's a more familiar story: the rich (private investors) get richer whilst the public (the taxpayer) get poorer. Like the Skye Bridge, for example. Toll charges indiscriminately soak visitor and local alike, but are guaranteed to fatten private investors' purses for years to come.

The people of Dunkeld and Birnam, on opposite banks of the River Tay, once had the same problem. The Duke of Atholl built the bridge that joins their communities in 1809 and for 70 years a toll was charged for crossing. Dunkeld people paid to meet trains in Birnam; Birnam people paid to go to church in Dunkeld. Either way, the laird won. Locals coughed up for nearly half a century before complaining and the riots that broke out in 1856 had to be quelled by the military. Even then, it was not until 1879 that the Duke gave up his rights to the County Council.

Cross the bridge free of charge today and join me in Dunkeld, number one on my hit-list of best-loved Perthshire hot spots; not only because of its grace and tranquillity, but also because it is a splendid jumping-off point for getting out and about in these airts. Those who like bags of up with their out and about have a number of Munros within easy range – to the west, Ben Chonzie, Schiehallion, Carn Mairg, Carn Gorm, Meall Garbh and Ben Alder, with the marvellous peaks of Glen Tilt and Drumochter to the north.

But Dunkeld also offers a splendid array of less taxing expeditions, all of which expectantly await well-shod hoofs. This is the ideal place to introduce little legs to the joy of hillwalking. It is also the place to begin to practise winter hillwalking skills. Provided you are properly equipped, follow the usual precautions and tell someone where you are going and when you expect to return, you should come to no harm. The terrain is wild and rugged but you are never far from safety.

The Tourist Information Centre (TIC) is in The Cross, one of Dunkeld's 'little houses'. These were built when the town was destroyed by fire in the aftermath of the Battle of Killiecrankie in 1689. Government troops defending the town set the houses ablaze when fighting off a Jacobite army. The TIC (Tel: 01350 727688) is open from April until October and will supply you with guidebooks and pamphlets about the area. Outwith that period, contact: Perthshire Tourist Board, Lower City Mills, West Mill Street, Perth PH1 5QP. Tel: 01738 627958; Fax: 01738 630416.

Popular Dunkeld and Birnam walks include: the Town Heritage Trail, the Cathedral and the famous Dunkeld Larches; the walk through the forest up the River Braan to The Hermitage and the Falls at Rumbling Bridge; the view point on Birnam Hill (366m) and the hike up to Cave Crags on Craig a' Barns. However, if you have the time and the inclination, there is a longer, 11-mile route which will give you a super day out and is a walk for all seasons, winter or summer.

Using OS Map 52, Aberfeldy and Glen Almond, park at the north end of Loch of Craiglush (Grid Ref: 047447). Find the track on the north side of the A923 Dunkeld to Blairgowrie road and follow it north through Drumbuie Wood. This leads to the south end of Mill Dam (Grid Ref: 031462). Bear right, round the east side of Mill Dam, and after about half a mile bear right again at a fork in the track (Grid Ref: 032472). The way now contours round the lower edge of Deuchary Hill (509m) and leads comfortably to Riemore Lodge and Loch Ordie (Grid Ref: 035500) after approximately three miles.

If you are an angler, pay your respects here to the loch that gave its name to one of Scotland's most famous trout flies: a bushy, brown, silver-and-grey concoction, guaranteed to mightily please fisherman, if not always fish. Circuit Loch Ordie, or track the south shore past Lochordie Lodge to the outlet stream at the southwest end. Follow the path south now to find Dowally Loch (Grid Ref: 018475) and Rotmell Loch (Grid Ref: 022471) with its sentinel rowan tree. Two further, 'private initiativeless toll bridge and angst-free' miles will bring you back to the road at Loch of Craiglush.

86. HIKING BOOTS AND BRANDY

Tramp with me today through Ogilvie country in magnificent Glen Clova in the county of Angus. In 1432 Sir William Ogilvie, Treasurer of Scotland, was granted permission by King James I to fortify his Tower of Eroly, the present site of the Castle of Airlie. James had returned home after 18 years captivity in England, determined to tame the lairds who had usurped his power during his enforced absence.

Nae luck, though. On 20 February 1437, James paid for his pains with his life. The Earl of Atholl, Robert Stewart and Robert Graham murdered him in Perth. Mind, they also paid a fiercesome price: they were professionally tortured, pinched with hot irons, then hanged. Politics were more 'immediate' then, although today much the same result is achieved by diplomatic manoeuvering behind closed doors.

Manoeuvre to the start point of this walk by parking at the Clova Hotel (formerly the Ogilvie Arms) at the head of the glen (OS Map 44, Ballater, second series, Scale 1:50,000, Grid Ref: 326732). Our objective is a circuit of the hills to the east of the glen, via Green Hill (867m) (Grid Ref: 348758) and round the horseshoe corrie to little Loch Brandy (Grid Ref: 340755). The track is well-marked and easy to follow – just unrelentingly steep.

If you are accompanied by a canine friend, keep him/her on the lead. There are numerous notices at the foot of the hill warning walkers to keep proper control of their dogs. One notice explains that stray dogs will be shot on sight. When we last hiked this way, I secretly eyed Ann's thug-like Yorkshire terrier hopefully. Sunlight warmed my back as I fell into line behind The Manager. She always blazes the trail, given that her map-reading skills are more highly developed than mine. At least, that is what she claims.

Making our way past the school next to the hotel, we followed the narrow track, climbing between Ben Reid and Rough Craig up the hill. On the crest of the first ridge, bear left. Ahead you will see the Corrie of Clova (Grid Ref: 326755) and The Snub (Grid Ref: 335755). We paused for breath on The Snub. I often pause for breath these days, although I refer to it as 'admiring the view'. Glen Clova and Glen Doll lay below us, enveloped in mist. The River South Esk twisted and turned like a silver ribbon through well-tended tiny fields. Driesh (847m), the most easterly Scottish Munro, reared its head above the green forests of Glen Doll.

The track leads up The Snub, then circles round the top of the dark corrie where the eastern horizon is dominated by the massive bulk of Ben Tirran (896m). As you begin to turn south, you will arrive at a junction in the path. Hang a left here and scramble to the top of Green Hill, then return to the path which leads gently down to sparkling Loch Brandy.

If you wish a longer day out, follow an alternative stalkers' path from the top of Green Hill southeast to the Craigs of Loch Wharral (Grid Ref: 355745). Following this route, at Rough Craig (Grid Ref: 351734) you may descend directly to the B956 near Inchdowrie House and walk a roadside mile back to the start point, or work westwards round Brown Holm (Grid Ref: 342736) to regain the outward track.

A scattering of rocks at the south shore of Loch Brandy provides shelter and an ideal spot for lunch – which, if you are so inclined, you may catch yourself from the clear waters of the loch. Loch Brandy contains large numbers of very pretty, small, wild brown trout. Hundred-foot-high cliffs surround the loch. If you decide to have a cast or two, do so from the shore. Even in midsummer, snow is not entirely unknown in these airts and the water is freezing.

The pleasurable glens of Angus, Isla, Prossen, Ogil, Lethnot, Esk and Clova offer some of the most exhilarating walking in Scotland. There are more than 60 hills here over 610m in height, enough to keep you fit and busy all your life. Those surrounding Loch Wharral and Loch Brandy are my special favourites. They are accessible and welcoming in almost all weather conditions and just about the right length to properly stretch both mind and body. Even nicer, at the end of the day, is descending from Green Hill in the full and certain knowledge that refreshment awaits in the warm embrace of the old Ogilvie Arms.

87. BEN VORLICH PERTHSHIRE

The late Vincent Price, star monster of a million horror movies, was highly suspicious of climbers and hillwalkers: 'I once went on a climbing expedition as a holiday and found the real reason climbers rope themselves together. It stops the sensible ones going home.' I think of Mr Price often, particularly when seeing my finger in front of my face becomes a problem. The trouble is that sometimes my companions see things differently. What appears dangerous to me might seem to them a perfectly acceptable thing to do. Consequently, much of my hillwalking is done in the company of individuals who share my belief that it is always better to be safe rather than sorry. If in doubt, don't. I remember abandoning an assault on Ben Vorlich (983m) and Stuc a'Chroin (977m) a few years ago. My companion, my cousin Bruce Reynolds, and I had laboured manfully through a storm until halfway up Coirre Buidhe. As conditions deteriorated, we paused to consider our situation: 'What do you think?' I asked, frozen fingers crossed behind my back. Bruce responded promptly. 'Abort,' he replied. 'Let's go down and try Inverarnan.' It was blowing a blizzard by then and I did not relish the prospect of another climb. I asked tentatively, 'How high is Inverarnan?' Bruce spluttered: 'Climb? What are you talking about, you idiot, Inverarnan is a pub at the north end of Loch Lomond!'

If I had to nominate one person to care for my best interests on the hill, then Bruce would be that man. He is vastly experienced, an expert map reader and a kind and considerate companion. But even he has the occasional mishap. He is a member of the Glasgow Moray Club, motto: 'Hill Rock, Snow and Ice.' Joining the club one morning for a day out, Bruce slipped in the car park and banged his head. Given that the club motto said nothing about car parks, he continued with the climb.

Later, enjoying rest and recuperation at the Inverarnan Inn, his companions pointed out that he was bleeding from the head. Bruce was rushed to hospital from whence he eventually emerged heavily head-bandaged and balaclava-bound. At the next club outing, their New Year Day Munro 'first foot', Bruce arrived at the start point looking like a survivor of the Charge of the Light Brigade. His fellow club members were similarly attired; also sporting bright multi-coloured balloons attached to their wrists. Thus prepared they set off, much to the astonishment of assembled onlookers.

Ben Vorlich, which means the 'hill of the bay', is one of Scotland's busiest Munros and in reasonable weather conditions presents few problems for hillwalkers. The view from the top more than repays the effort involved in getting there: north over Ben Lawers and Rannoch Moor to Glencoe and the Mamore Forest; east to the Wee Kingdom of Fife and Lomond hills; south and west to Ben Lomond, the Campsie Fells and the Arrochar Alps.

Find your way round Ben Vorlich and Stuc a'Chroin by using OS Map 57, Stirling and The Trossachs; Map No 51, Loch Tay, second series, Scale 1:50,000. Park at Ardvorlich (Grid Ref: 633231) on the minor road that margins the south shore of Loch Earn. Follow the path up Glen Vorlich for one mile to the junction with the track up Coire Buidhe. This leads up the hill to the north ridge of Ben Vorlich and thence on to the summit (Grid Ref: 631189). By following the fence posts down to Bealach an Dubh Choirean you can also climb Stuc a'Chroin (Grid Ref: 619175), avoiding the crags by angling right to locate a narrow path. There and back involves a round trip of some nine miles including steep climbs. Allow six or seven hours for the journey and make sure you are well prepared.

After abandoning our assault on the mountain, Bruce and I hurried off in search of a bit of TLC. The Inverarnan Inn provided this and much, much more. It is a gem of a pub, wonderfully welcoming, and we happily thawed out in front of a roaring fire whilst steaming gently over a cold beer. As my circulation returned, the morning blizzard became a matter of little consequence. After all, we had been sensible, and there was always tomorrow.

88. LOCH KATRINE

It is a few years since I last suffered from saddle sores, cycle, that is, not cuddy, but this morning I think we should, as Norman Tebbit once ominously advised, get on our bikes. Well, some of us, because the Trossachs offer many options: gentle walks and cycle-rides by the shores of Loch Katrine, as well as vigorous hikes into the surrounding hills. Something for everyone and a composite day out amidst splendid scenery for all the family, young and not so young alike.

Use two OS Maps: 57, Stirling and The Trossachs and 56, Loch Lomond, both second series, Scale 1:50,000. Whilst you and like-minded companions tackle the craggy twin-summits of Ben Venue (Grid Ref: 474064), less altitudinously inclined clan members can amble west from The Pier, on bike or on foot, to visit Rob Roy MacGregor's birthplace at Glengyle (Grid Ref: 387383). The old house still stands by the shore, and has the MacGregor initials, GM, and the date, 1704, above the door. Rob's mother lies asleep in the graveyard here. Rob himself is interred further north with two of his sons, on the Braes of Balquhidder.

The bike brigade should contact Joe and Hazel Norman of Trossachs Cycles to hire their mounts (Tel: 01877 382614, Fax: 01877 382732). Family parties are made particularly welcome and child seats are provided for little ones whose legs have yet to grow long enough to reach the pedals. Safety helmets are free of charge and, where required, a roof rack may be available to help transport the bikes to the start point of your expedition.

Mountain bikes are also available for hire, although – and I know I am going to regret saying this – I think they are an abomination and should be banned from the high hills. So there.

The road round the shores of Loch Katrine ends at Stronachlachar (Grid Ref: 402103) and there and back is a fair distance, some 20 miles, but there is no rule which dictates that you must do the whole route. Do as much as you please and enjoy the walk or ride. On your way, near Portnellan (Grid Ref: 402123), don't miss the Black Isle in the loch. Rob MacGregor once kidnapped and imprisoned the Duke of Montrose's rent collector there during a cold spring. After several weeks' captivity, when the duke refused to pay any ransom for the poor man, MacGregor released him. Minus the £300 in rents he was carrying at the time of his abduction.

As you return to The Pier, pause at Brenachoile (Grid Ref: 480100) and say a small prayer for the soul of Dr Archie Cameron, the brother of Cameron of Lochiel, who was involved with his sibling in Bonnie Prince Charlie's disastrous rebellion of 1745. Archie cared for the wounded on the bloody field of Culloden. For that 'crime' he was hunted down and eventually arrested at Brenachoile. He was rewarded for his humanity by being hanged at Tyburn in London in 1752.

There are two principal routes to the summit of Ben Venue (729m). One starts near the Loch Achray Hotel (Grid Ref: 503064), the other from the shores of Loch Ard at Ledard (Grid Ref: 460023) on the B829 Aberfoyle–Stronachlachar road. Sort out transport arrangements in advance and link them up, walking from Ledard in the south over Ben Venue to the Loch Achray Hotel in the north, a distance of approximately four and a half miles. The going is good to muddy, but there is a convenient track most of the way.

The only section which requires care, and, depending upon the weather, some hands-and-knees work, is on the approach to the highest summit, which is topped by a stone shaped like a human hip bone. The adjacent summit, a short step southeast and two metres lower in height, has a trig point. Leave this summit to the south and tramp down to the start of the forest path in Gleann Riabach (Grid Ref: 474050). This will lead you comfortably back to the Loch Achray Hotel.

Both expeditions, cycle and hike, are perhaps most worthwhile during the early months of the year. At this time, visitor pressure on the Trossachs is much less than during summer and autumn months and, consequently, the area is more peaceful. Granted, you will have to keep an eye on the weather, particularly on Ben Venue, but in reasonable conditions you will come to no harm.

89. BEN VENUE

We were in serious trouble. The rest of our group, members of the Moray Club, Glasgow's friendliest climbing club, had vanished. We were on our own and I was close to panic. I looked at my companion, my cousin Bruce Reynolds, and, trying to appear calm, asked: 'Well, Bruce, what do we do now?' He smiled bravely: 'Don't worry, I will think of something.' Getting lost is embarrassing enough, but getting lost in a multi-storey office block in the middle of Glasgow, which also happens to be the Regional Headquarters of Strathclyde Police, is absolute ignominy – two allegedly experienced outdoor types, stumbling around dimly lit corridors, going up and down in lifts various getting nowhere fast.

Earlier that evening we had been counted in to attend a talk given by George Oswald of Ben Alder Estate. Afterwards, Bruce and I stood talking about the points George had raised: access to the hills, the importance of collaboration and cooperation between estate owners and public. By the time we had finished chatting, the lecture theatre was deserted. Our attempt to find the way back to reception ended 30 minutes later, I think on the fourth floor, when we called a halt to consider the best course of action. Bruce came up with the answer: find an open office and telephone the front desk. Eventually, we found an unlocked door and a telephone. 'Go on then, Bruce,' I said, 'there's a phone.' 'Oh no,' he replied. 'I thought of the idea, you make the call.'

I picked up the handset. 'Good grief,' came the outraged response when I finally made contact. 'Is that where you are? Don't move.' A few moments later a less-than-calm policeman appeared before us and escorted us down to reception. Shown to the front door, we shambled off down Sauchiehall Street in search of a pint. I glanced back. The 'polis' was staring at our retreating backs, shaking his head in disbelief.

Ben Venue (727m), by Loch Katrine and Loch Ard, is a lot more user-friendly, even in bad weather, and this graceful Trossachs hill is one of my favourite Lowland walks. The hill is rarely crowded in spite of being within range of half the population of Scotland and the vista from its twin summit peaks is magnificent.

Ben Venue is also a great place to introduce newcomers to the gentle art of hillwalking. Ann, my wife, is an expert in this field. I often hear her chatting to some unsuspecting woman, generally after a friendly dinner. 'Do you like our Scottish hills?' Manners being manners, the victim generally concedes that Scottish hills are indeed a joy to behold. Ann has them kitted out and above 610m quicker than you can say 'Auchtermuchty'. The last time she struck was a few years ago, when I had the pleasure of meeting Anton Rodgers, television star of *Fresh Fields* and *May to December*. Whilst Anton and I fished Lake of Menteith, Ann took Anton's wife, the actress Elizabeth Garvie, up Ben Venue. 'Do you think they will be all right, Bruce?' Anton asked as the weather closed in during the afternoon. ' No,' I replied. 'In fact, knowing Ann's idea of a gentle walk, I wouldn't be surprised if we never saw either of them again.' The ladies arrived back, half an hour late, wet, tired, but utterly exhilarated from their day out.

Ben Venue may be climbed from either Loch Katrine in the north, via the Goblin's Cave and Bealach nam Bo, 'the pass of the cattle', or from Ledard Farm by Loch Ard to the south. The Ledard Farm approach is longer, but in my opinion the more attractive route, particularly in autumn when the woodlands are decked in gold and russet in readiness for winter.

I bear my most enduring memory of Ledard Farm on the second finger of my right hand. Before crossing the burn, I came upon a goat with its horned head stuck in a fence. With devotion far above and beyond the call of duty I freed the brute. Whereupon it bit me, before mincing off as though getting stuck in a fence was an everyday occurrence, part and parcel of being a goat.

Park by Loch Ard on the B829 by the track to Ledard Farm. The route is well signposted, past the farm, through the woods and up the hill. The track can be muddy. From the *bealach* at Beinn Bhreac, the way ahead is obvious. Care is required during the final approach, particularly in bad weather. The highest top is the first of the twin peaks, to the north of the track.

The Ledard Burn is one of Scotland's most attractive streams, a constant source of delight, tumbling white-foamed through the forest on the lower slopes, rowan and heather-banked as you climb higher. The track to Beinn Bhreac (700m) margins and streams and once on the bealach, Ben Venue invites you in along an irresistible ribbon-path across the side of the hill.

Ann told me later that as she and Elizabeth Garvie scrambled to the top of the mist-shrouded summit, Elizabeth stopped and exclaimed, 'My God, if my agent could see me now he would have a heart attack. In fact, if he ever finds out he probably will have a heart attack.' But they at least knew where they were, and would not have to confront the wrath of the Strathclyde polis in order to find their way down.

Use OS Map 57, Stirling and The Trossachs, second series, Scale 1:50,000. Start of northern approach: Grid Ref: 503063 (The Loch Achray Hotel); southern approach, Grid Ref: 461023 (Ledard Farm); Beinn Bhreac Grid Ref: 459059; Ben Venue Grid Ref: 475064.

90. DRUMGOYNE AND THE EARL'S SEAT

George Buchanan (1506–1582) is not one of my favourite historical characters. He was a self-opinionated bigot. He benefited financially from his relationship with Mary, Queen of Scots, then betrayed her. After the murder of Mary's husband, Henry Darnley, Buchanan conveniently 'confirmed' that the infamous Casket Letters, implicating Mary in the murder, had been written in her hand. Worse, as tutor to the young King James V1, he poisoned the boy's mind against his mother. Consequently, James did nothing whatsoever to prevent the judicial execution of Mary in the great hall of Fotheringhay Castle on 8 February 1587.

Buchanan was born in the village of Killearn, where a slim obelisk commemorates his less than lily-white life. I paused there recently to pay my disrespects on the way to climb nearby Drumgoyne Hill (525m) and Earl's Seat (710m), in the Campsie Fells. Use OS Map 64, Glasgow, second series, Scale 1:50,000, to find your way around. There is nothing quite like the steep frontal assault on Drumgoyne to engender angst for alleged wrongs, no matter how long ago they might have occurred. By the time I had reached the top I was in a positive lather of righteous indignation over Buchanan's duplicity.

The Campsie Fells, although in Glasgow's 'back yard', are rarely crowded. During my hike, once clear of Drumgoyne I saw only two other walkers. This was my first expedition to these airts and the round trip, there and back, was an easy seven miles. I was delighted by everything I saw and am determined to return as soon as I possibly can. This vast expanse of golden moorland offers excellent walking and is ideal for a weekend outing for all the family. There is nothing too taxing and a well-defined track will keep you safe and sound all the way.

Even nicer, the start point is at the front stoop of a distillery, the birthplace of the redoubtable Glengoyne single malts. Three distillations are on offer: 10-year-old, 12-year-old and the incomparable 17-year-old.

Arrange your day accordingly: hike first, taste later. Park across the road at Grid Ref: 526825 on the wide grass verge adjacent to the A81 Strathblane to Killearn road. A private road leads east, past white-painted cottages then uphill through a dank wood by Blairgar House (Grid Ref: 531829). Once past Blairgar, cross a meadowsweet field to the stile over the fence at the foot of Drumgoyne Hill.

Drumgoyne (Grid Ref: 541828) is a volcanic plug and the ascent is unrelentingly steep. However, once you have overcome the climb the rest of the walk is a comfortable dawdle. Descend north from Drumgoyne and pick up the line of a well-marked track that winds northeast to reach the high plateau of the fells at Garloch Hill (573m) (Grid Ref: 553837). From this crow's nest, the cultivated orderliness of Flanders Moss sweeps north over forests and fields to the high peaks of the Trossachs, Ben Venue, Ben Ledi and Ben Vorlich. To the west, Loch Lomond scythes a wild blue arc round the foot of the Luss Hills and Arrochar Alps.

A further mile east brings you gently to the trig point on the summit of Earl's Seat, where three fences meet. Lunch time, and time also, on a good day, to catch a glimpse of the Island of Arran to the west. From this distance, Arran's 'sleeping warrior' outline is all the more dramatic, like a silver-grey giant lying at rest, his head cushioned on a pillow of white clouds. Also prominent to the northwest is the vast bulk of Ben Lomond. I never see Ben Lomond without remembering the late November day when I was hit by an unexpected whiteout near the top which sent me scurrying off the mountain in record time.

The return to the start point may be varied by following a number of circuitous routes, via Little Earl (Grid Ref: 565829) and Graham's Cairn (Grid Ref: 557829), but once off the track walking is tedious and hard-going. The moor is wet and soggy in places, particularly in the vicinity of Clachertyfarlie Knowes (Grid Ref: 557834). I added a fair few steps to my journey skirting marsh pools and bogs to reach the grassy summit of the Knowes. It is probably best to return by the outward route. This is no hardship, because the vistas you missed on the way out will enliven your journey home, as will the prospect of a pit stop at the distillery. I doubt if dour George Buchanan would approve of such merriment. But he rarely approved of anything, other than his own self-importance.

91. LAKE OF MENTEITH

Don't miss the boat. Hurry along to Port of Menteith to spend a few quality hours exploring the romantic island of Inchmaholme, the largest of three islands which grace the Lake of Menteith. Sailings to Inchmahome normally stop at the end of September, but they are being kept going this year during October as part of the Scottish Tourist Board's splendid 'Autumn Gold' programme.

But I'm damned if I know why Menteith should be called a 'lake'. The most likely explanation is that it was dubbed so by Victorian visitors and the name stuck. Our new Scottish Parliament should unstick it and give Menteith its prerogative of 'loch', if for no other reason than as a mark of respect to Robert Cunninghame Graham, the first president of the Scottish National Party, who lies buried with his wife on Inchmahome. They must birl every time they hear someone mention the word 'lake'.

Don't go to Inchmahome if you love painting. You might never leave. The priory on the island is an artist's dream despite the pristine surrounding lawns, neatly maintained by the owners, Historic Scotland. The priory was founded in 1238 by Augustinian canons, 'black friars', at the behest of Walter Comyn, Earl of Menteith. Robert the Bruce was a regular visitor and his daughter, Marjorie, married Walter Stewart, a descendant of Comyn. Marjorie was the 'lass' that brought the Scottish crown to the Stuart family.

The 'lass' that signalled the end of the Stuart Dynasty, Mary Queen of Scots, also knew Inchmahome. As a child of barely five years old, she was taken there in 1547 for safekeeping during King Henry VIII's 'rough wooing of Scotland'. Unable by sweet reasonableness to obtain the betrothal of his sickly son Edward to Mary, Henry sent his lackey, the Earl of Hertford, north to burn the Scots into submission. Mary spent three weeks on Inchmahome before being bustled off to France and, ultimately, to her meeting with an English headman's axe at Fotheringhay 40 years later. Much has been made of Mary's time on Inchmahome and, if all is to be believed, she must have been a most remarkable child; busy planting trees, gardening, and, when not doing so, learning Latin and various other languages from the incumbent Abbot Still. When I think of my own granddaughter Jessica, who is the same age, I suppose it could be true. Jessica digs in the garden, plants flowers and knows a lot of Gaelic words, but then I would say that, wouldn't I?

I defy anyone not to feel instantly at ease the moment they set foot on Inchmahome. The isle is 'full of noises, sounds, and sweet airs, that give delight and hurt not'. The grey stones of the priory speak of peace. Centuries-old trees, now resplendent with myriad shades of autumn, russet and gold, soothe the soul. The clear blue waters of the loch lap white, pebble-dashed shingle shores. Mystical swans glide silently by. With 'tiny-eyed caution', wrens, chaffinches and tits alight on the forest floor to eat.

I suppose I shouldn't be churlish about the well-tended nature of the island. For hundreds of years, Inchmaholme was carefully tended by the Black Friars, cloisters, chapter house, gardens and trees et al. Nothing shows this more clearly than the coppiced woodlands; essential then to provide not only wood for the single fire which was allowed to warm their religious endeavours, but also to provide building material and, no doubt, gardening tools.

The daily affairs of the community were discussed in the chapter house. There the canons sat on a cold stone bench, built into the inner wall, which helped to ease the physical burden of their business deliberations. Today, the most significant and beautiful effigy on the island rests on the floor in the middle of the Chapter House: a stone memorial to Walter, the first earl of the Stuart line, and his countess. They lie in eternal rest, each with a comforting hand on the other's shoulder.

The most enduring picture I have, however, is of the little queen. Walking in the woodlands, playing among the red and brown September leaves; sitting by a roaring fire in the Warming House in the evening and listening to the melodious sound of the canons at their devotions; digging busily in her garden, throwing stones into the waters of the loch. As I walk the pathways where she must have walked, I hear her childish laughter and remember her future sadness and Scotland's enduring shame for turning a blind eye to the judicial murder of their queen.

92. PARROT HUNTING ON BEN CLEUCH

After two months free-range on Ben Cleuch (720m), it had to be either a very sick, or a very dead, parrot. News of the bird, an escapee rosella parrot, native to Australia, was reported at the end of September. As I prepared to begin my hike up the mountain, I was determined to watch out for its distinctive red head, yellow-and-green body and blue wings. Could I recapture the poor creature?

The walk starts in Tillicoultry, in the 'Wee County' of Clackmannanshire, at the end of Ochil Hill Road, just past the whitewashed facade of The Woolpack Inn. The route is signposted as a 'right of way', north to Blackford on the A9 in Strathallan. As I heaved on my boots prior to setting off, a cumbersome lorry stopped in the narrow street by the bridge where the Daiglen Burn tumbles down to meet the River Devon.

The driver called across 'Hey, Jimmy, can you tell me where . . .' I stopped him short. 'Sorry mate, my first time in Tillicoultry.' Sod's law, isn't it, that any time you stop to ask the way, you find yourself speaking to a completely clueless stranger? But I liked Tillicoultry. It has a clean, fresh, well-organised sparkle about it, guarded by the graceful bulk of Ben Cleuch, the highest of the gentle Ochils.

Clutching OS Map No 58, Perth and Kinross, second series, Scale 1:50,000, and my walking stick, I set off happily from Grid Ref: 913977, warmed by the sun of a perfect autumn morning. A shorter walk encircles tree-lined Tillicoultry Glen and the route follows this path up neatly maintained steps. As you go, count the wooden seats by the side of the track carefully. At the fifth seat, leave the well-trodden way through the bracken and strike directly uphill. If you don't do so, you will eventually find yourself down in the glen facing a brutal frontal assault of Ben Cleuch.

This would be a pity, because the 'right of way' is a marvellous walk, wandering north between King's Seat (643m) and The Law (638m). The Gannel Burn burbles below and as you gain height a tremendous vista awaits: smoke rising lazily from Tillicoultry chimneys; matchstick-sized golfers below, busy spoiling a good walk; the blue splash of Gartmore Dam; a patchwork of fields, pricked by the tiny gold dots of straw bales. Beyond New Sauchie, Keilarsbrae and Alloa, the silver thread of the River Forth meanders east past the dark pall of Grangemouth to the spikes of the Forth Bridges. The ancient town of Stirling straddles the plain, its castle dominating the surrounding countryside. To the south, the horizon is lined by misty grey southern upland hills: Pentland, Moorfoot, Lammermuir, Coulter and Campsie.

After two and a half miles, the route reaches a saddle in the hill at Maddy Moss (Grid Ref: 922010). Turn left here. I did, and was soon enveloped in cloud. It started to rain, heavily. Fortunately, the track ahead was easy to follow, but the wind was cold and biting. I stopped to pull on an extra sweater and waterproofs and consult the compass. Walking 'blind', after a further mile or so I reached the unnamed top at Grid Ref: 914002.

Care is required in misty conditions, since the route follows the edge of a deep corrie dividing the top from the summit of Ben Cleuch. It is easy to lose height and become disorientated. A convenient fence line will keep you safe. If you miss the track, walk north to find the fence. In doing so, you will cross and regain the comfort of the path. I continued to climb, curious about the sudden appearance of large white stones. The clouds lifted. The stones, which were in reality sheep, got up and ambled off. Before me lay my goal, the cairn on Ben Cleuch (Grid Ref: 902007).

Just below the summit, on the north face, there is a commodious, stone-built shelter. Lunch time. From here, a well-worn, wide path hurtles you back down the hillside, over The Law (Grid Ref: 919996) to the head of Tillicoultry Glen where Gannel Burn and Daiglen Burn meet in white-foamed flow. Filigree harebells nodded greeting and red berry-bedecked rowans bobbed in the breeze. The homeward part of this splendid seven-mile tramp is along the Tillicoultry Glen walk.

I did not need a compass and map to find my way to my final destination, the Woolpack Inn. Comfortably ensconced behind a rewarding pint, I mused on the sad fate of the lost parrot. If the bird was still alive, then I hadn't seen it. I did, however, see another bird – a very smug-looking, well-fed sparrowhawk.

93. KING'S SEAT

It takes a 'lang spoon to sup wi' a Fifer', as those dining with Chancellor Gordon Brown quickly realise. But it requires an even longer one to sup with a Yorkshireman. A few years ago, whilst being driven round Limekilns Estate near Dunfermline by Lord Elgin, the laird, my companion, a native of Castleford, quipped, 'Have you lived here long, My Lord?' I glanced at the abbey through the trees. Written round the tower in stone are the words 'King Robert the Bruce'. After a moment, our chauffeur smiled and replied courteously, 'Well, about 700 years, actually.' I waited for the inevitable response. '700 years? Then you'll almost be one of the locals by now?'

The Kingdom of Fife has been at the centre of Scotland's historical and political life since time immemorial. Dunfermline Abbey was founded in the latter years of the eleventh century. The body of Robert the Bruce was buried there in 1329. King James I was born in Dunfermline in 1394, luckless King Charles I in 1600. Nearby, in Culross Abbey on the shores of the Firth of Forth, are alabaster effigies of the Bruce family.

The Ochil Hills lie to the northwest of Dunfermline. Their tops provide an arresting view over what was once the industrial heartland of Scotland. The silver flow of the River Forth grows into the blue firth, guarded by the Bass Rock. The bulk of Stirling Castle and the slender pinprick of the Wallace Monument dominate the western plain. Grampian Mountains rear to the north. Auld Reekie glowers over all from below the Pentland Hills.

There are a number of fine walks through the Ochil Hills. Find them on OS Map 58, Perth and Kinross, second series, Scale 1: 50,000. One of my favourites begins near Glendevon at Grid Ref: 951052. This is an all day hike of approximately ten miles and it takes about five or six hours, depending upon how long and how often you choose to ' stand and stare'. The going is easy, but once off the beaten track, on the high moorland, it can be soggy, particularly after heavy rain.

Follow the road southwest to Lower Glendevon Reservoir (Grid Ref: 940044) and skirt the shore to reach the dam wall at Upper Glendevon Reservoir at Grid Ref: 924042. From this point, hang a left and follow the track past Backhills Farm (Grid Ref: 915035). As you climb the hill by Broich Burn, the glen narrows and is engulfed by Crodwell Hill (553m) to the west and Middle Hill (496m) to the east. The path quickly degenerates into little better than a sheep track.

Thus, once you 'break out' onto the upper plateau on Maddy Moss (Grid Ref: 924009), the contrast is exhilarating and rewarding; one moment dark and forbidding, the next all sweetness and light with a view of half of Scotland waiting to greet you. The high point of our journey lies one mile southeast: King's Seat Hill (643m), towering over the town of Dollar and grim Castle Gloom (Grid Ref: 060993), which stands forlornly between the Burn of Sorrow and the Burn of Care. The castle was renamed 'Castle Campbell' by an Act of Parliament in 1465. Amongst the list of illustrious visitors to Castle Campbell is Mary, Queen of Scots, her arch-enemy, John Knox, and last but not least James Graham, Marquis of Montrose, who seriously knocked it about a bit in 1645 on behalf of the deposed King Charles II.

King's Seat Hill is the ideal place for a 'crow's nest' lunch. Thereafter, tramp due north and descend to near the source of the Burn of Sorrow (Grid Ref: 934008). Hike northeast from here to find the top of Tarmangie Hill (645m) (Grid Ref: 941014). A forestry plantation home obscures the route. March the forest edge to find a convenient fire break and follow it down to locate a comfortable track (Grid Ref: 949025) which leads to the south end of Glensherup Reservoir (Grid Ref: 966043).

The monotony of blanket forestry soon gives way to a 'proper' wood, alive with birdsong, and the chance to pause and ruminate on a splendid arched bridge (Grid Ref: 965056) spanning the crystal-clear waters of the infant River Devon. At the main road, the A823, turn left. Half a careful mile will bring you back to the start point. Refresh yourself in a local hostelry, but remember to have your 'lang spoon' ready. In these airts, you never know when you might need it.

94. TENTSMUIR FOREST

On 3 May 1679, twelve angry men ambushed the Archbishop of St Andrews, James Sharpe, at Magus Muir near Pitscottie in Fife. John Balfour of Kinloch was the ringleader. He and his zealous covenanting co-conspirators dragged the episcopalian prelate from his coach and hacked him to death. A monument to Sharpe stands in a forest at the side of the B939 Pitscottie to St Andrews road. Every time I pass, I remember with horror some serious hacking I myself carried out nearby. I had been invited to make up a golf four on the Old Course and was anticipating the event with as much enthusiasm as Sharpe must have felt when he faced his killers. My love of the royal and ancient game far exceeds my ability to play it. I was so nervous that it took me nearly a minute to balance the ball on the tee prior to battle. I then hacked my way round the hallowed sward. By the time I staggered onto the 17th tee I wanted to die, more so after I sliced my ball into the dining-room of the hotel overlooking the fairway.

As I hiked miserably off to retrieve it, I noticed a famous figure observing my wrack. It was Lee Trevino, leaning on the wall, chin couched in the comfortable triangle of his hands. He never said a word, but as I slouched shamefacedly past he shook his head sadly. I have never forgotten the look on his face.

Which is why Tentsmuir Forest, north from St Andrews across the muddy estuary of the River Eden, is always so welcoming. Not a green, fairway or golf ball to be seen. Just splendid isolation and the chance to enjoy a good walk unspoiled. Use OS Map 59, St Andrews and Kirkcaldy, second series, Scale 1:50,000, to find your way round.

A vast expanse of sand has been formed here over the centuries by silt and sediment washed down from the River Tay, Scotland's longest and most loquacious stream. The impact of the river flow also affects the north shore of the firth, at Barry/Buddon links and at Carnoustie. The planting of Tentsmuir Forest has helped stabilise the southern sands whilst those to the north are being steadily eroded.

Neolithic people lived and worked at Tentsmuir more than 4,000 years ago. In the Middle Ages, these remote lands were reputed to be the haunt and hideout of brigands and pirates. The Forestry Commission owns Tentsmuir today. So not much change there, then?

Tentsmuir covers an area four miles north–south by one and a half miles east–west. It is unique in that it is a growing dune system. The sand deposited by the River Tay at Tentsmuir Point is blown inland by the wind, thus increasing the land area in size. In 1940, a defensive line of anti-tank obstructions was built on the shore. They are now more than 800 yards inland. Morton Lochs Nature Reserve, at Grid Ref: 462264, is a favourite roosting place for birds. But one of the most spectacular ornithological treasures here is the sight and sound of the thousands of winter visitors that crowd Abertay Sands (Grid Ref: 520273), lying offshore from Tentsmuir Point; sanderlings, little stints, dunlins, plovers, common scoters, eider ducks and up to 8,000 pink-footed geese. Just as spectacular are the dune's wildflowers; sea rocket, sea sandwort, the delicate pink of common storksbill, bird's foot trefoil, sand spurrey, thrift, the ubiquitous willow herb and, during August and September, clouds of ivory-coloured grass of Parnassus.

A good start point is the parking place at Grid Ref: 499241. The broken road you follow to reach it is replete with 'official' traffic barriers and, as several notices warn, they are locked at night. At the parking place, modern-day 'pirates' who relieve you of hard cash for the privilege of doing so captain a wooden hut. I object to this. After all, the Forestry Commission is funded by the taxpayer, so why should we have to fork out twice?

Whatever, from the parking place you can set off to explore Tentsmuir, the sands and the nature reserve, along a series of well-marked paths and trails. How long you choose to hike for is a matter of personal choice. Just make sure that if you have taken your car to the start point you get back before closing time. Tentsmuir is a splendid place to walk, regardless of wind and weather, and it is guaranteed golf and hacker free. Enjoy.

95. WEST LOMOND AND LOCH LEVEN

Three for the price of one this morning. A boat-ride to Castle Island in Loch Leven, bird counting at Vane Farm, and a tramp to the top of West Lomond (522m). This expedition provides an exciting day out for all ages and stages of physical fitness. Pack OS Map 58, Perth and Kinross, second series, Scale 1:50,000 to navigate round. Get afloat at Grid Ref: 128017 near Kinross House. The sail to Castle Island takes eight minutes and the ferry runs from 9.30 a.m. until 5.30 p.m. Booking is not required. For further information contact the Tourist Information Centre at the Service Area at Junction 6 on the M90 Motorway (Tel: 01577 863680).

When I first visited Lochleven Castle, it was undeveloped. Everything is pristine now, with manicured lawns, signposts, gift shop, display panels, the whole bang-shoot of tourism. I liked it better the old way: a broken tower amidst a tangle of briar and bramble. A family of mallard were the only occupants then, apart from Mary, Queen of Scots. I had a chat with her. At least, I did in my imagination. The queen was imprisoned here after the debacle of Carberry Hill in 1567. The following spring, with the help of her admirer, Willy Douglas, Mary escaped. Willy remained with the Queen until the very end, on Wednesday, 8 February 1587, when she was beheaded at Fotheringhay Castle.

Return to Kinross and drive south down the B996 to its junction with the B9097. Hang a left here towards Kinglassie. Vane Farm, a domain of the RSPB on the shores of Loch Leven, is two miles distant. The best time to descend on Vane Farm, particularly if you have youngsters with you, is from 10 a.m. to 1 p.m. on Saturday, 29 May 2001. A Breeding Wader Survey is taking place then with the opportunity of spotting lapwings, redshanks, snipe and curlews. Go along and help with the count.

There are nature trails in the woodlands to the south. During May, summer migrants return, including willow warblers, blackcaps and garden warblers. Watch out also for spotted woodpeckers, tree pipits and spotted flycatchers, as do the resident raptors, buzzards, peregrines, kestrels and sparrowhawks. Hundreds of frogs and toads start to emerge from their ponds during May and there are carefully positioned hides which allow you to view the wildlife without disturbing their daily business (Tel: 01577 862355).

Our main work today, the ascent of West Lomond, starts from the car park at Grid Ref: 227063 to the west of Falkland Palace. As a teenager, the Earl of Angus held King James V prisoner at Falkland. James eventually died there in 1542, shortly after receiving news of the birth of his daughter, Mary, at Linlithgow. The dying monarch is reputed to have said, prophetically: 'Farewell, it cam' with ane lass and it will pass with ane lass.' John Knox, Mary's arch-enemy, visited the area in 1559, determined to root out every vestige of Catholic idolatry. He is reported to have said: 'We reformed them.' Meaning that his sanctimonious black-gowned followers burnt everything in sight.

An excellent track, bounded by a dry-stone wall, leads west from the car park giving easy access to the hill. If you fancy some serious climbing, you can find this at Craigen Gaw (Grid Ref: 203073) to the north of the path. Otherwise, amble to the shoulder of the hill and then reach for the summit. Once there, you will find a strange, camouflaged, rectangular sentry box, surmounted by an aerial – at least, it was there when I last hiked this way. I have no idea what purpose it serves and there is no evidence of a door. Anyway, I knocked loudly, just in case some poor soul was locked inside, but of answer came there none.

Other, more ancient people knew the summit intimately. Neolithic people built a huge burial cairn on the top of the hill, 4,000 years ago. It has been severely damaged over the years, but in its original form it could have had a diameter of 30m. All that remains now are scattered stones and a sense of serenity. Serenity also pervades the panoramic view from West Lomond: the Angus Glens and Cairngorm tops to the north; Ben Lawers and Ben Lomond westward; the stub of Largo Law, Edinburgh and the Pentland and Lammermuir Hills to the south. At the foot of the hill lies graceful Loch Leven, swained by tree-covered Castle Island and the sad shade of Mary, Queen of Scots.

96. LARGO LAW AND ROBINSON CRUSOE

One of the most significant lowland heights I had yet to Scale was Largo Law (290m). It dominates the southern fringe of the Wee Kingdom of Fife and is visible from miles around. If ever a hill asks to be climbed, then Largo Law is that hill. With that thought in mind, I set out to do so on a brisk December day at the end of the last millennium.

Which is where my troubles began. I couldn't find a way up. All obvious routes were barred by notices warning the public to keep out. Use OS Map

59, St Andrews and Kirkcaldy, second series, Scale 1:50,000, to pinpoint exactly where local landowners don't want you to tread. When it comes to allowing public access, lowland lairds are no more accommodating that their Highland brethren.

The track leading northwest from the A915 to Lahill Craig (Grid Ref: 436048) is, according to a prominent signpost, private. At Auchindownie (Grid Ref: 421056), somebody has built a high roadside chain-link, barbed-wire-topped fence for 90 metres. It is impassable. I called at Wester Newburn (Grid Ref: 441052), to ask if I could walk through the farm to access the hill. Nobody answered my knock. Rather than spend the day going round in dangerously decreasing circles, I abandoned the Law and opted instead for plan B, a tramp along the beach from Lower Largo to Elie, a splendid there-and-back journey of ten miles. But if any Largo Law farmer, or the local tourist board, can throw some light upon why it should be so difficult to find a welcoming route to the top of this famous Scottish hill, then I would dearly like to know.

I discussed this with Robinson Crusoe (aka Andrew Selkirk) in Lower Largo. Did he decide to run away to sea in 1695 because of overbearing landowners? He stands on a stone plinth above the doorway of his father's house, hand shading his eyes, endlessly searching the far horizon. The English spy and writer Daniel Defoe immortalised Selkirk in his book *Robinson Crusoe*, based on the taciturn seaman's exploits, particularly the years he spent as a castaway on the island of Juan Fernandez in the Pacific Ocean. Selkirk was abandoned there after quarrelling with his ship's captain.

Another Scottish seafaring hero of mine, Sir Andrew Wood, was also a native of Lower Largo. Between 1489 and 1504, Wood, in his galleons the *Yellow Carvel* and the *Flower*, fought and won a series of famous battles in the Firth of Forth against usurping English invaders. Even as a retired landlubber, Wood maintained his love of being afloat: he had a canal dug from his home to church so that he could be rowed to worship in appropriate style. Sir Andrew was buried in the churchyard in 1515.

The style of today's walk is just as impressive. Turn left before the sea in the centre of Lower Largo and follow the narrow road to where it ends near a convenient car park. A short walk will bring you to the beach (Grid Ref: 427250) and the wide crescent of sand reaching east to Elie. The beach is backed by golden marram grass-covered dunes that play host to a number of rare and beautiful plants, including grass of Parnassus and early purple orchids. Red-billed oyster-catchers, curlews and dunlins poke and probe for food along the wave-washed shore.

At the end of the beach, after splashing across Cocklemill Burn (Grid Ref: 460009), a circuitous track leads round Shell Bay past Kincraig Point (Grid Ref: 465997) and into Elie. Lunch at the flourishing boat-bobbing harbour (Grid Ref: 499996), where there are windsurfers, sailboards, dinghies, canoes and pedalos for hire. Elie is a popular summer holiday resort, but it is still a working harbour, where the descendants of Selkirk and Wood continue to brave the waters of the Firth in search of lobster and crab.

The quickest way home is via the line of the disused railway track. Find it just north of the golf links (watch out for flying balls) at Grid Ref: 490003. It leads directly back to Lower Largo via the ruins of Mount Pleasant (Grid Ref: 464019). However, if the weather is fine, it is hard to resist the lure of the beach and return by the outward route. In Lower Largo, pay your last respects to the ever-watchful Mr Crusoe, then repair for refreshment to the hotel named after him on the seafront. Who knows, perhaps they might even be able to tell you how to access Largo Law!

97. KINGHORN LOCH

I was a good but lazy swimmer, and learned my trade in the sea at Kinghorn in the Wee Kingdom of Fife. For many years the royal burgh on the shores of the Firth of Forth was our regular holiday resort; reached after an exciting, steam-belching train ride from Waverley Station, Edinburgh, clattering through the vast, red-painted arches of the majestic Forth Railway Bridge.

Kinghorn was a central part of family life and we all loved the intimate character of the small seaside town. My parents eventually bought a top-floor flat in a grey tenement building on the harbour front, and, in due course, our own children splashed and danced in the salty waves that washed the golden beach. Time was of little consequence, simply the distance between sea-sprayed rocks and lunch. These were endless days, an enchanted journey amidst boundless horizons, and my love for much that I now hold dear was born there: our precious landscape; Scotland's flora and fauna; pride and pleasure in the independent nature of our people.

One of Scotland's most significant monuments stands by the road on the cliff near Pettycur, one and a half miles west of Kinghorn; a tall obelisk marking the beginning of Scotland's ruin, commemorating the site where

King Alexander III was killed in a storm on 12 March 1286, after falling from his horse. Scotland without a king 'lay in as much perplexity as a vessel in the midst of the waves of the ocean without oarsmen or helmsman'. Alexander's daughter, married to Eric II of Norway, had died and her child, Margaret, the infant Maid of Norway, was successor to the Scottish crown. However, Margaret died in Orkney on her way to claim her inheritance.

The rest, as they say, is history. Centuries of strife, internally and with England, a rapacious neighbour, intent upon subjugation, culminating in the Act of Union in 1707 and the end of Scottish independence. As I stand before the memorial, I recall words from *Liber Pluscardensis*: 'Woe to the folk of Scotland, for here is the beginning of all sorrow.'

But not for small boys. As we grew older we ventured further afield. There is a wonderful cliff path leading east from Kinghorn towards Kirkcaldy. A few minutes' walk brings you to an isolated cove with clear, green water over a sandy bottom, ideal for swimming. The track eventually arrives at the old tower of Seafield, perched above the black rocks of East and West Vows. Kinghorn Loch, north of the golf course and the B923 road, is a bird sanctuary, hosting many species of duck and diver. I saw my first great crested grebe there, and marvelled at the clockwork progress of moorhens and coots as they marshalled broods of downy chicks through the tangle of lochside rushes.

Another favourite expedition was to the beach at Lower Largo, between Methil and Elie, a two-mile crescent of sand-backed dunes and the chance to play games based upon *Robinson Crusoe*. The statue of Andrew Selkirk, the real castaway, stands above his door, hand raised, hopefully scanning the horizon – wondering, perhaps, if it is time to learn to swim?

The best way to visit Alexander's Monument is by car. To reach the cove and Seafield Tower, take the track that branches right, halfway up the brae from the harbour, before the railway bridge. For Lower Largo, park at the harbour by the hotel and walk east up the main street past Andrew Selkirk's house to reach the east end of the beach.

Use OS Maps 66, Edinburgh and 59, St Andrews and Kirkcaldy; second series, Scale 1: 50,000. Kinghorn Grid Ref: 270869; Alexander's Monument Grid Ref: 254864; Seafield Tower Grid Ref: 280885; Kinghorn Loch Grid Ref: 259873; start of Lower Largo walk Grid Ref: 422027.

98. TINTO HILL

Range over Tinto Hill (707m) near Biggar this morning. As winter days lengthen, the view from the massive, tumbled summit cairn sparkles with spring's freshness. At Tinto's feet, the River Clyde lies like a silver thread; skirting Culter Fell, wending its way past Symington and beneath Wolfclyde bridge to reach the graceful little village of Thankerton. When I passed on 15 March the river was bristling with busy anglers, celebrating the opening of the trout fishing season.

The thumb of conical Quothquan Law (325m) stubs the flood plain below Tinto. To the north, Ben Lomond (974m) rears skyward, buttressed by the Arrochar Alps and the peaks of Perthshire and Argyll. West, across the bleak sweep of the grey Strathaven and Darvel moors, Goat Fell (874m), the head of Arran's 'Sleeping Warrior', lies at rest. To the south, waves of green hills crowd the horizon; Lowther, Manor and Ettrick hills leading towards Broad Law (840m) and Merrick (843m), the highest peaks in Southern Scotland.

Tinto Hill, approximately 30 minutes drive from Glasgow and 45 minutes from Edinburgh, is one of the most dramatic and yet most easily accessible Scottish mountains. It is bordered to the east and northeast by the A73 Abington to Lanark road. The B7055 Winston to Douglas Water road lies to the south. Additional minor roads give access from the north and west. Therefore, you have no excuse whatsoever for not dragging out the hiking boots and getting to grips with this welcoming ben.

Use OS Map 72, Upper Clyde Valley, Scale 1:50,000, second series, to find your preferred route to the top, but the car park at Fallburn (Grid Ref: 965374) is a useful start point. This offers a six-mile round trip with the delights of the Fallburn Inn waiting to receive you at close of play. A track leads from the car park over the first top, Totherin Hill (479m), to the summit (Grid Ref: 952343). Introduce yourself to The Dimple, immediately south, then descend to Scaut Hill (586m, Grid Ref: 966346) and Wee Hill (385m) at Grid Ref: 978350. From Wee Hill, hike northwest back to the car park via Park Knowe (Grid Ref: 970367).

The top of many of the peaks in this area are sites of prehistoric hill forts; at Candybank, Quothquan, Park Knowe, Chester, Cow Castle, Nisbet, Devonshaw, Black Hill, Bodsberry and, the best preserved example, Arbory Hill near Abington. The name 'fort' suggests that these structures were entirely military in function, but this is not so. They were in fact embryonic villages, built within defensive perimeters to protect their communities from the unwelcome attention of aggressive neighbours. They can be dated back to around the eighth century BC and were probably used for 1,000 years.

Stop at Park Knowe and trace the outlines of its oval shaped fort. The remains of the two stone walls that contained the 61m by 52m village can still be seen. However, keeping up with their neighbours who lived on the tip of Quothquan Law was not really an option for Park Knowe residents, as the fort on Quothquan was substantially larger, initially measuring 122m by 76m and later extended by the addition of a 91m by 61m enclosure. Whatever, it must have been a busy place, even before Agricola arrived to civilise our ancestors. Or try to.

We Scots are a thrawn bunch. Taking us to water does not necessarily imply that Jock Tamson's bairns can be induced to drink. Just below the surface of our national id lurks an instinctive, deep-rooted suspicion of gift-horses, no matter how grand or how well-groomed they might be. The people of Lanarkshire have more than their full measure of this conceit, hardened by centuries of opposition to concepts which they refused to either accept or adopt. 'Bloody' Claverhouse is still vilified in these airts, as much as the memory of Richard Cameron, Covenanter and preacher, is revered.

However, as the days lengthen and wildflowers blossom in the hedgerows, I am reminded of another son of Scotland, the poet Christopher Murray Grieve, 'Hugh MacDiarmid'. He lived for a number of years at Brownsbank, to the north of Biggar, and on my descent from Tinto Hill I stopped to pay my respects to the memory of this great Scottish nationalist. His poem, 'Water Music', written for William and Flora Johnstone, illuminates this wonderful landscape:

> Wheest, wheest, Joyce, and let me hear
> Nae Anna Livvy's lilt,
> But Wauchope, Esk, and Ewes again,
> Each wi' its ain rhythms till't.

I regularly swanned about Swanston at the foot of the Pentland Hills near Edinburgh as a youth. I swooned a lot as well, in the 'T' Woods, in the depths of adolescent love, when I had my first kiss. Come to think of it, Swanston and the Pentland Hills played a huge part in my formative years. It awakened in me an awareness of the finer things in life: the great outdoors; the history of my native land; poetry and literature; hillwalking and trout fishing; birds, both feathered and otherwise; and, of course, the supreme importance of Scotland's alternative national game, 'gowf'. Most weeks, to the utter disgust of the long-suffering green-keeper, I hacked my way round Swanston Golf Course with a handful of hickory-shafted clubs. The first-ever piebald blackbird I saw was in the garden of the Swanston cottage, where Robert Louis Stevenson used to spend his youthful summers. The first trout flies I lost were snagged by jagged rocks on the bed of the infant Water of Leith when I fished near Balerno.

Eight principal peaks cling here to the hem of Auld Reekie's southern skirts: Scald Law, Carnethy Hill, West Kip, The Mount, East Cairn, West Cairn, Byrehope Mount and Craigengar. All rise to over 457m in height, the tallest being proud Scald Law (579m). Two notable rivers are born in the Pentland Hills, the Water of Leith and the North Esk. More than a dozen lochs and reservoirs blue-stamp these green hills and bronzed moorlands and a spider-web network of public rights of way and tracks give access to the innermost soul of this quiet, secluded land.

In spite of being on the doorstep of Scotland's capital city, within striking distance of more than 3 million of Jock Tamson's bairns, the Pentland Hills remain peaceful. It is possible to walk all day without seeing anybody else, particularly towards the southern end of this 15 mile-long range of hills. A footpath from Garvald (OS Map 72, Upper Clyde Valley, Grid Ref: 098493) will introduce you to a grand seven-mile circular tour taking in the Covenanter's Grave on Black Law (Grid Ref: 080521), The Pike (Grid Ref: 061521), Bleak Law (Grid Ref: 064513), Mid Hill (Grid Ref: 070499) and the cairn on Dunsyre Hill (Grid Ref: 070490).

The car park at Nine Mile Burn (OS Map 66, Edinburgh, Grid Ref:

177577) is a convenient start point from which to explore the dramatic little ridge on West Kip (Grid Ref: 178606) and Scald Law (Grid Ref: 192611). If you can arrange transport at the other end, then a splendid four-mile hike starts at Flotterstone (Grid Ref: 234630) on the A702 Edinburgh to Biggar road. Walk north round Glencorse Reservoir and at Grid Ref: 215640, find the track which leads north over the west shoulder of Capelaw Hill to Bonaly Tower (Grid Ref: 215677) and Colinton. When the Logan Burn was impounded to create Glencorse Reservoir, a church was flooded. In stormy weather, from beneath the waves, you can sometimes hear the doleful toll of its sunken bell. Well, that's what is said, but although I have listened long and hard over the years, I confess that I have never heard a single ding or dong.

The quick canter up to the top of Caerketton Hill (Grid Ref: 238662) from Swanston Village (Grid Ref: 240674) remains one of my favourite Pentland outings. Cars are banned from the village, but may be left in a car park adjacent to the entrance to the golf course. Wander uphill by the burn to visit the 'T' Woods, then climb steeply to the summit to examine the remains of a Neolithic cairn, probably built some 4,000 years ago and still covering an area of approximately 15m in diameter. Head due west now, along the crest of the ridge, to find Allermuir Hill (Grid Ref: 227662). Descend west from Allermuir to pick up the track leading north by the side of the Howden Burn. This will lead you gently round the north side of the hill and back, in time for tea, to your start point at the village. A happy round trip of about four miles. When I revisited Swanston last summer, I paid my respects to Stevenson's Cottage and to the places I knew and loved so well. As I ruminated by the garden wall on times past, a flash of white caught my eye. It was a piebald blackbird and I felt as though I had come home.

100. SKIPPING OVER THE KIPS

The Pentland Hills have been part of my life for as long as I can remember. I first committed the 'sin' of golf at Swanston, a Pentland course reputed to be the preferred territory of mountain goats. Most of my time there was spent raking about in gorse bushes searching for lost golf balls. To stave off the imminent prospect of bankruptcy, my father banished me until I had learned to 'Watch where the damned ball lands!'

These gentle hills are the lungs of Auld Reekie; a place where dour citizens can wander all day without encountering a single MSP, bagpipe player or urgent inducement to attend some state-of-the-art cultural beanfeast. The Pentlands, by comparison with, say, Ben More Assynt in Sutherland, may be busy, but they still provide relative peace and a chance to escape the dust and angst which palls the foot of the Royal Mile, where Caledonia's parliament building is, phoenix-like, rising (?).

Swanston village was also a magnet for me because the poet Robert Louis Stevenson stayed there as a youth. I saw my first-ever albino blackbird in his back garden and also discovered my first girlfriend at Swanston. We used to lurk amidst the bluebells and whisper sweet nothings into each other's lugs in the shade of the T Woods. Her name was Wendy Brown. Where is she now? I also found Habbie's Howe, the famous pub, now sadly gone, at Nine Mile Burn. Allan Ramsay, in *The Gentle Shepherd*, wrote:

> Gae faurer doon the burn tae Habbie's Howe,
> Where a' the sweets o' spring and summer grow,
> An' when ye're tired o' prattling side the rill,
> Return tae Ninemileburn, an' tak a gill.

The Manager and I, both before and after we were married, took Ramsay's advice regularly. The deal struck between us was always the same: no pleasure before pain. A brisk canter to the top of a Pentland peak, then, and only then, a 'gill' at Habbie's.

One of our favourite walks starts from the car park at Habbie's Howe (Grid Ref: 178577); a splendid, six-mile hike to the top of the highest Pentland summit, Scald Law (579m), then back via the line of a Roman road. OS Map 65, Falkirk and West Lothian, will guide you round the route. At the gate onto the hill, follow the Scottish Rights of Way Society signpost to Balerno, by Monks Rig and Braid Law. The track climbs gently north whilst the Monks Burn gurgles brightly on your left.

It is easy to picture these hooded Cistercian divines tramping the path. This was the route they used from their monastery at Newhall, in the woods to the south of Habbie's Howe, to visit a holy chapel on the north shore of Loganlee Reservoir, where Howlets House (Grid Ref: 190620), 'the house of the owls', now stands. I followed their footsteps and stopped at the Font Stone (Grid Ref: 174592) where they slaked their thirst, drinking rainwater from the hollowed-out centre of the stone.

At the road junction (Grid Ref: 175604), march straight on and assault the steep face of West Kip (550m), the Pentland's second-highest peak. As you approach the top, the track narrows and in wet weather, or in high winds, tackle this part of the walk with caution. Descend from West Kip and tramp over the grassy saddle to gain its near neighbour, East Kip. The way ahead now follows a good path which leads easily up the north side of the hill to the trig point on the summit of Scald Law (Grid Ref: 192611).

Hike the rim of the wide corrie that links Scald Law to the top of South Black Hill (Grid Ref: 192603). There is a vast tumble of stones here that provide welcome shelter from the wind. Enjoy your lunch, and a panoramic vista: the Bass Rock and Berwick Law, the Lammermuir and Moorfoot Hills, and, far below, the distinctive, concentric rings which mark the site of Braidwood hill fort (Grid Ref: 193596), occupied by our ancestors more than 2,000 years ago.

Descend from South Black Hill and say hello to ghosts of times past. The Roman road, their principal route between the Solway Firth and Cramond on the Firth of Forth, runs to the south of the Braidwood at Eight Mile Burn. The true line of the road has long since been ploughed up, but every time I pass this way I swear that I can hear the sound of clinking metal kilts and the cursing of weary soldiers.

101. BLACKNESS CASTLE

When I sported a neckerchief and woggle, topped off by the statutory floppy, wide-brimmed brown hat, a favourite weekend campsite was in the woods to the west of Hopetoun House, near South Queensferry. My Scout Patrol, the Otters, of which I was illustrious leader, hiked there from Edinburgh hauling a trek-cart – an over-grown, two-wheeled barrow into which we crammed tents, cooking utensils, food and personal effects. I recently drove the route and realised just how much things had altered, not least the volume of vehicles encountered along the way. Today, we would be yanked off to the nearest police station and charged with causing a traffic hazard before we had covered the first mile. Even the minor roads were car-crammed. I barely recognised the once-peaceful little village of Dalmeny. But the woods were unchanged. The same birds sang from the same statuesque copper and silver birch trees. Red-speckled trout still splashed in the small stream. The view from the shore of the Firth of Forth towards the dark bulk of Blackness Castle was just as dramatic. Even now, a stone's throw from the centre of Auld Reekie, that well-remembered, tangible sense of solitude welcomed me. That corner of my memory remained intact.

Make your own trek to Blackness and find this pleasure: an easy five-mile walk from the fourteenth century castle along the foreshore to the woods, returning across parkland to examine another splendid monument, The House of the Binns, where General Tam Dalyell raised the Royal Scots Greys in 1681. This is a splendid hike, ideal for every member of your patrol, except, that is, for 'man's best friend'. Dogs are not allowed on the house policies.

Find the walk on OS Map 66, Falkirk and West Lothian, second series, Scale 1:50,000. Park near the yacht clubhouse in Blackness Village at Grid Ref: 053801. An intimidating road leads northeast, hugging the edge of Blackness Bay to reach the castle at Grid Ref: 057803. James III stationed his forces at Blackness in 1488, as he prepared to confront the insurrection which finally lead to his mysterious murder after the rout at Sauchieburn a few months later.

By 1543, the castle was being used as a state prison. The Scottish Chancellor, Cardinal David Beaton (1494–1546), was incarcerated there for a month in that year because of his opposition to plans to marry the infant Mary, Queen of Scots to Prince Edward, the son of Henry VIII of England. Three years after his release Beaton was murdered in St Andrews Castle, allegedly as the result of an English-inspired plot.

Cromwell's armies knocked Blackness about a bit in 1650, during their conquest of Scotland, but the castle was restored again in 1660 when Charles II also restored legal mirth and jollity to his kingdoms. During the French wars, between 1759 and 1815, Blackness was a prison for captured Frenchmen, but by 1870 it had lost much of its prestige and was reduced to being Scotland's principal ammunition dump.

After paying your respects to the castle, return to the village to find the start of the Firth-side track along Wester Shore Wood (Grid Ref: 055799). The Forth Bridges dominate the eastern view; complete, when I last passed, with vast, brilliant lights on top of the central arch of the Railway Bridge counting off the days to go until the new millennium. Who dreams up these daft schemes? Can't they think of anything better to do with our money?

When you arrive at the mouth of the burn (Grid Ref: 080793), hang a right and escape into the woods. Find the track at Grid Ref: 076786 and, skirting Midhope and Hawthornsyke, cross the parklands to The House of the Binns (Grid Ref: 051785). Muse en route about Roy Rodgers – famous USA cowboy film star and his trusty stead Trigger. The late Willie Drysdale, a keeper on the estate, met him. Willie told me: 'He may have been the cat's pyjamas with a six-shooter but he couldn't hit a barn door with a twelve-bore.'

The House of the Binns is open from May to September, the parklands from 1 April to 31 October. Entry to the house and gardens is £3.90 (adult), £2.60 (child), and £10.40 for a family party. However, serving members of the Royal Scots Dragoon Guards, the successor regiment of General Dalyell's 'Greys', are admitted free – provided they are in uniform. Anyone trying to avoid these charges will be hustled down the street and locked up in Blackness Castle. You have been warned.

102. INCHCOLM

Walk on water today, from Queensferry aboard the *Maid of the Forth* to the romantic island of Inchcolm. The jetty below the russet cantilever of the Forth Railway Bridge is quieter today than it was in my youth. Then it bustled constantly with the business of transporting people, goods and chattels north to the Wee Kingdom of Fife. Three boats worked the passage, the *William Wallace*, the *Robert the Bruce* and the *Queen Margaret*. Often waiting vehicles were parked three-deep and the line sometimes stretched back up the hill leading into the town. Drivers could wait for two hours or more before boarding. Now, traffic speeds over the watery gap on the Forth Road Bridge, Europe's longest suspension bridge.

Queensferry was named after Queen Margaret (1045–93), the Hungarian-born wife of Malcolm Canmore. Their son, King Alexander I (1078–1124), sailed from Queensferry in 1123 but a sudden storm blew his vessel down the Firth. The royal party escaped certain death by making a safe landing on the rocky island of Inchcolm. There they found a hermit living in a stone-built cell, who fed and watered them until the storm abated and they could continue their journey. The King determined to build a priory on the island in thanks for his deliverance. The hermit, in order to continue in his self-imposed solitude, presumably moved on to a less busy billet. He must have mused: 'Well, there's gratitude.'

Alexander died before he could fulfil his promise and it was left to King David 1 (1080–1153), the sixth son of Malcolm and Margaret, to carry out his elder brother's wishes. The first church has been subsumed into later buildings but part of the nave survives, as does the Hermit's Cell, wonderfully positioned in a corner of the well-tended garden to the north west of the Abbey. The twelfth-century bell tower is also largely intact, as are the cloisters and, most impressive of all, the thirteenth-century polygonal chapter house. The most illustrious Abbot of Inchcolm was Walter Bower (1385–1449). Writing in his small study that abutted the bell tower, Bower completed the great history of Scotland, *Scotichronicon,* which had been begun by his ecclesiastical colleague, John of Fordun, a Kincardineshire priest who died in about 1384.

The best kick-off time from Queensferry is 10.45 a.m. and the trip lasts approximately three hours. This gives plenty of time to explore the island and the splendid ruins of the still-graceful Abbey. There are no eateries ashore, so pack a picnic. Also pack binoculars to ogle the wide variety of birdlife on the island and tenement-tall ships plying their trade up and down the Firth. Well-marked tracks will take you round the island, which is in the care of Historic Scotland. Find out more about Inchcolm and other Historic Scotland properties at www.historic-scotland.gov.uk on their website. Check sailing times with the ferry operators on Tel: 0131 331 4857. They also run sealife cruises that specialise in whale spotting, and listening to the clicks and whistles of dolphins recorded on special underwater microphones.

No doubt the Augustinian friars in their black gowns clicked and whistled a bit themselves during their tenure. For almost the entire period of the glory days of the Abbey, it was riven by the brutal and debilitating Wars of Independence between England and Scotland. The island was visited with fire and sword on a number of occasions and such was the danger that it was seldom occupied during the summer months of the 'fighting season.' Bower wrote: 'When the stormy winter weather was at hand and the corn gathered into the barn and the fear of English raids less menacing, the abbot and the brethren, together with the servants and all their gear, went into residence on the island.' However, it was not the English that put an end to the Abbey, but fellow Scots themselves: the religious zealots of the Reformation in the sixteenth century. Happily, and probably because it was so isolated, the Abbey largely escaped the fate of many other Scottish 'monastic' churches. Instead of being razed to the ground, it became the property of James Stewart, Lord Doune. But by 1578, the last of the Black Friars, Dominus Johne Brounhill and Dominus Andro Anguss, had gone. Well, maybe, because you know, I could almost swear that I heard the rustle of robes and the scuffle of sandals on stone as I wandered in their footsteps and the sonorous chant of the 'Sanctorum Piisime Columba' echoing softly round the old grey walls.

103. EDINBURGH AND ARTHUR'S SEAT

I was born and brought up in Edinburgh and wear the 'Auld Grey City' like a garment round my soul. I was educated in Edinburgh at Scotland's oldest seat of learning, the Royal High School, founded in 1120 under the Abbot of Holyrood. There I was thoroughly boiled in Bannockburn and the Battle of Stirling Bridge and imbued with the poetry of Burns and the stirring novels of our famous former pupil, Sir Walter Scott. Edinburgh is one of the most beautiful cities in the world and a walk through 'The Athens of the North' is an exciting adventure. For me, it is not only a walk through Scottish history but also a walk through my childhood years. What was time then? The distance between the top of Arthur's Seat and the hot chiding awaiting when we arrived home late for dinner.

My quick way to school was over Calton Hill and this is an excellent start point for an Edinburgh walk. There is an entrance 60m up Blenheim Place. Find your way round using a street map of the city. The hill is an ancient lava flow, steep-cragged to the south and smoothed by ice to the north, ideal for summer sledging on school drawing boards. Calton is graced by 'the disgrace of Edinburgh', an unfinished monument of classical proportions, the building of which ended when funds ran out.

The path round the side of the Observatory, above Leith Street, is also an ideal place to watch the last-night sentiment of the Edinburgh International Festival. Castle lights dim, leaving only topmost turrets illuminated. A lone piper laments. Then the blaze and sparkle as fireworks scatter and burst, brightening the star-specked sky. Nelson's Column crowns Calton Hill, an ugly monument to Trafalgar's posthumous victor. The firing of the One O'Clock Gun from Edinburgh Castle is timed at the Column. As one o'clock approaches, a ball slowly ascends a mast to the top of the tower. When it falls, half a mile away, the gun fires. Which is why I never mastered the niceties of algebra. From my classroom window, I could see this inevitable daily sequence. Much more interesting.

Steps lead down the hill to Waterloo Place by St Andrew's House, packed full of government bureaucracy busy administering Scottish affairs. At the east end of Princes Street stand these grand lumps, the old Central

Post Office and the North British Hotel. I don't care how often they change the name of the hotel; it will always be the NB to me. Registrar House, a magnificently proportioned Adam building, eyes them warily from across the street, guarded by a statue of the Duke of Wellington, horse-mounted, arm outflung, pointing towards danger from Portobello. Across Princes Street, past Waverley Bridge, squats the Scott Monument, like a huge wedding cake waiting to be sliced. Sir Walter sits serenely under his arches, book on lap, studious hands on marble pages, frequently red-nosed with paint wickedly daubed on the great man's face by irreverent pranksters.

Scotland's National Gallery, a few yards further on, is a favourite stopping place of mine. Not the one fronting Princes Street, but the one behind, where admission is free. I could never afford the other, and consequently spent my time round the corner. Raeburn's portrait of Mrs Scott Moncrieff, the Rembrandt self-portrait, Monet's poplars, Chardin's flowers and McTaggart are amongst my best-loved residents here.

A road known as The Mound leads from the galleries up to the Castle and High Street. The Nor' Loch used to protect these northern walls and it was formed in 1448 when the east end of the valley was dammed. After it had been drained, the mound was built to give access to the New Town, built to ease the crush of tenements clustered down Royal Mile from Castle to Holyrood. A Royal Mile of history leads downhill from the Castle past still-impressive tenements, called 'lands' in their days of glory. The higher your station, the nearer to ground level you lived; but the same entrance was used by mighty lord and humble servant alike and Scottish social distinctions were much formed by these meetings on the stairs. It was hard to be impressed by your neighbour, regardless of his position in society, when you were accustomed to seeing him rolling home pickled six nights a week.

An amazing array of intellectual ability flourished in the High Street during the eighteenth and nineteenth centuries. Allan Ramsay, founder of the Select Society, a literary elite. His son, also Allan, the portrait painter, and his pupil, Naysmith. Philosopher David Hume. Adam Smith, author of *The Wealth of Nations*. William Creech, publisher of the Edinburgh Edition of Burns's poetry and of course, Scotia's bard himself. However, amidst all the bustle of High Street my most treasured place is round the back of St Giles' Cathedral. This is an evening sanctuary of peace and solitude shadowed and softened by lingering sunlight, watched over and guarded by the statue of Corollus Secundus, Emperor of Rome, on his mighty horse.

At the foot of the hill stands the palace of Holyroodhouse, residence of Scottish monarchs until the Union of the Crowns in 1603, surrounded by the well-kept acres of Holyrood Park, crowned by the proud 'lion' of Arthur's Seat. The Picts built one of their largest forts on top of the hill, enclosing some 20 acres, and Arthur's Seat is easily climbed. But perhaps the most famous site in the park is the 'Hutton Section' at the south end of the Salisbury Crags. James Hutton (1726–1823) was born in Auld Reekie and studied medicine at Edinburgh University. He is best known as the author of *A Theory of the Earth*, the cornerstone of modern geology, and he developed his theory whilst examining the rock structures that comprise the crags. Hutton showed how the crags were formed: not by cold precipitation from the sea, but by the intrusion and cooling of hot molten rocks during volcanic activity. Get hot today by scampering over the crags or the 308-metre summit of Arthur's Seat. Retrace your steps to Holyrood Palace and return to Blenheim Place by walking up Regent Road. At the traffic lights at the top, cross over and follow the cobbled street directly ahead of you back to the start point.

104. THE WATER OF LEITH

You don't need an Ordnance Survey map for this walk, just the bus and the ability to follow signposts – from Balerno to Leith Docks in Auld Reekie. This is a gentle 12-mile amble along good paths by the banks of the Water of Leith, via Currie, Juniper Green and Slateford, past Murrayfield Stadium, Roseburn and Dean Village to Stockbridge; thence by Powderhall and Bonnington, to where the stream flows through the rejuvenated environs of the old town of Leith to greet the Firth of Forth.

Park the car in Leith near Tower Street. Tramp back to Bernard Street Bridge. Hang a left and find your way to the bottom end of Leith Walk, the 'fit o' the walk' in local parlance. Catch a no. 22 bus up Leith Walk and get off at Elm Row. Cross London Road and wait for a no. 44. This will take you out to Balerno and the start of the adventure. Should you find yourself in Portobello you have gone the wrong way. Avoid doing so by asking the driver, as you embark, 'Does this bus go to Balerno?'

I was born and brought up in the Old Grey City and wear memories of these days like a comforter round my soul. The Water of Leith was an everyday part of my life. Where I saw my first brown trout, splashing in the shallows. Where I hunted for white-billed coots' nests and hand-fed mute swans. Where my brother and I used to peer over the fence at Powderhall, fascinated by the bustle and bright lights of the greyhound-racing stadium, visible from the footpath if we stood on tiptoe.

Few European capital cities can boast of a trout stream running within a stone's throw of the city centre. Once vastly polluted, over the years the Water of Leith has been greatly improved in terms of water quality and amenity value due to the sterling efforts of the Water of Leith Conservation Trust (Tel: 0131 455 7367). The Trust also built the walkway and although there are short sections still to be completed, follow the signposts and you will reach journey's end without mishap.

Prior to setting out, arm yourself with a copy of *A Guide to the Water of Leith Walkway*, available from the Trust Heritage Centre, 24 Lanark Road, Edinburgh EH14 1TQ. Each section of the walk is described in detail and points of interest noted. Downstream from Balerno, for instance, are stone retaining walls where Dougal Haston, a native of Currie and the first Scot to reach the summit of Mount Everest, trained.

The section of the walk between Juniper Green and Slateford is enchanting. It is hard to imagine the busy life of a great city close by. The river here flows through a wonderful deciduous forest, where elms, ash and willows overhang deep pools. There are also Spanish chestnuts, hornbeams, Atlantic cedars and copper beeches. Pause at the hexagonal grotto near Redhall, built in 1750 by the famous landscape gardener Robert Bowie and constructed from stones from the four airts of Scotland.

Slateford is a good place for lunch, where an inviting pub overlooks the river. Refreshed, cross Lanark Road to visit the Heritage Centre. Between the Heritage Centre and Gorgie work is continuing on the path. Ask for directions from Trust staff. The walkway is pristine again from Balgreen onwards. At Dean Village, the river runs through a deep gorge spanned by Thomas Telford's magnificent bridge, built in 1832. The stream here produces some large trout, fish of up to and over 2lb in weight, a nod and a wink from the West End of Princes Street.

Inverleith Park and Canonmills were part of my adolescent territory, particularly the Colonies, a row of houses built during the period 1861–1911 to provide healthy homes for workers. I knew a bewitching girl who lived there and spent ages at Canonmills bird-watching – the feathered kind. Robert Louis Stevenson fished for trout here. Frederick Chopin stayed nearby when he visited Edinburgh in 1848. And then there is Powderhall Stadium, where the hero of *Chariots of Fire*, Eric Liddell, raced in 1922.

Finish your race by the old Signal Tower, built in 1686 and used during the Napoleonic Wars to flag ships lying in the Firth. If you have timed the expedition efficiently, repair immediately to one of the excellent eateries which have sprung up in The Shore area of Leith in recent years. The perfect end to a perfect day.

105. CRAMOND TO SOUTH QUEENSFERRY

One of my best-loved walks near Edinburgh is from the village of Cramond to South Queensferry and back, a distance of ten miles along the shores of the Firth of Forth. Cramond 'Caer' Almond, the fort on the River Almond, was an important Roman garrison town and excavations have revealed much of the signs of early occupation by these methodical invaders of Scotland. The white-walled Cramond Inn provides a focal point for the village and is well known for the excellence of its food and drink.

Robert Louis Stevenson, author of *Treasure Island* and *Kidnapped*, was a frequent visitor to the old inn and, at the other end of the walk at South Queensferry, there is an equally famous watering hole, the Hawes Inn, built in 1683. Stevenson dreamed up the plot for *Kidnapped* whilst staying at the Hawes in bedroom no. 13, 'a small room, with a bed in it and heated like an oven by a great coal fire'.

It was low tide when I last walked this way. The River Almond lay exposed, mud-flatted between tree-lined banks dotted with small sailing boats. A group of youngsters in kayaks ploughed up and down, yelling with delight when one of their companions capsized. Visitors wandered happily in the warm sun. For centuries, a small boat, sculled back and forth on demand by a ferryman who lives in a cottage on the west bank, has provided passage over the Almond. I stood by the steps leading down to the river, looking hopeful, and in a few minutes the ferryman appeared. On the west bank I set off along the path through magnificent woodlands peopled with ancient trees. A few hundred yards on I turned right, down to the shingle shore, to revisit Eagle Rock. The shape of an eagle has been chiselled in the stone, a Roman eagle, reputed to have been the work of the garrison stationed at Cramond.

Walking along the Firth is like a journey in and out of history. The sea is scattered with passing ships: ponderous tankers; a Rosyth-bound Royal Navy frigate; oil-drilling platforms; pleasure craft. The Romans would have passed this way, dreaming of their loved ones at home and sun-drenched Italian plains. An RAF fighter plane screams low over Inchcolm, shaking the ruins of the island's ancient abbey, founded in 1123. Barnbougle Castle loomed ahead, built in the thirteenth century by the Moubray family and ideally placed for smuggling. Then there is Hound Point, haunted by the ghost of Sir Roger Moubray's dog, Baskerville, still howling for his dead master who was killed during the Crusades.

Dalmeny golf course interrupts the cool woods, precisely manicured in well ordered calm. A notice warns me to take care, presumably from flying golf balls, but the greens and fairways are empty this morning. Time to visit Dalmeny House, home of the Primrose family, Earls of Rosebery who have lived here for more than 300 years. I never think of Rosebery without reciting to myself the lines Robert Burns once gave a previous Lord and Lady Rosebery to say:

> Rosebery to his Lady says,
> My hinnie and my socour,
> Oh, shall we do the thing ye ken,
> Or shall we tak our supper?
> Wi modest face, sae fu of grace,
> Replied the bonnie lady,
> My Noble Lord, do as you please,
> But supper isna ready.

The parents of the present Lord Rosebery divided their time between Mentmore and Dalmeny, 'driving north with two dogs, a cat, a parrot, about 12 staff, three cars and a horse box full of luggage every August in time for the grouse shooting and the Edinburgh Festival'.

Dalmeny House is the work of the fourth Earl, who, one year before the Battle of Waterloo, commissioned the architect William Wilkins to prepare plans for a new house. Barnbougle, the old house, was 'much neglected'. Lady Rosebery recounts a story, in her guidebook to Dalmeny, of how the third Earl was once drenched by a wave breaking through the dining-room window of Barnbougle. But the Earl maintained that what had been good enough for his grandfather was good enough for his own grandchildren.

From Dalmeny I walked on to the Forth Bridges and Queensferry. Sir John Fowler designed the railway bridge in 1890 and in its day it was one of the wonders of the modern world. Even now, the imposing structure dominates the feather-like span of the new road bridge. Before the road bridge was built, passage across the Forth was by ferry, established in the twelfth century by Queen Margaret. In my young days Queensferry's narrow streets were always packed with waiting cars. Crossing the Forth could take anything up to three hours, shuttled below the bridge by side-paddle steamers: the *Queen Margaret*, the *Robert the Bruce* and the *Sir William Wallace*.

Time for a closer look at the Hawes Inn before the return to Cramond. You must be back at the River Almond before 7 p.m. from April to

September or before 4 p.m. during the winter months. Otherwise you might end up having to swim for your supper and who needs that?

106. CULZEAN CASTLE

Breaking and entry is not one of my regular pastimes. I blame Tony Sykes for getting me into such an exposed position. I first met the redoubtable Sykes, who hailed from Bridge of Weir, whilst serving Queen and Country in Southern Arabia. On our return to civilian life, Sykes lived for a time at Knutsford, near Manchester, and I visited him there. Carefully following the directions he had supplied, which was my first mistake, I thought I would surprise Tony and his wife, Isobel, by arriving unannounced. Having found the house I rang the bell and waited. No answer. I quietly let myself in, crossed the deeply carpeted, well-furnished front hall and paused to consider further action.

A tall, smartly dressed woman suddenly appeared carrying a tray of drinks, and we stared at each other in amazement. 'What the hell do you think you are doing?' she demanded. As I spluttered, a door opened to reveal half a dozen dinner guests, one of whom was menacingly clutching a poker. I was in the wrong house.

I am still uneasy in strange houses and never more so than when visiting stately homes and castles. As I tiptoe round neatly set dining tables or stare curiously at freshly made beds and pristine drawing rooms, I know I am an intruder and expect every moment to hear again that dread cry: 'What the hell do you think you are doing?'

Culzean Castle, near Auld Ayr, that town of 'honest men and bonnie lassies', is no exception. The dining-room is particularly intimidating, laid for 12 guests, clearly expected to arrive at any moment, and I can hardly stand a second in The Best Bedroom: an 1813 Lefevre portrait of Napoleon hangs above the marble fireplace. One glance from the Little Corporal sends me scurrying from the room. Another, more modern soldier is remembered at Culzean: Dwight D. Eisenhower, Commander of Allied Forces in Europe during the Second World War. Part of the castle was gifted to Eisenhower for his lifetime as a mark of respect to the D-Day supreme commander. The general's desk, chair and Presidential Standard are displayed in an alcove in his room. Americans like flags.

But Culzean, owned by the National Trust for Scotland, is enormously popular, and upwards of 300,000 people visit the castle each year; poking and prying into the nooks and crannies of Clan Kennedy life, past and present. Nor can they be wrong, for Culzean is a marvellous example of how 'the other half lives', ancient and modern, and the National Trust are justly proud of their lowland flagship property. Most visitors confine their activity to the castle and in doing so miss much of the real magic of the place, because Culzean is not just house and castle, but is also the centrepiece of the surrounding estate. The Trust have fully restored the walks and gardens and it is still possible to find peace and seclusion, 'far from the madding crowd', even during the height of the season. The fifth Marquis of Ailsa gave Culzean Castle to The National Trust for Scotland in 1945, along with 532 acres of land, and the estate was declared Scotland's first country park in 1969. The fascinating series of walks round the estate make it an ideal place to introduce little ones to the delights of the great outdoors.

The Home Farm, part of Robert Adam's (1728–92) grand Neoclassical/Gothic design for Culzean, has been converted into a visitor centre: information area, exhibition, auditorium, schoolrooms, restaurant, shop, and base for the excellent park ranger service. The rangers organise events linked to guided walks and their Young Naturalists' Club embraces an outstanding range of activities and is immensely popular.

Six walks have been plotted for visitors. The longest, three hours, takes you round the boundary of the estate via the shoreline where you can investigate univalve and bivalve shells, seaweed, rock pool animals and birdlife. More than 155 bird species have been recorded at Culzean and a full checklist is available at the visitor centre.

Warm April days at Culzean are dream-like. The woodland is full of the busy chatter of nest-building; wild hyacinths and daffodils carpet the forest floor; roe deer and red squirrel do what roe deer and red squirrel do in the spring. Culzean is always welcoming, regardless of who may or may not be coming for dinner, invited or otherwise.

Location: OS Map 70, Ayr and Kilmarnock. second series, Scale 1:50,000. Culzean Castle Grid Ref: 233102. All the walks are clearly identified and described in the Culzean Country Park Walks brochure. It is possible to extend them into a single walk of four and a half hours by combining walks two and six.

107. CROOK INN

The Crook Inn was the first Scottish hostelry to be licensed. Legalised drinking began there about 1604 and the inn beside the A701 Moffat to

Penicuik road has been going strong ever since. It certainly was when I stayed there in August, and very enjoyable it was too, comfortable, welcoming and relaxed. Find the Crook Inn at Grid Ref: 111263 on OS Map 72, Upper Clyde Valley, second series, Scale 1:50,000. You will also find a magnificent array of inviting hills. None are physically taxing and there are more hills here of over 2,000ft in height than anywhere else in Scotland. The highest is Broad Law (839m), followed by Dollar Law (817m), Hart Fell (808m), Culter Fell (748m) and Tinto Hill (707m). But for me, hiking is not about 'elevation'. It has as much to do with peace and solitude. These gentle green hills are rarely busy and you may walk all day without meeting another soul.

After breakfast, as a seven-mile-long introduction to the area, pack lunch and walk from the back of the hotel to the line of a disused railway. John Best of Leith built it in 1896 to carry men and materials for the construction of Talla Reservoir. The labour force, mainly Irish and 300-strong, spent much of their hard-earned pay drinking at the Crook. Best had a financial interest in the Crook and he boasted that most of the money he paid out on Friday afternoon was back in his pocket by Monday.

Climb by way of a small burn to reach the top of Crook Head (450m) at Grid Ref: 100267. From here there is a glorious summit walk of some two miles over Nether Oliver Dod (510m) to Upper Oliver Dod (490m). As you descend from Upper Oliver Dod, at Grid Ref: 084248, you will meet a good track leading to the village of Tweedsmuir. Take care as you cross the main road. It is invariably busy with traffic. Walk down to the village over the humpback bridge across Talla Water; a tributary of the River Tweed made famous by John Buchan's poem 'Fisher Jamie', written about an angling friend killed during the First World War:

> He lo'ed nae music, kenned nae tunes,
> except the sang o' Tweed in spate,
> or Talla loupin' ower its linns.

As you enter the churchyard (Grid Ref: 101245), on your left is a tombstone that commemorates 30 men who died during the construction of Talla Reservoir. An older stone in the northeast corner remembers John Hunter, martyr and Covenanter, 'Cruelly murdered at Corehead by Col James Douglas and his party for his adherence to the word of God and Scotland's Covenanted work of Reformation, 1685.'

Leave the churchyard and follow the road to Talla Water. Cross over and pick up the line of the disused railway again, below the thickly wooded slopes of Cockiland Hill (422m). The track was lifted a few years after the completion of the reservoir in 1905, but every time I walk this way I swear I can still here the chug-chug of the engine, the 'Pug', loud with Irish laughter as she laboured up the slope to Talla. The old railway line crosses the River Tweed on a bridge now used to carry a water pipe (Grid Ref: 105251). The Tweed is a modest stream here, close to her beginnings by Annanhead. Three of Scotland's most significant rivers rise nearby: 'Annan, Tweed and Clyde, rise a' oot' o' ae hillside.' But my favourite is the Tweed, the 'Queen of Scottish Rivers'. Blindfold, I would recognise the scent and sound of Tweed anywhere.

Follow the railway line back to Crook Inn, crossing to the west side of the A701 at Grid Ref: 109260. You should by now be ready for refreshment. Robert Burns was, after meeting Willie Wastle's wife at Linkumdoddie, a few miles north from the inn. He wrote his less-than-polite description of the woman whilst in the bar of the Crook Inn: 'sic a wife as Willie had, I wad na gie a button for her.'

I would 'gie' rather more than a button for some of the 1920s Art Deco furnishings that ornament the Crook Inn, particularly the bathrooms. They are quite stunning, with their straight lines, bright colours and decorative tiles and mirrors. Perhaps finest of all are the ladies', which is where I came unstuck trying to explain exactly why I was lurking around inside to a less-than-receptive female audience outside. The angst I experienced was enough to drive a poor hillwalker to drink, and it did.

108. HOMAGE TO TIBBIE SHIELS

Tibbie Shiels Inn at the south end of St Mary's Loch in the Ettrick Forest has been cosseting world-weary souls for more than 200 years. The inn is named after the original owner, Isobel Richardson, who was born in 1783 near Ettrick Kirk. Tibbie married Robert Richardson, a mole-catcher on Lord Napier's Thirlestane Estate. When Robert died suddenly in 1824 leaving Tibbie and their six children virtually destitute, she set up in business as an innkeeper, catering for the anglers who fished the loch.

Some of Scotland's most notable literary figures stayed at the inn; Sir Walter Scott and his son-in-law John Gibson Lockhart; Professor John Wilson, who wrote in *Blackwood's Edinburgh Magazine* as 'Christopher North'; angling author, Thomas Todd Stoddart and his friend, James Hogg, 'The Ettrick Shepherd'. Although she never remarried, in later years Tibbie said: 'Yon Hogg, the Shepherd, ye ken, was an awfu' fine man. He should hae tae'n me, for he cam coortin for years, but he just gaed away and took another.' Tibbie outlived them all and died aged 96.

The inn is as welcoming and friendly today as it was when Tibbie ruled her roost. It is also an ideal base from which to explore the surrounding hills and moorlands; green Lowther and Galloway hills to the west and south, Moffat, Ettrick and Manor Hills to the north and east. But for me, the Manor Hills are the real prize, 20 tops of over 2,000ft in height where you may walk miles all day without meeting another soul. The highest peak is Broad Law (839m), closely followed by Cramalt Craig (830m) and Dollar Law (817m).

This morning, however, our goal is Black Law (696m), to the north of St Mary's Loch. You will need OS Map 73, Galashiels and Ettrick Forest, second series, Scale 1:50,000 to find your way round. There and back is an exhilarating ten miles. The going is easy but, nevertheless, be well prepared for whatever the weather might bring. Early spring is a wonderful time to make this walk, when the air is champagne-charged and the wind like a whetted knife hurries you up the hill. First primroses blush in sheltered corners, mountain hares nervously note your passing, the call of curlews haunts your footsteps.

Park at Grid Ref: 266240 and walk north past Kirkstead. The path follows the course of Kirkstead Burn into the hills and ends at Dryhope (Grid Ref: 245262). Bear left here and continue along the line of the burn. The way ahead climbs between Layer Knowe to the north and Conscleuch Head to the south, reaching the final haul to the summit of Black Law (Grid Ref: 219275). At this point you will find the fence marking the Peebles–Selkirk boundary. This fence runs from Megget Stone, north over Broad Law, Cramalt Craig and Dollar Law, ending on Dun Rig. In poor weather conditions this fence is an invaluable aid to direction finding.

From Black Law, walk half a mile northeast to the unnamed top at Grid Ref: 225280. Descend east and tramp the broad summit plateau for two miles to reach Deepslack Knowe (Grid Ref: 259273). Turn south now and locate the track which leads downhill between South Hawkshaw Rig to the left and Dryhope Rig on your right. A mile and a half will bring you back to the A708 Moffat–Selkirk road. Turn right along the shore of St Mary's Loch to reach the start point.

Return now to Tibbie Shiels Inn for rest and recuperation. Whilst doing so, consider what it used to be like when Scott and his friends stayed there:

> The old-fashioned kitchen was the model of what a kitchen ought to be; it had such an air of cosy warmth and welcoming hospitality. In the vast open fireplace were glowing peat embers, the kettle sang on the hob, the white-faced grandfather's clock ticked beside the 'bink', and was there ever anything so quaintly picturesque as the box beds with their sliding doors? But best of all was Tibbie's

spinning-wheel on one side of the hearth, and Sir Walter Scott's armchair on the other.

And what of the object of Tibbie's unrequited love, James Hogg, who must have tramped more miles across these hills in a day than most of us do in a year? He sits in stony silence overlooking the loch where he and his drouthy companions spent so many happy hours fishing together. His shepherd's crook is in one hand, in the other, a scroll inscribed with the words from his wondrous poem, 'The Queen's Wake': 'He taught the wandering winds to sing.'

109. CRAMALT CRAIG

A fiery cross burns bright in the Highlands, at least among the Munro-bagging fraternity, that illustrious group of climbers and hillwalkers who have scaled all of Scotland's mountains above 3,000ft in height. A recent reassessment has added eight more summits to the present score of 277. Consequently, those who had fondly imagined that their self-imposed task was complete will have to lace up their boots again and head for the hills. Sir Hugh Munro compiled the first list of 3,000ft-plus peaks in 1891, and thus gave birth to the 'habit' that bears his name. The Rev. A.E. Robertson had climbed them by 1901 after 'a desultory campaign of ten years'. Since then, more than 1,000 vigorous baggers have followed in his footsteps. The Scottish Mountaineering Club honourably mentions the names of all Munroists in the book *Munro's Tables*. There are two other mountain classifications: Corbetts, 221 in number, hills between 2,500ft and 2,999ft named in honour of J. Rooke Corbett. And Donalds, Percy Donald's 87 Scottish Lowland hills of 2,000ft and above. But you never hear of Corbett Baggers, or Donald Baggers. Doesn't have the same, lofty, ring as Munro Bagger, I suppose, maybe because it sounds more like a description of travelling salesmen or a demented attempt to eat in every fast-food shop in Scotland.

Whatever, a mountain is a mountain, regardless of its height or classification, and many of the lower peaks are every bit as splendid to climb as their more altitudinous brethren. Also, they are often less intimidating, more user-friendly and approachable by those who simply seek a fine day out, rather than another 'tick' in the Tables. The same rules apply, however, as far as safety is concerned: proper clothing, stout boots, emergency wet-weather gear, food, and a compass, map and whistle.

The Manor Hills near Peebles offer such an opportunity; supremely beautiful peaks, remote and welcoming, gently rounded and giving splendid mile after happy mile of high-level walks above the 749m contour. The highest of the Manor Hills is Cramalt Craig (830m), approached from Manorhead by the banks of Manor Water, and my wife and I paid our respects to it a couple of weeks ago on a warm, lazy, bee-buzzing day.

The hill is shown on OS Map 72, Upper Clyde Valley, second series, Scale 1:50,000. Park at Grid Ref: 199286 and follow the road south towards Manorhead. Skirt round the white farm buildings and cross Ugly Grain Burn to gain the hill. Climb past the small conifer plantation and, as you go, look out for delicate, cream-coloured cow wheat growing strongly amidst the profusion of yellow tormentil and bright purple bell heather.

Half an hour will bring you to the line of the Thief's Road, a reminder of the days when these Border lands were the lawless preserve of steel-bonneted reivers and rogues. From this point, direction finding is made easy by a convenient fence. Follow the fence onto Fifescar Knowe and then southwest to the top of Dun Law (Grid Ref: 258511). Cramalt Craig lies ahead, with the hump of Broad Law (839m) and its bristling radio beacon beyond.

We lunched by the cairn on Cramalt Craig with a pair of ravens for guests, then retraced our fence-line steps back via Dun Law and Fifescar Knowe, to ascend to the summit of Dollar Law (817m) where we found that Mr Ben McMahon had beaten us to it. I know this because he had spray painted his name on the side of the trig point:

'Ben McMahon, 2.7.'97.' I presume he also left the empty crisp packet in the hole on top of the trig point? If he wants it back, I have it. All he needs to do is give me a call. I couldn't remove the graffiti.

The descent from Dollar Law also follows a fence line, but this leads into some pretty severe, breast-high, uncomfortable bracken. Avoid this by bearing right near the bottom of the hill, through magnificent banks of wild thyme. With luck, you should pick up a muddy but very welcome sheep track that leads back to the Manorhead road and the car park.

This walk takes about five hours, depending on how often you stop to enjoy the panoramic views and, apart from the initial steep ascent to Fifescar Knowe, the going is easy. The total distance there and back is approximately seven and a half miles. Distance and time enough to work up an honest thirst, which may be adequately attended to at the end of the day in Peebles.

110. NEIDPATH CASTLE

Old Q, William Douglas, fourth Duke of Queensberry, was a gambling buddy of 'Priny', the weight-challenged Prince of Wales, during the later years of the eighteenth century. His peccadilloes earned him the sobriquet 'Star of Piccadilly' and Old Q was never out of debt. He rarely visited his ancestral lands near Peebles, but he trashed them ruthlessly to hold off his creditors; most famously, in about 1795, by selling the magnificent woodlands that surrounded his castle at Neidpath on the banks of the River Tweed. Sir Walter Scott took two inveterate travellers there to ogle the ruins in 1803: William Wordsworth and his sister, Dorothy. The poet was horrified and spontaneously delivered himself of 14 lines of pompous doggerel: 'Degenerate Douglas! O the unworthy lord!' and more in a similar vein, as stunted as the roots of the raped trees themselves: 'Leaving an ancient dome, and towers like these Beggar'd and outraged . . .' Sir Walter also wrote about Neidpath. His 'Maid of Neidpath' recounts how the Maid's father banished her lover. When she came close to death with grief, he summoned him home. The Maid was so ravished by despair that her beau failed to recognise her. Thus, in the romantic fashion, she promptly died. Scott's poem is way over-the-top and it was left to another, T. Campbell, to do the subject justice:

> In vain he weeps, in vain he sighs;
> Her cheek is cold as ashes;
> Nor love's own kiss shall wake those eyes;
> To lift their silken lashes.

I have sighed and wept here many times, and my cheek has been cold as ashes; not with love, but with despair at being unable to tempt any Tweed trout or salmon to grab my carefully presented flies. The process of fishing, however, has brought me an understanding of the beauty of this most peaceful part of the river, from Lyne Footbridge downstream to Peebles, and I carry the sweet scent and smell of Tweed in my soul to this day.

Discover this joy for yourself by walking the banks of the river; a wonderful, easy, seven-and-a-half-mile stomp from Tweed Bridge in Peebles, west to Manor and Lyne, returning to the old market town along the disused railway via Neidpath Castle. Dr Beeching 'did' for the line in the 1950s when he modernised Britain's railway system, in much the same way as John Knox 'modernised' the Scottish Church in the mid-1500s, by reducing most of it to ruin.

Park in Peebles at the south end of Tweed Bridge (OS Map 73, Galashiels and Ettrick Forest, second series, Scale 1:50,000, Grid Ref: 251404). Walk back across the bridge and down to a path by the river which leads upstream to Victoria's Bridge (Grid Ref: 242404). Cross the bridge then walk south to join a minor road, the 'back road' to Manor. Turn right and follow this route up to the viewpoint at the top of the hill near Edderston Farm (Grid Ref: 241396). Take a right again here, and follow the road down to the bridge across Manor Water (Grid Ref: 231394). This handsome, horseshoe-shaped structure was designed by one of Old Q's ancestors, William Douglas, the first Duke of Queensberry and built by his son, William, Earl of March, in 1702. Not that they paid for it. Being canny Scots, they made sure that the construction was funded out of the revenues of Manor Church. The Duke had been Lord Treasurer of Scotland and knew how to save a bob or three.

The best way to view the bridge is from below. Cross over and loup the gate on your right to gain the stream. At the south end of the new bridge across Tweed (Grid Ref: 229395) take the steps down to the river bank and walk upstream for one mile to find Barns Tower (Grid Ref: 217391), built in the aftermath of the Battle of Flodden (1513) and once the home of William Burnet, the 'Hoolet' – the Scots word for an owl; a polite name for a thug or a gangster who worked mostly at night. Track the avenue of lime trees, then follow the path through the woods down to the river to cross the Tweed by Lyne Footbridge (Grid Ref: 206399).

In Lyne Station, at the railway bridge, climb up to the rail-less track and hike east to reach Neidpath Castle (Grid Ref: 236405) after two and a half happy miles. The fourteenth-century castle, with its 3.4-metre-thick walls, dank pit-prison and magnificent Laigh Hall, was converted into a tower house in the seventeenth century after being knocked about a bit by Cromwell's crusaders. End your 'crusade' by yomping the final mile to Peebles along the north bank of fair lady Tweed, 'Queen of Scottish Rivers'.

111. MELROSE AND THE EILDON HILLS

This article has been seasonally adjusted to take into account the underlying effect of mist and mellow fruitfulness. In other words, a wonderful autumnal walk from Melrose over the Eildon Hills, returning to base by the banks of the River Tweed via Newstead. Pack OS Map 73, Galashiels and Ettrick Forest, second series, Scale 1:50,000. You don't really need it, because once 'up' the way ahead is obvious, but, nevertheless, be safe rather than sorry.

Begin at Melrose Abbey by paying your respects to Robert Bruce. His heart is buried there. Just his heart; the rest of Bob's bits and pieces lie at Dunfermline Abbey in Fife. When the great king died in 1329, his hawk and lady fair comforting his demise, the heart was removed from the body and placed in a silver casket. Bruce had instructed James Douglas, his faithful lieutenant, to carry it with him on a Crusade to the Holy Land. However, Douglas, not one to pass up the chance of some pre-emptive Moor-bashing, was killed along the way during a scrap in Spain. The casket was taken back to Melrose Abbey and interred. Recently, the casket was dug up for care and maintenance and, at a simple ceremony presided over by Scottish Secretary Donald Dewar, reburied, topped off by an emotive memorial stone upon which are inscribed the words 'A noble heart may have nane ease gif freedom failye.' What better words could be inscribed upon the hearts and minds of the prospective members of our soon-to-be-realised Scottish Parliament? What finer sentiment could inform their daily deliberations? Will they, I wonder, be a credit to the memory of the man who fought so long and so hard for Scotland's freedom?

Melrose Abbey was founded in 1136 and for 400 years played an important part in the nation's affairs. King David I (1008–1153) granted the monks vast lands for their sustenance: 'Eildon, Melrose and Darnick, together with the royal lands and forest of Selkirk and Traquair with pasturage for sheep and cattle, wood for building and burning and rights of fishing in the Tweed.' The Earl of Hertford burned the abbey in 1544; during the time of the 'Rough Wooing' of the infant Mary, Queen of Scots by Hertford's bullyboy master, King Henry VIII of England. By 1590, Jo

Watsonn, 'pensionarius de Melrose', was the sole member of the convent and when he died in that year the glory days of the abbey ended.

The start of the Eildon Walk is signposted near to the centre of town. Park by the station building, now an excellent restaurant, and then follow the B6359. After passing under the railway bridge, hang a left. A well-marked path leads directly onto the lower slopes of the hills. Make for the distant white flag pole and then climb to the saddle between North and South Eildon. After visiting the south cairn (422m), hike north to the next summit (404m). Your only companions will be larks and meadow pipits, but be aware that you are treading in the footsteps of the Selgovae tribe. They had their home here long before the Romans clanked over the horizon. More than 300 settlements have been identified and, if you look carefully, you may still see their outlines today.

Gnaeus Julius Agricola 'subdued' the Selgovae, evicted them from the hilltop fortress and, in its place, built a signal station. Descend north from the summit to find the little hamlet of Newstead on the line of the Roman Road, Dere Street, where there was a substantial military base which could accommodate two legions and 500 cavalry, a total of up to 10,000 soldiers. What they did in their spare time, when the NAAFI was closed, is a matter of speculation, but no doubt they fished for salmon in the Tweed; probably with greater success than anglers now, given the decline in Scottish salmon numbers.

This part of the walk, by the Tweed, is a sheer joy; the sweet scent of the river, the russet-and gold of autumn leaves, the urgent splash of *salmo salar*, surging to upstream spawning grounds. After you pass the sawmill on your left and before the suspension bridge over the river, leave the bank and walk back into Melrose. Time for tea and a bun, and then, perhaps, another pilgrimage to say hello to the shades of Sir Walter Scott at Abbotsford? He lies at rest at that other magnificent Border Abbey, Dryburgh, a few miles from Melrose. I like to think of him deep in conversation with King Robert, concordant hearts at ease.

112. WINE AND PORTMORE

I can't remember not knowing Valvona & Crolla's Edinburgh emporium in Elm Row. As a youth, I passed by on my way to and from school; catching a tram (I cannot lie, it was a tram) at the top of London Road to go to primary school at Jock's Lodge and, latterly, on my way to the old Royal

High School on Calton Hill. Whether or not the shop was closed, with grey shutters down, or open and busy with the sound of a dozen different dialects doing business, it didn't matter. It was always exciting to pass by – a universe of exotic scents and sights assailed the senses. In later years, for special picnics, my wife and I would buy wine, bread and cheese from Valvona & Crolla prior to setting out for a weekend walk. Several hundred miles away in North Sutherland, as I write these words, I have the same feeling of anticipation as I had the moment I stepped inside the narrow front door of the shop. This culinary Aladdin's Cave is an institution. To visit Auld Reekie and not pay respects to Valvona & Crolla would be unimaginable.

One of our favourite locations for consuming the goodies we purchased was Portmore Loch, 20 miles or so south from Edinburgh to the east of the A703 road to Peebles. The loch is busier now than when we first walked there, having been developed into a commercial trout fishery, but a few strides soon brings peace and solitude. Find Portmore on OS Map 73, Galashiels and Ettrick Forest, second series, scale 1:50,000. Park at Grid Ref: 259508. This is the start point for an invigorating six-mile hike over the wild Moorfoot Hills, returning through ancient woodlands of beech, sycamore and oak via the site of a dramatic Pictish hill fort.

This is a walk for all seasons, winter or summer, but you will still need a compass and map and full-service hiking gear in case of bad weather. From the car park, strike due east up Loch Hill to the knowe at Grid Ref: 270501, then climb directly to the cairn on Jeffries Corse (611m) at Grid Ref: 281495. On a fine day, the view north is splendid. Arthur's Seat and the dark outline of Salisbury Crags guard Edinburgh Castle, enfolded by the Pentland and Lammermuir Hills. Across the Firth of Forth in Fife, Largo Law pinpricks the horizon. Below lies the ever-expanding dormitory sprawl of Penicuik, 'the hill of the cuckoo'. Much of the landscape to the south is blanketed with forestry plantations, regimented rows of inappropriate taxpayer-funded Christmas trees. Only the top of Totto Hill (Grid Ref: 310455) remains uncovered. But the remainder is still virgin land; wave after wave of gentle, rolling hills, sweeping westwards in a sea of unending tranquillity. In all the years I have walked this way, I have never once met another soul. The Moorfoot Hills may not have the rugged grandeur of the Highland peaks and glens, but they offer seclusion and an unhurried calm that has long since disappeared in many more famous places further north.

The moorland surrounding the top is wet, soggy and hard going, but the ridge itself consists of soft, springy turf that is a delight to walk over. Do so, to reach Dundreich (622m) at Grid Ref: 275491. From here, there is a birds-eye view of the Pictish fort marked on the OS Map as Northshield Rings (Grid Ref: 257493). Continue south to Milky Law (Grid Ref: 264480) and descend to Boreland (Grid Ref: 257480). Follow the track north from Boreland and, just before reaching the south shore of Portmore Loch, hang a left to climb the hill and explore Northshield Rings.

Three concentric circles of ramparts and ditches enclose an area 73m by 6.4m. These forts were more villages than defensive structures, fortified only as much as was required to keep out unwelcome neighbours. Lunch here, amidst the shades of times past. Listen for the laughter of children. Leave Northshield and pick up the track that leads northwest into the woods. The contrast between the open hill and the enclosed woodlands is dramatic, particularly on a stormy day. The way through the woods ambles comfortably back to the north end of Portmore Loch, by the man-made dam that created the water some 150 years ago. Finches and tits flit amidst branches, alighting on the forest floor to eat 'with tiny-eyed caution'. Scatter a Valvona & Crolla crust and a rind of cheese to keep them happy.

113. NOT SWIMMING AT NORTH BERWICK

Call me a wimp, but as a boy I never could muster up enough courage to dive into the cold waters of the old outdoor swimming pool at North Berwick. Toes, feet and ankles were as far as I got. It was the coldest place in Christendom. In 1591 nearly 100 people, mostly impecunious old women, were tortured in the Burgh. They were accused of witchcraft; specifically, drumming up a huge storm that ravaged ships bearing King James VI and his entourage as they sailed past on their way to Norway, where James was to marry Anne of Denmark. James's written works were greatly admired, including an awesome book, *Daemonologie*, published in 1588, on the murky world of demonology. In the 150 years following his birth more than 4,000 frightened souls were burnt as witches. Having been condemned, they were 'ducked' and then 'worryit'; the euphemism for strangulation prior to being burnt at the stake. The King took a personal interest in the trial of the North Berwick witches, all of whom were put to death.

The town is friendlier today, a popular holiday destination. You need two maps to find your way round: OS Map 66, Edinburgh, and OS Map 67, Duns and Dunbar, both second series, scale 1:50,000. And probably golf clubs, if you are so afflicted; the links course here is one of the best in Scotland. If you have little ones, lug along a bevy of buckets and spades for sandcastle building. Our walk is in two parts: a quick canter to the top of North Berwick Law (187m, Grid Ref: 655843) for an overview of the situation, followed by a happy six-mile beach and cliff-top stroll to visit the gaunt ruins of Tantallon Castle (Grid Ref: 597851). We will also call in at the newly opened Scottish Seabird Centre by the ruins of the twelfth-century Auld Kirk near the harbour.

The Law is a volcanic plug, surmounted by the jawbone of a whale and a watchtower dating back to Napoleonic times. Up and down takes about an hour and the vista from the top is stunning. The sea-girt outcrops of Fidra, Lamb, Craigleith and the Bass Rock stub the wave-capped waters of the Firth of Forth. Beyond the Isle of May lie the gold-fringed shores of the Wee Kingdom of Fife, Largo Law and the blue-grey Lomond Hills. Well-tended fields skirt The Law, while to the west is a wood planted in 1707 to commemorate the Union of Parliaments. Local lore has it that when the trees die, the Union will die also. The trees look decidedly shaky to me.

Return from The Law to Melbourne Road and park near the Auld Kirk (Grid Ref: 555855). Walk onto the beach; tramp east. At the end of the beach, at the back of the sand dunes, a path leads up the side of the hill to Rugged Knowes (Grid Ref: 570855). From there, follow the cliff line round the golf course to where it meets the A198 road (Grid Ref: 585851) above Canty Bay. Half a mile further brings you to Tantallon Castle. When I first visited it as a boy, we simply walked in. Now you pay to enter. I object to paying to explore part of my historical heritage; we already pay for the upkeep and preservation of our national treasurers through taxation. Asking us to pay again is, in my view, an insulting rip-off. For centuries, the red-stone castle on the cliff was impregnable. Perched more than 30m above the sea, Tantallon belied all attempts to subdue it until General Monk arrived with his cannon in 1651. Over a period of 12 days he battered the castle into submission. The ruins are pretty much as he left them.

Return to the start point by the outward route in time for tea and puffins at the Seabird Centre. Cameras placed on the Bass Rock and under the sea at a number of locations relay pictures to viewing screens in the Centre. They provide spectacular images of puffins, gannets, kittiwakes and other birds busy doing what they do best: catching and eating fish, squabbling and squawking, breeding and tending their chicks. Tend to your own chicks in the snack bar attached to the Seabird Centre. A platform has been built above basalt rocks. Muse here over tea and scones about witchcraft – and wimps afraid of cold water.

114. CRICHTON CASTLE

Back to basics was fact rather than fancy in our first home. Rose Cottage had all the elements associated with the name, honeysuckle and roses round the door, but it lacked such amenities as running water, electricity or an inside toilet. Indeed, the loo was a bucket under a bench seat, carefully disguised in an ancient yew tree at the bottom of the garden. Oil lamps lit our winter evenings and a trip to the yew on a cold spring morning was a wondrously invigorating way to start the day. Splash-tub baths and running-on-the-spot to keep warm promoted a degree of fitness not apparent amongst our better-heeled contemporaries, whilst collecting well water engendered everlasting propriety in the use of natural resources. But we were content, in spite of the lack of allegedly essential accoutrements.

Our baby son thrived. We had two kittens, named after respective mothers-in-law for easier kicking, and a rusty old sheepdog, Spud, retired from active duty on the Pentland Hills. For entertainment we had a battery-operated gramophone, 200 records, three yards of books and the beneficence of youth.

Rose Cottage nestled in the small village of Fala Dam, 15 miles south from Edinburgh. It had been in my wife's family for years. Fala Dam was perfect for lovers of the great outdoors, offering easy access to Moorfoot and Lammer Hills and to the 'empty quarter': Fala Moor, an expanse of damp moorland across which Charles Edward Stuart and his Highland army slogged in 1745 on their road south to Derby. Mary, Queen of Scots also tramped the moor after her escape from Borthwick Castle in 1567. She stopped at Cakemuir on her way to Dunbar to change from her disguise as a pageboy, before meeting her lover, James Hepburn.

I had done a fair bit of tramping round Fala long before I bumped into my own intended. As a Scout and patrol leader of the Otters, I got my gang lost there on more than one occasion during Midlothian adventure hikes. Later, as an embryonic artist, I cycled from Edinburgh to sketch the stark ruins of Crichton Castle which stands on a hill overlooking the silver River Tyne.

One of my favourite walks begins at Crichton, west of Pathhead, 'Pawtheed' in local parlance, on the A68 road south to Soutra Hill. Crichton church dates from 1449 and was established by that arch-schemer, William Crichton, Lord Chancellor of Scotland in the middle years of the fifteenth century; a man described by Sir Walter Scott as being 'as destitute of faith, mercy and conscience as of fear and folly.' His contemporaries no doubt said the same, but not when Sir William was listening.

The castle is a short walk from the church and the most significant visible feature is the magnificent Italianate stone facade in the central courtyard; built by the last Earl Bothwell, Francis Stewart, around 1585 on his return from a visit to Ferarra in Italy. But Francis Stewart 'made his life one continuous orgy of violence and uproar', and when his estate was forfeited in 1593 the glory days of Crichton and the castle were ended.

Invisible, but never far from my mind when I wander the ruins, are the shades of young William Douglas and his brother, David. Grim Chancellor Crichton entertained them in his castle in November 1440, prior to conducting them to Edinburgh to meet the boy-king, James II. After dinner in Edinburgh Castle, Crichton placed a black bull's head on the table, the sign of death. In spite of the King's pleading, after a mock trial, the brothers were beheaded on Castle Hill.

Find Crichton Castle on OS Map 66, Edinburgh, second series, Scale 1:50,000. Crichton Grid Ref: 388620; start of walk Grid Ref: 380616; Crichton Castle Grid Ref: 380611; Borthwick Castle Grid Ref: 370597; Loquhariot Grid Ref: 370609. Park by Crichton church and follow the signpost to the castle. Leave the castle by the west side of the stable building and walk down to the River Tyne. A muddy path leads south to Borthwick Castle through woodlands by the banks of the little river. It crosses the ribbed-track of the old Waverley Line railway to a hill overlooking Borthwick Castle: a gaunt, double-towered structure dating from 1430, briefly the home of Mary, Queen of Scots and her rapacious husband, James Hepburn, fourth Earl of Bothwell, after their star-crossed marriage in 1566. Cromwell's troops paid Borthwick a visit in 1650 and left their calling card on the south wall of the outer defences, hence the cannonball marks.

The castle has been wonderfully restored and is now an excellent hotel. The Great Hall retains the massive, barrel-vaulted roof and a majestic, hooded fireplace. Mary and Bothwell spent their last nights together round the spark of the Great Hall's log fire and the hotel boasts adjacent bedrooms named after them. Would that poor Mary had kept to her own bed. As it was, she lost her heart to Bothwell and, 21 years later, her head to her cousin Queen Elizabeth, in a far less welcoming great hall at Fotheringhay.

After viewing Borthwick church and castle, go north from the village to cross Gore Water. Turn left at the road junction and within 50 yards, on the north side of the old Waverley Line, pick up the track over the fields to Loquhariot. Turn right on the road walk back towards Crichton. As you climb the hill to the village, you may bear right through the woods to reach the car park after an easy five-mile historical ramble.

115. BLACKHOPE SCAR

The Borders author Judy Steel recounts a story that captures the raw, independent spirit of the people who live in the shadow of the Moorfoot Hills. An illustrious Edwardian lady, travelling by rail from Fountainhall to Lauder, asked the station-master for directions to the Lauder train: 'It's ower the brig,' he replied. 'I need assistance,' she demanded crossly, 'I have a tin chest.' The station-master responded unceremoniously: 'I dinna care whether you've a tin chest or a brass arse. It's ower the brig to Lauder.'

My introduction to the sharp edge of the Borders tongue came early when, as a boy, I used to fish the silver streams which scar the lonely Moorfoot glens. A local angler, intent upon taking a fish home for supper, got his 'fly' caught in the branches of a rowan overhanging the pool. I climbed up to retrieve it and found not a fly of fur and leather, but a large, bare, viciously barbed treble hook; to be ripped through the water blindly, in the hope of impaling an unsuspecting fish. 'What sort of a fly do you call this?' I asked. 'It's a Scott Jock,' he barked. 'Now get yourself away and leave me in peace.'

Peace is the one thing you will most decidedly find in the Moorfoots. It is possible to walk here all day without meeting another soul. As more and more people take to the high tops, Scotland's altitudinous peaks have become little other than names to be 'ticked off' in a Munro Bagger's almanac. But these gentle hills continue to offer silence and serenity, that special sense of contentment that is only to be found in a landscape devoid of hordes of humans. This is a landscape free from those more intent on histrionics than on the joy of walking through the paradise garden beneath their feet.

One of my favourites, and a Happy New Year walk, enfolds the crystal-clear waters of the infant South Esk. The glen and its surrounding hills are the perfect place to work off post-festive season excess; well within reach of both Glasgow and Edinburgh and ideal for a short, winter day out in the wilds. It is also ideal for little legs, because there is a good Esk-side track all the way to the head of the glen. Those of a more adventurous turn of mind, weather permitting, may then return to the start point along the broad summit plateau to the east of the stream.

Find the glen on OS Map 73, Galashiels and Ettrick Forest, second series, Scale: 1:50,000. Park at Grid Ref: 293528, by Gladhouse Reservoir, at this time of year temporary home to vast flocks of visiting geese from the Arctic and a wide variety of other waterfowl. Skirt Moorfoot Farm and follow the track south to greet the Esk at Gladhouse Cottage (Grid Ref: 295515). Across to your left, on the side of the hill, stand the gaunt, mysterious ruins of Hirendean Castle (Grid Ref: 299512). Little is known about the provenance of Hirendean, but it was probably associated with a monastery, long since vanished into the mists of time, which used to stand near Moorfoot Farm.

As easy tramp from Moorfoot Cottage will bring you to the end of the path after a brisk step of approximately two-and-a-half miles. Either return by the outward route or climb the course of the diminishing burn into the steep-sided V of Long Cleave (Grid Ref: 305481). The South Esk has its birth here and the second highest point in the Moorfoot Hills, Blackhope Scar (651m, Grid Ref: 315484), lies ahead; the highest Moorfoot honour is claimed by Windlestraw (659m), which lies to the east of Glentress Rig on the B709 lnnerleithen–Heriot road. If you fancy geographical tricks, it is possible to stand on Blackhope Scar near the trig point, where a quartet of fences meet, with one foot in Peebleshire and the other in Midlothian.

The way home from Blackhope Scar lies northwest via the summit of The Kips (Grid Ref: 541501). The going, in inclement weather, is rough-to-miserable, but on a sharp January day, with snow dust crusting the moor, it is an exhilarating adventure. Half a mile further north from The Kipps you will discover the source of an armlet of the River Esk (Grid Ref: 304507). which stumbles back down to the welcome shelter of Hirendean Castle and its sentinel clump of storm-tossed trees.

The round trip is some seven miles. How long is the journey? In the deep mid-winter, will you be there by candlelight? Yes, and back again.

116. LAMMER LAW

For the first year of our married life my wife, Ann, and I lived in a cottage at Fala Dam, a small village 15 miles south of Edinburgh close to the Lammermuir and Moorfoot hills. We lived the simple life: no running water, no electricity and no inside toilet, just a bucket in an old timber-built shed disguised by a yew tree at the bottom of the garden.

Changing circumstances moved us from Fala, but the memories linger; smoke drifting in cold winter's air, the riot of roses and honeysuckle that was summer, the smell of heather and bog myrtle on the moors; the ever-present sound of Fala Burn 'loupin ower its linns'. So it was like visiting an old friend when I passed the village again, on my way to Gifford and Longyester, intent on walking the Lammermuirs. I parked by Longyester Farm cottages and surveyed the soft shoulder of Lammer Law, rising 538m before me, grey, blue and green against the horizon. Squared banks of conifers line the fields, windbreaks against Lammer storms and welcome shelter for sheep and cattle. Clearing the shelter of the woods, I caught the full force of the wind howling downhill. Butterflies and moths were keeping a low profile that morning. Scabious, tormentil and buttercups tossed and bobbed in the gale.

The track over Lammer Law is an old drove road, used for centuries to take cattle and sheep to the great southern markets. Whole families would make the long journey; lean husbands, wives, children and dogs, chattering and yapping, herding complaining herds and flocks over the moors. The Romans knew this land and called the inhabitants the Votadini. These ancient Picts peopled the Lothians for a thousand years with hill forts and settlements. I looked towards graceful Trapain Law, their capital, where, in the early years of this century a group of workmen discovered an astonishing array of Roman silver and Pictish treasures. Tarpain was a sophisticated town enclosing an area of 40 acres.

I caught a glimpse of Hopes Reservoir, leaden, sparkling at the foot of Bulihope Law, dotted black by a hopeful fishing boat. At the top of Lammer Law the sun sailed clear from behind the dark clouds and the glories of the Lowlands crowded round: Arthur's Seat, a lion crouching over the Auld

Grey City of Edinburgh; the blue line of the Pentland Hills; Sir Walter Scott's rounded Eildons and, closer, as though waiting to be stroked, the gentle Moorfoots. I hurried on towards Tollishill round Hog Hill and Windy Law to reach my goal, a single standing stone and the outlines of a Pictish fort ringing the top of a small hill to the west of Tollishill Farm. Vast pylons strode across the hill like figures from H.G. Wells's *War of the Worlds*, stark and menacing in the mist. A rabbit scurried over the track, pursued by a bad-eyed stoat. Death in the heather.

Passing under the humming hydro wires, I reached Tollishill. The outline of the fort is clearly visible: concentric rings, commanding a 360-degree view. These forts were as much working villages as defensive structures. Gates were barred and spears sharpened only in time of communal danger, generally from the acquisitive aspirations of overbearing neighbours. The single sentinel standing stone is by the side of the road on the edge of a little wood.

I retraced my steps up Crib Law, shadowed by a hungry herring gull and two minister-black crows, wind pushing me home. Before Lammer Law a deep scar cuts into the hill and I struck right, over the moor, to Bleak Law by Sting Bank Burn. On the summit of Bleak Law a tumbled cairn centres a criss-cross of sheep tracks that lead through heather and ferns down to a red-rust-roofed shed at the foot of the valley. Sting Bank Burn bustles into Hopes Reservoir through a wood of alder, silver birch and hazel. Although Hopes is man-made, it is old enough to have an established, settled look, which is not diminished by the neo-Gothic water tower and trimmed lawns surrounding the south end.

A dipper, black-and-white best-bib-tuckered, kept me company along the outlet burn. The hills around Hopes are scattered with evidence of the Pictish endeavour. The ghosts of 1,000 years kept step with my squelching sodden boots as I tramped the last easy miles along tree-lined lanes back to Longyester.

Use OS Map 66, Edinburgh, second series, Scale 1:50,000. Longyester Grid Ref: 545651; Blinkbonny Wood Grid Ref: 537642; Lammer Law Grid Ref: 524618; Crib Law Grid Ref: 525598; Tollishill Farm Grid Ref: 519581; Bleak Law Grid Ref: 538616; Hopes Reservoir Grid Ref: 547622; Hope Farm Grid Ref: 559638.

117. ST ABBS AND COLDINGHAM

Childhood memories live deep in adult minds. Of summer rambles, winter snow-fights, school squabbles and seaside holidays. A cupboardful of dreams opened and awakened by half-forgotten familiar sights and sounds. The seaside village of St Abbs in Berwickshire lay before me, bathed in autumn sunlight, boat-bobbing and exactly the same as it had been on my first visit more than 50 years ago. The lifeboat station perched on the edge of the harbour wall. The same row of brightly painted cottages crested the hill. I noted the bedroom window where my brother and I had waited, breathless with impatience, for the sound of stones rattling on our window telling us that Jake Nisbet had come to take us to sea. I see him now, white stocking tops turned down over Wellington boots, huge grey-speckled jumper and dark blue cap. Jake was our hero, full of tales of whaling days in the South Atlantic and endless patience with the excited chatter of two small boys. That was our first family holiday after the First World War and they were two of the most memorable weeks of my life. I thought of that holiday as I paused above Wuddy Rocks and looked down on the harbour. The entrance is narrow. I remember Jake telling us how to negotiate the rock-bounded channel. As I watched, a small clinker-built boat edged cautiously out. I thought of my relief on a windy night, sailing home with Jake, cold and shaken by rough seas, when we found the harbour mouth.

My walk that day had started in the nearby village of Coldingham, at the old cross erected by Lord Home in 1815 to celebrate Napoleon's defeat at Waterloo. A priory was founded in Coldingham in 635 and a church built on the priory site in 1135, renewed in 1220. This structure survived until 1648 when Oliver Cromwell paid it an ungentle visit. Coldingham was one of Scotland's most important religious centres in the Middle Ages, a constant source of English–Scottish dispute. A major restoration programme was completed in 1954 and the church is now one of the most attractive and best maintained in Berwickshire.

Just past the Anchor Inn, a hedge-lined road leads out to Coldingham Loch, once the preserve of the House of Usher, the Scottish brewing family, and now owned by Dr and Mrs Douglas Wise. They manage the loch as a trout fishery and wildlife haven. The first rainbow trout to be introduced to Scottish waters were stocked into Coldingham in about 1950. A track skirts the loch and leads to dramatic cliffs that are amongst the highest in Britain and the site of a Pictish hill fort. The perfect place for lunch and a chat with your ancestors.

After lunch, I tramped eastwards along the cliff-top track to Pettico Wick Marine Nature Reserve. You don't see much of a marine nature reserve from land, but I am glad it is there. St Abb's Head towers above the bay, topped by a lighthouse and separately placed foghorn. This is the St Abb's Head Nature Reserve, 200 acres of wonderful wildflowers and wildlife. A path winds south from St Abbs to Coldingham Bay with its crescent of golden sand where my brother and I swam. I marched down, stripped off and plunged in for a commemorative splash. The water was just as cold as I remembered, but a vigorous hike up the hill to Coldingham Village restored circulation.

You need OS Map 67, Duns and Dunbar, second series, Scale 1:50,000 for this walk. Park in Coldingham Village and walk north past Anchor Inn to the B6438, which is on your right. Walk out to Coldingham Loch, angle through the woods along the east shore of the loch to reach the cliff path and Pictish hill fort. Follow the cliff path down to Pettico Wick to join a tarmac road that leads to St Abb's Head.

Behind the lighthouse, the cliff path continues to St Abbs. Exit from the village along the front of the fishermen's cottages above the harbour, via a path that takes you into Coldingham Bay. From the bay, walk west past the caravan site back to your car. The walk is only eight miles and easy going, but allow plenty time for stopping because there's lots to see. Take care in wet or windy weather and keep back from the cliff edge.

Key points: Coldingham Grid Ref: 902659; Coldingham Loch Grid Ref: 896684; hill fort Grid Ref: 898688; Pettico Wick Grid Ref: 907691; St Abb's Head Grid Ref: 910694; St Abbs Grid Ref: 918673; Coldingham Bay Grid Ref: 917665.

118. MERRICK

As our politicians bombard us with pre-election promises and the media is full of in-depth analytical policy reviews, many of Jock Tamson's bairns may be confused. Who is telling the truth? Is there any such thing as political truth? Does a single vote really matter? Or does it just encourage them in their madness? If you doubt the probity of this ruction and waver between one decision or the other, then this is the time to head for the hills where you may consider your position 'far from the madding crowd'.

Do so above Loch Trool in the Galloway Forest Park and you will be in good company. An earlier pro-devolutionist, Robert Bruce, wrestled with similar problems here in April 1307 and in the process gave a bunch of his opponents a terminal headache. Bruce and his desperate band of supporters were hiding in these hills when news was brought of an approaching English force led by Aymer de Valence, the Earl of Pembroke. The Bruce greeted them by rolling huge boulders down onto their unsuspecting heads from the heights of Mulldonach Hill (557m). The mangled remains of de Valence's force were buried by the shores of the loch. Thereafter, Bruce galloped off to achieve gory fame and Scottish independence at the Battle of Bannockburn seven years later. His victory in Glen Trool is commemorated by a huge stone, 'The Bruce's Stone', overlooking the head of the loch.

To the north of Loch Trool, a few miles distant, where the hill is glacially-gashed between Buchan Burn and Loch Enoch, the escarpment takes on the shape of an unsmiling human face (OS Map 77, New Galloway and Glen Trool, second series, Scale 1:50,000, Grid Ref: 437846). This feature is known as the 'Grey Man of Merrick'. Granite-faced Mr Merrick no doubt allowed himself a rare, wry, smile as he listened to the noise of the stramash down in Glen Trool and approved of its outcome.

You also will approve of the outcome of an expedition to Merrick (842m) in the 'Little Highlands of Scotland'. This is the supreme hill of the Southern Uplands, bested only in height by Goatfell (87m) on the Island of Arran, which is clearly visible from the summit. As are the Mountains of Mourne in Ireland, the purple hills of the Lake District across the wide sands of the Solway Firth and Ben Lomond and the tumble of mightier Scottish peaks to the north.

Begin your thoughtful day at the car park (Grid Ref: 417803) near Bruce's Stone. Allow six hours for the walk and be wary of the weather – notoriously fickle in these airts. The going is rough-to-terrible at the lower levels, particularly on the way home, so be prepared, compass-and-mapped and ready to weather all contingencies. Once up the walking is easy, over springy turf across a broad, safe plateau that leads to the summit cairn. Get up by following the left-hand side of Buchan Burn, a perfect highland stream, banked by heather clumps and red-decked rowan. The stream sings and chortles all the way to the ruined cottage at Cul Sharg (Grid Ref: 416819). A signposted track leads from the back of the cottage, through the conifer plantations, onto the south face of Benyellary (720m) which is the southern gateway to Merrick.

A drystane dyke welcomes you at the top. Hang a right here and follow the dyke north to the summit of Benyellary (Grid Ref: 415389). Merrick looms ahead, one and a half miles distant, and the track dips into a saddle at the source of the Gloan Burn before rising gently to the white-painted trig point on Merrick (Grid Ref: 428854). Time for lunch, a chat with Arran's 'Sleeping Warrior' hills and a joke with Paddy's Milestone, Ailsa Craig, gloriously isolated in the blue waters of the Firth of Clyde to the west.

Descend from Merrick at Grid Ref: 420853, plotting your route ahead before you do so. Make for the south end of Loch Enoch (Grid Ref: 445850); over 100ft deep and now virtually fishless due to the effects of acid rain, as are most of the waters you will pass on the way home. Continue south over the Rig of Enoch (Grid Ref: 435835) to Murder Hole (Grid Ref: 439830) at the west end of Loch Neldricken, made infamous by Samuel Crockett (1859-1914) in his novel *The Raiders*.

A farther half-mile south, at the west end of Loch Valley (Grid Ref: 445817), brings you the welcome relief of an excellent although muddy track which contours round the east side of Buchan Hill to the Bruce's Stone and the start point. By now you should have resolved any problem you might have had in connection with our democratic process. Probably when the Grey Man of Merrick gave you a wink and a nod as you squelched by. Remember The Bruce.

119. HERMITAGE HILL

I have been much exercised by water this morning, or rather by the lack of water. Like many North Sutherland homes, we have a private supply and from time-to-time our pipes clag up. Unidentifiable things get stuck in mid-flow. Or the inlet pipe to the header tank becomes blocked with heather and peat. The worst such incident happened last winter. We spent a whole week microwaving snow, in between lugging slopping buckets kitchenwards from an adjacent stream. With that in mind, I clambered up Hysbackie Brae in bright April sunlight and soon located the source of our problem: the pipe had sprung up from the stream. Breathing a huge sigh of relief, I re-instated it and hurried back home to collect copious brownie points from a grateful spouse.

Still, is there such a thing as a 'bad breeze'? As I poked around I heard and saw the first wheatear of our northern spring; fresh from Africa's distant shores, dolled up in his breeding finery, proudly puff-breasted and chattering crossly at me from the top of a drystane dyke. As far as I could gather, the bird seemed to be telling me to be up-and-about the glorious business of exploring my native land; that it was time to banish winter blues, drag out the hiking boots and head for the high tops, hills and moorlands.

A good place to begin is by visiting Hermitage Castle, the 'strength of Liddesdale'; a gaunt Douglas stronghold built in the thirteenth century to protect the southwestern approaches of the realm from rapacious English attack. The castle lies some 12 miles south from Hawick, close to the B6399 Hawick–Newcastleton road. It is dominated by Hermitage Hill (403m) to the north and Din Fell (529m) to the south. The castle is at Grid Ref: 497960. Use OS Map 79, Hawick and Eskdale, second series, Scale 1:50,000 to find your way around.

When the weather is uncertain, this is a perfect place for an early season walk, suitable for legs of all lengths. Park at the bridge over Hermitage Water (Grid Ref: 495960). Exercise first, and then pay your respects to the dark ruins. This is not a taxing walk, there and back takes about two hours. But the ground is rugged so be well-shod and prepared with suitable wet weather gear and compass and map. Cross the bridge and strike directly uphill, taking the less steep route by bearing slightly northeast. You may descend by returning the same way, or, more fun, come down the south west slope of the hill to the small burn that leads via Old Braidlie (Grid Ref: 479970) to the road and back to the car park.

The benefit of making the climb prior to investigating the castle is the vista from the summit of Hermitage Hill. The strategic importance of the fortress is immediately apparent. Any invading force by-passing the castle would leave itself open to a counter-attack from the defenders secure behind its intimidating grey walls. The vastness of the surrounding countryside is overwhelming; a landscape redolent with the history of Border feuds, a buffer between the blood-soaked Debatable Lands to the south and relative civilisation to the north.

Sir James Douglas, the Black Douglas, one of Robert Bruce's most reliable supporters who fought with him at Bannockburn (1314), once owned the castle. But perhaps the most famous, or infamous, owner was James Hepburn, Earl of Bothwell; would-be king of Scotland, lover and eventually husband of sad Mary Queen of Scots. Mary visited Bothwell on 15 October 1566, leaving her sick bed in Jedburgh and riding the 50 miles there and back in a day to comfort Bothwell, who had been wounded in a

Border affray. Tongues wagged furiously in Auld Reekie when the story became known, to the delight of Mary's enemies.

Hermitage is held in trust for the nation by the Secretary of State for Scotland and in times past you could wander freely round the castle. But times change and there is now a charge for doing so. Granted, a modest charge, but, as a Scot, I object to paying to visit something which is, essentially, already mine. I wonder just how long it will take Scotland's lairds to start doing the same before they allow us access to 'their' hills? A tariff based upon mountain heights? All heart, aren't they, these protectors of our precious environment – enough to make even a wheatear weep. Remember that you read it here first.

120. LAST TRAIN TO RICCARTON

There is one railway route in Scotland, the Waverley Line, which is entirely safe and guaranteed no delays, no damaged track and no signal failures. In fact, no trains, no track, no signals at all, because the line was closed in 1969. Sir David Steel, then a humble backbencher in the Westminster Parliament, rode the last through train on the night of 6 January. The following morning a section of the track was lifted.

My wife, Ann, The Manager, has close links with the Waverley Line. She spent several childhood years at Riccarton Junction, an exchange station and village servicing the railway that lies deep in the border hills south from Hawick. Her mother was a schoolteacher there during the last war and Ann loved the moorlands and hills surrounding her home. Over the years we have seen station buildings, marshalling yards, turntables, signal boxes and railway workers' houses decay, become ruins and disappear. The open landscape encompassing Arnton Fell (446m), Stitchel Hill (318m) and Leap Hill (471m) is now smothered with blanket forestry. Shepherds have gone from the moor. All that remains to mark the passing of this once-vibrant community is the old schoolhouse on the hill.

But it is an ill wind. The disused railway line provides comfortable walking and there are easy paths leading from it to the top of Arnton Fell. However, you still need hiking boots, wet-weather gear and OS Map No 79, Hawick and Eskdale, second series, Scale 1:50,000, to find your way safely round. Make a nostalgic visit to Riccarton Junction during the course of this eleven-mile, six-hour adventure.

Begin by parking on the B6399 Hawick–Newcastleton road near

Whitropefoot (Grid Ref: 512980). Walk down the road to the bridge over Whitrope Burn and look out on your left for the 'Border Forest Park' notice board. Follow the signpost to Ninestone Rig by tramping the outside edge of the forest. After 15 minutes, cross a stile into the conifers and march on to visit an ancient stone circle at Grid Ref: 519974. Continue northeast from the stone circle for approximately one and a half miles to reach the disused railway track. The Waverley Line, between Hawick and Carlisle, was the 'brain child' of Richard Hodgson, Chairman of the North British Railway Company. Work started in 1858 and traversed some of the wildest country in Scotland. A tunnel had to be driven 1,152 metres through Limekilnridge and the route had sharper curves and steeper gradients than any other track in Britain.

As you walk south along the line of the railway, which even yet is graced by a grand display of ubiquitous willow herb, spare a thought for the men who constructed the track. They were mostly itinerant, hard-drinking Irishmen. The story is told of a local shepherd who intervened in a pay-night fight between two of them. In the scuffle, the shepherd and one of the Irishmen fell into a ditch. His erstwhile opponent called down in alarm and asked, 'Michael, is that man attacking you?'

Unless you are a 'railway buff', it is hard to recreate in your mind the layout of Riccarton Junction (Grid Ref: 540978). The name has long since vanished even from the OS Map. But The Manager knows, and points out to me places she knew as a child: where the village swing was hung from an accommodating tree; the bridge over a stream which she 'helped' build; the station-master's house; the 'refresher', a canteen on the station platform.

Reach the summit of Arnton Fell by turning right uphill at the first gate across the track south from Riccarton at Grid Ref: 524936. A convenient wall guides your steps. The top is treeless and offers a wonderful vista over green Liddesdale hills. The grey bulk of Hermitage Castle, 'The Strength of Liddesdale', glowers south at the foot of Hermitage Hill (403m) towards lands of 'The Auld Enemy'. To the east, lights from the windows of Riccarton Schoolhouse still pinprick evening's coming.

Hike north along the broad ridge of Arnton Fell to Grid Ref: 530968 before descending between Blackwood Hill and Bell Hill to cross Roughley Burn (Grid Ref: 521965). In spate conditions, this can be difficult. I recall once wading the stream with The Manager on my back, for which feat I received brownie points in abundance. Climb the east slope of Ninestone Rig to rejoin your outward path. As promised, no delays, no damaged track or signal failures, just home safe and sound.

121. THE GREAT CHEVIOT

A walk abroad this morning, through the 'unchristened country' of the Border Reivers to greet Great Cheviot (815m) in the Northumberland National Park. This land blurs the psychological boundary between Scotland and England. It is a land where family names bear the imprint of centuries of feuds, thuggery, and thieving: Hume, Kerr, Forster, Ridley, Rutherford, Scott, Elliot, Turnbull, Fenwick, Armstrong, Charlton, Robson, and Storey. Our band of 'raiders' consisted of my wife Ann, and Hareton, a ten-month-old terrorist Yorkshire Terrier and myself. We were fulfilling a long-held ambition born out of decades of travel through the Border hills between England and Scotland. Although we lived in Northumberland for many years and, as youths, made the Scottish Borders our friend, we had never climbed to the summit of this most famous of all Cheviot peaks.

For 300 years, from the time of Edward I (1239–1307) until the Union of the Crowns (1603), those who lived here were virtually a law unto themselves, encouraged in this intransigence by the Kings of England and Scotland in order to furnish them with an excuse for armed incursion into each other's realms. Going safely to bed at night was no guarantee of a safe awakening the following morning. Life was lightly held and anything not securely nailed down was considered fair game for all. I was reminded of this when we parked at the end of the road from Wooler to Langleeford on the banks of Harthope Burn. A notice warned us to beware of ' car thieves'. Some things never change. Until excise duties between England and Scotland were standardised in 1855, these hills were a refuge for thieves and smugglers. Contraband goods were landed at the port of Boulmer to the east of Alnwick, by rascal characters such as Blind Will Balmer, Wull Faa, the gypsy king of Kirk Yetholm, and Isaac Addison, landlord of the Fishing Boat Inn at Boulmer in 1820.

Daniel Defoe (1660–1731), author, English government spy, and general meddler in the affairs surrounding the Union of Parliaments in 1707, visited Great Cheviot in 1728. He wrote an account of his ascent of the hill on horseback which is pure tabloid journalism: 'We rode up higher still, till at length our hearts failed us all together and we resolved to alight . . . the ground seeming to descend every way from the edges of the summit.' Must have been one of Defoe's bad days. The ascent is in fact safe and straightforward.

A well-marked track rises from the stream to gain the summit of Scald Hill (548m) after an easy one and three quarter miles. Thereafter, crossing two stiles, the rounded bulk of Great Cheviot lies ahead, the way forward following a deeply scarred indentation in the northeast face of the hill. The route joins the Pennine Way near the top and the track has been trodden into a quagmire of peat holes and black sludge, best avoided in all but the driest of weather or in the grip of a hard frost. The summit cairn sits in a sea of peat in the middle of a vast, featureless bog. Stone slabs have been laid on top of the peat to form a safe pathway and we rested on the plinth of the cairn to have lunch. I was reminded of scenes from the First World War Battle of Passchendaele (1917), when heavy rain and bombardment turned the battlefield into a nightmare, water-filled swamp. Had a stark hand appeared through the peat around the cairn on Great Cheviot, I would not have blinked an eye.

It is only when you leave the summit plateau, southwest along the stone walkway to Cairn Hill (776m), that the view opens to show the gentle folds of the Border hills; loud with the cry of curlews, larks and meadow pipits, spreading wave-like into the far horizon.

We descend south from Cairn Hill by Scotsman's Knowe to find the source of Harthope Burn. The descent over tufted, ankle-breaking ground requires care and it is not until the burn is reached that the walk is eased by convenient sheep tracks.

A ' proper' track by the burn helped us home; past Harthope Linn where the golden, peat-stained stream tumbles 7.6m into a deep, dark pool. We paused at Langleeford Hope to pay our respects to Sir Walter Scott, who stayed there in 1771 and was much taken with not only the beauty of his surroundings, but also with the beauty of the girl who brought him his morning goat's milk. Back at the start point, ours was the only vehicle left in the parking area. I wondered, had latter-day reivers been busy?

You will need two OS Maps to find your way round: Map 74, Kelso, and Map 80, The Cheviot Hills; both second series, Scale 1:50,000. Park at Langleeford Grid Ref: 949220; Scald Hill Grid Ref: 929219; The Cheviot Grid Ref: 910205; Cairn Hill Grid Ref: 904195; Scotsman's Knowe Grid Ref: 905187; start of track by Harthope Burn Grid Ref: 901191.

122. HADRIAN'S WALL

Time to play soldiers. March with me along the great wall that Emperor Hadrian built in AD 122 across Cumberland and Northumberland to keep us Scots in our proper place, beyond the pale of Roman civilisation. The wall was 70 miles, 80 Roman miles, in length. It started in the west at Bowness on the Solway Firth and ended at Wallsend to the east of Newcastle. The structure was massive, built mainly of freestone blocks with a rubble core, 5.4m in height and up to 2.7 thick, flanked by a defensive ditch 11m wide and 4.5m deep. There were 80 'milecastles', between which were placed 320 watchtowers. No doubt the wall pleased its builders mightily and it must have scared the living daylights out of the locals. Which is exactly what the Romans intended. Nobody messed them about with impunity.

The parts of the wall that remain today are still fiercely impressive. The best-preserved section lies between Chollerford, to the north of Hexham, and Greenhead near Haltwhistle. For many years we lived close to the wall, in an old house overlooking the River South Tyne. Indeed, I am convinced that the small, squat, monumental stone in the centre of our rose garden had been filched from the wall by previous tenants of our property.

Which is exactly what happened to great chunks of Publius Aelius Hadrianus's battlements. Over the centuries, farmers and others illegally used the stones for their own building purposes. But the biggest act of vandalism occurred in the years following 1745, in the aftermath of Bonnie Prince Charlie's ill-fated rebellion. A seriously worried government allowed the use of vast quantities of Mr Hadrian's stone to build the foundations of a new Military Road (the present B6318) which parallels the wall to the south.

OS Map 87, Hexham and Haltwhistle, second series, Scale 1:50,000, will guide you round. One of our favourite walks starts at the car park adjacent to the Twice Brewed Inn (Grid Ref: 752668) (Tel: 01434 344534). The name, 'Twice Brewed', harks back to the building of the Military Road. Apparently, the toiling labourers were dissatisfied with the strength of the beer they were served and demanded that it be brewed again, hence 'Twice

Brewed'. Next door to the Inn, at Once Brewed, is a Northumberland National Park Information and Visitor Centre (Tel: 01434 344396) and a Youth Hostel. Why Once Brewed? Well, the Youth Hostel is unlicensed and, consequently, drinks such as coffee and tea are once brewed, rather than twice. Well, that's the story. Make the Park Centre your first call, it is packed with detail about the central section of the Roman Wall and details of other walks in the area.

Leave the Centre and tramp north up the minor road for half a mile to find the wall (Grid Ref: 751676), which is divided by this road. Hang a left and follow the wall west up to where it reaches its highest point on Whinshields Crag (345m) at Grid Ref: 742676. Continue west to Shield on the Wall (Grid Ref: 728667). The cottage here was the home of Mr Stott, who retired to it after a lifetime's work building fishing rods for Hardy Brothers in Alnwick. He made me a wonderful cane trout rod which has been in constant use ever since.

Another mile west along the craggy top leads you down to dramatic Milecastle 42 (Grid Ref: 716667). Immediately to the west are the remains of the Roman fort of Aesica at Great Chesters (Grid Ref: 704669). Return to Milecastle 42 and the Twice Brewed along the line of the vallum, an earthen mound that protected the southern approach to the wall. This is not a long walk, albeit wild enough on a windy day, approximately five miles, and it should leave plenty of time to visit two of the most stunning forts associated with the wall: Housesteads (Grid Ref: 790690) and Vindolanda (Grid Ref: 771663).

Housesteads covers five acres and used to support a garrison of 1,000 soldiers. The remains of their living quarters are superbly displayed: gateways, latrines, a barrack block, granaries, hospital and the Commanding Officer's house. Vindolanda boasts an open-air museum and reconstructions of the wall and one of the wall's turrets; also a Roman temple, house, shop and other items excavated here. By this time you should have built up a worthwhile drouth. *Contendere alqo* quickly with me and slake it at the Twice Brewed Inn.

123. HITCHING A RAILWAY RIDE IN NORTHUMBERLAND

Begin this morning with a nostalgic trip on a proper train. Ride along England's most elevated narrow-gauge railway, from Alston in Cumbria to

Kirkhaugh in Northumberland. The route crosses a splendid three-arch stone viaduct as it chugs and puffs its way to the end of the line. Get off at Kirkhaugh and tramp home over wild moorlands via Grey Nag (656m) and Tom Smith's Stone (631m), a journey of about seven miles. In the hills you need OS Map 86, Haltwhistle and Alston, second series, Scale 1:50,000, to find your way round – the train knows its own way.

The Newcastle & Carlisle Railway Company opened the original line in 1852 as a branch line running between Haltwhistle in the Tyne Valley and Alston. The South Tyneside Railway Preservation Society has restored part of this line, closed in 1976, by constructing a 2ft-gauge railway along the old trackbed. The route was officially opened by the Earl of Carlisle in May 1984 and carried more than 10,000 passengers in its first full season and tens of thousands more since. The railway is operated by members of the Society, who voluntarily provide maintenance, cleaning, drivers, guards, signal and ticket office staff. The station building hosts the local Tourist Information Centre, a bookshop and tearoom. Park at Alston Station (Grid Ref: 719467) on the banks of the River South Tyne. The town itself is unique and worth exploring, with its old market cross and steep, cobbled main street. Alston was once a centre of lead mining in the area and the remains of these mines with their distinctive chimneys dominate the landscape.

Clan Sandison also dominated this landscape for a number of years when we lived in a rambling haunted house near Bardon Mill. The Newcastle to Carlisle railway line ran along a high embankment at the foot of our garden and the rattle of passing engines were part of our daily life. Also part of our life was walking in the surrounding hills. Mr Hadrian's Roman Wall was a few minutes north and we regularly marched, smartly, to the highest point at Whinshields Crag (345m, Grid Ref: 735673). Another favourite walk was from Wilimotswick (Grid Ref: 770635) up to the ruined buildings at Penpeugh (Grid Ref: 766620) on Ridley Common. Bishop Nicholas Ridley (1500–55), Bishop of London, was born at Wilimotswick, although some say he was born in the house where we lived. Which could account for our ghosts. Nicholas was burned at the stake for heresy, encouraged in this extremity by his fellow sufferer, Bishop Hugh Latimer: 'Be of good comfort, Master Ridley, and play the man. We shall this day light a candle by God's grace in England, as I trust shall never be put out.' Hard to be of good comfort when you are on fire.

The walk back from Kirkhaugh (Grid Ref: 695499), after leaving the train, will almost certainly set your spirits on fire. The hills here, although not grand in the Scottish Highland sense of the word, are wonderful. Better still, they are infrequently visited so, more likely than not, you will have them to yourself all day. Cross the A689 Brampton to Alston road and angle round the north side of the hill to find the ruin at Grid Ref: 682509.

From the ruin, climb due south to Great Heaplaw (481m) at Grid Ref: 684486, then southwest up the broad shoulder of Whitley Common to ascend Black Hill (527m) (Grid Ref: 679477). Grey Nag (Grid Ref: 665475) lies one mile to the west over gently rising ground. A further comfortable mile southwest brings you to Tom Smith's Stone (Grid Ref: 652464). Here you may indulge in geographical tricks and stand with one foot in Northumberland and the other in Cumbria. If that's what turns you on.

If it does, you can compound your enjoyment on the way home because the route follows the county boundary line. Descend southeast from Tom Smith's Stone steeply down to find the Woldgill Burn. After a happy half-mile, Woldgill joins Gliderdale Burn and the stream eventually bumps into the Pennine Way at Grid Ref: 696474. Hang a right and follow the Pennine Way to the A689, thence back to Alston.

To properly enjoy Alston and its environs, indulge in a weekend break. Contact the Tourist Information Centre (Tel: 01434 381696) for accommodation details. For train times, contact the South Tyneside Railway, The Railway Station, Alston, Cumbria. Tel: 01434 381696. And be assured, unlike the rest of the UK's less-than-blessed privatised rail system, Alston trains do run on time.

124. ALLENDALE DAYS OUT

The Manager and I had a canny three-day break recently, staying at the King's Head Hotel in Allendale, Northumberland. The cost was canny as well, a total of £150 for both of us. This old Northumbrian market town is famous for its New Year's Eve tar barrel ceremony. Forty men dressed out-rageously and led by the local band march round the village carrying flaming barrels of tar above their heads. As the clock strikes midnight, the barrels are thrown into a huge bonfire blazing in the middle of the square. The bells of St Cuthbert's Church then ring in the New Year as hundreds of people roar out 'Auld Lang Syne'.

We did a fair bit of roaring ourselves, celebrating a family wedding and exploring the surrounding countryside over well-marked rights of way. This is designer walking, relaxed going along good footpaths and through luxuriant fields and wildflower-decked woods. One of the hallmarks of walking here is searching for the fantastic stiles built over the drystane walls that dominate the landscape. There are also reminders of the dale's industrial past, when Allendale was an important lead-mining centre such as the remains of two finger-like mine chimneys on the edge of Dryburn Moor.

Allendale Parish Council has published an excellent series of pamphlets describing 20 walks, varying in length from three to eight miles. It is available for a small charge at the post office in the Market Place. With a modicum of judicious juggling, it is easy to combine selected walks into longer expeditions. It is also useful to have OS Map 87, Hexham and Haltwhistle, second series, Scale 1:50,000, to provide an overview. Although we lived in the area for several years, I still have problems finding my way round the maze of minor roads that quarter these wonderful fells and valleys.

One of the great pleasures of walking in Allendale is that once you have arrived there you can abandon your car. Ours never moved an inch from its parking spot outside the King's Head. After breakfast, we simply dragged on the walking boots, grabbed a route map and set off. If you wish, you might tramp a five-mile walk in the morning, return to the pub for lunch, and then continue with a second hike during the afternoon. Being more accustomed to lunching in the shelter of a cairn on top of a windswept Scottish mountain, this was a unique experience.

Our only regret was, what with the nuptials and all, that time was limited. On Saturday morning we left the village and walked down Peth Bank to the River East Allen. The path borders the east bank of the stream, passing along the way the entrance to a mine tunnel that was intended to run from Allendale to Allenheads, a distance of seven miles. The project was abandoned in 1896 as being too difficult. Brown trout splashed in the river as dippers hurried about their urgent business. At a wicket gate, the track winds up towards windy Hope Farm and on to Close Hole, before leading gently back into Allendale.

The following morning we set off again on a seven-and-a-half mile tramp from Allendale to Oakpool and East Allen. The first part of the route followed our previous excursion, then crossed the old stone bridge at Allen Mill. The footpath from Allen Mill to Oakpool is sheer delight. It wends over a fertile landscape that has remained largely unchanged for the past hundred years. At Bridge Eal, by a wooden stile, a derelict grey house guards the way. The cottage at the rear has the date 1836 inscribed above the top of a rear window. Further on, at Oakpool, the doocote bears the date 1815 and the barely discernible inscription: 'Let me fly in time of need, My young ones for to feed.'

With this thought in mind, we marched steeply uphill past Old Town, which is the site of a Roman fort. The route home from there winds and twists across grass fields. Keeping on the right of way requires care and attention. As always, when it comes to path finding, I left this matter in the capable hands of The Manager. Back in the King's Head, we warmed ourselves outside before the open fire in the bar, and, inside, with a large dram of Auchentoshan. The hotel has one of the finest collections of single malt whiskies I have ever seen. Who could ask for more?

For further information, contact: Margaret Taylor, King's Head Hotel, Market Place, Allendale, Northumberland NE47 9BD. Tel: 01434 683681.

125. WALKABOUT DOWN UNDER

A window-rattling storm rages round our cottage here in North Sutherland. Sheep huddle behind drystane walls. Supersonic crows, flying forward, whisk by backwards. The last rose of summer is heading out towards Iceland and our aristocratic Siamese cat refuses to expose even the tip of his elegant dark nose to the howling gale. Winter is knocking at our door.

This time last year The Manager and I were also airborne, although in greater comfort, heading east to Perth in Western Australia. The object of our visit was to get in some serious bonding with four of our eight grandchildren. I call them 'The Enemy'. It had to be done. There was no way out. My son sent the tickets as a wedding anniversary present. Part of the deal, however, was that we should have a week away on our own, somewhere remote, preferably near the sea. Which is how we came to discover one of the most magical beaches and one of the most dramatic walks we have ever encountered: at Coral Bay, the southern gateway to the Ningaloo Reef Marine Park which margins the shore of the Cape Range Peninsula, 800 miles north from Perth. And it was hot, hot, hot.

Aboriginal people lived at Coral Bay 32,000 years ago, but it is only in recent times that modern man has intruded in any numbers. Each sheep station established in the area in the early years of this century averaged 620,000 acres and was run by only four or five people. As communications improved, tourists began to arrive. The first hotel, which opened in 1969, quickly went bust and it was not until 1981 that Coral Bay established itself as an 'in' place for those who relish adventure. My first adventure was being 'done' for speeding after leaving Learmonth airport. Mortified, I thought my son would never forgive me if I was charged. 'Name?' the young policeman inquired, squinting up at me through darkened sunglasses. 'Bruce Sandison.' 'And have you got a middle name, Brucie?' he said. 'Yes', I replied, squirming, 'MacGregor.' I am sure I got off with only a warning because I was Scottish.

The reef is the big attraction at Coral Bay. People come from all over the world from March to June to swim with the whale sharks which gather there at that time. In July and August, humpback whales are seen, migrating north. From September onwards, grey reef sharks congregate and turtles arrive to mate. Manta Ray and squid are prolific. The reef is home to more than 500 species of fish: clownfish, gobies, angelfish, wrasses, parrotfish, firefish, snappers, catfish, rabbitfish and many more.

The calm bay in front of our comfortable, but basic, cabin was rarely busy, perhaps a couple of dozen sun-worshippers at a time – children splashing in the warm shallows, families trooping off to board pleasure boats, others booking snorkelling and scuba dive sessions with local operators. There are also tours in glass-bottomed boats which drift over the reef, allowing you to enjoy its myriad maze of startling colours.

In the Presbyterian belief that pain should precede pleasure, and to escape even Coral Bay's modest 'madding crowd', The Manager was determined that we should hoof it to more distant airts. Once on the beach, we walked north and within a few minutes were on our own. We hiked the shore for five miles, past Crayfish Rock where shoals of baby reef sharks played and round the headland into Boorubooja Bay. Ahead of us, the beach seemed to continue endlessly. We stripped off and dived into the coolness of the azure-blue ocean, then lazed on the sand.

A school of dolphins appeared, sheepdog-herding a shoal of flying-fish into a tight circle prior to feeding on them. The periscope-like necks of green turtles popped up above the surface as they swam by in search of mates. A huge Manta Ray rose bat-like from the depths and crashed back into the sea, the sound of its landing sending small lark-like birds fluttering to safety. Clouds of white terns billowed over the point.

Later, in the early evening, back in Coral Bay, I sat with a glass of best Australian red, watching the sun set into the Indian Ocean. A handsome young Australian couple walked by on their way to the headland to view the spectacle. 'Come on, Sheila,' he said, 'move your butt or we will miss it.' 'Keep your hair on,' she replied. 'It's only a bloody sunset.'